THE FIRST PRIMARY

The First Primary

*New Hampshire's Outsize Role
in Presidential Nominations*

DAVID W. MOORE AND ANDREW E. SMITH

University of New Hampshire Press

Durham, New Hampshire

University of New Hampshire Press
www.upne.com/unh.html
© 2015 David W. Moore and Andrew E. Smith
All rights reserved
Manufactured in the United States of America
Designed by April Leidig
Typeset in Minion by Copperline Book Services

For permission to reproduce any of the material
in this book, contact Permissions, University Press
of New England, One Court Street, Suite 250,
Lebanon NH 03766; or visit www.upne.com

Library of Congress Cataloging-in-Publication Data
Moore, David W.
The first primary: New Hampshire's outsize role in
presidential nominations / David W. Moore and Andrew E. Smith.
    pages cm
Includes bibliographical references and index.
ISBN 978-1-61168-466-7 (cloth: alk. paper)
ISBN 978-1-61168-798-9 (pbk.: alk. paper)
ISBN 978-1-61168-799-6 (ebook)
    1. Primaries—New Hampshire—History. 2. Elections—
New Hampshire—History. 3. New Hampshire—Politics and
government. 4. Presidential candidates—United States.
I. Smith, Andrew E. II. Title.
JK2075.N42M66   2015
324.273'1509742—dc23   2015004847

5 4 3 2 1

Contents

Preface

New Hampshire held its first presidential primary in 1916 and has held the first primary in the nomination process since 1920. It is a small state with only 1.4 million people, but anyone with an even a minimal interest in American politics is aware that New Hampshire is the most important contest in securing the presidential nomination. Why that is and how New Hampshire achieved this distinction is the subject of this book. We hope to provide the reader with a comprehensive history of the New Hampshire primary and a detailed portrait of the voters of New Hampshire.

David Moore came to the University of New Hampshire in 1972, founded the UNH Survey Center in 1976, and conducted New Hampshire primary polls between 1976 and 1992 at UNH. He then polled in New Hampshire as senior editor of the Gallup Poll from 1996 through 2004. Andrew Smith became director of the UNH Survey Center in 1999 and has been polling in the primary beginning in 2000 and heading into the 2016 election. Between us, we have more than forty years of experience studying and writing about the New Hampshire primary, which covers the entire post-reform period. Though our names are listed alphabetically, this book represents an equal collaboration in all phases of the project.

There have been numerous critics of New Hampshire's outsized role and calls to reform the nomination process. Many attempts to diminish New Hampshire's status through the process known as "front-loading" have occurred over recent decades.

Regardless of those efforts, the New Hampshire primary will continue to be critical for the next presidential nominees. In the months leading up to the 2016 primary, campaigns will post their best campaign staff to the Granite State, spend tens of millions of dollars campaigning there, and make more campaign visits there than to any other state, except perhaps Iowa. Understanding how this primary works is essential for anyone who wants to understand who will become the two next nominees.

In this book, we cover the history of the New Hampshire primary over the past century, from its beginning in 1916 to its likely role in 2016. We include the battles waged by other states to dislodge New Hampshire from its first-in-the-nation position and highlight the central role played by New Hampshire Secretary of State William Gardner, along with the state chairs of both major political parties, in prevailing over the challengers.

In order to give the reader a broader understanding of the impact that the New Hampshire primary has had in determining the nominee, we describe each of the primary battles since the "beauty contest" was first run in 1952. These vignettes provide the reader an insight into the candidates and issues in each primary contest, the critical turning points of the campaigns, and what factors were most significant in determining the outcome.

To further understand why New Hampshire votes the way it does, we take a look at the demographic characteristics of the voters. We also compare the Republican and Democratic primary electorates to those in other primary states to show how New Hampshire is different and why that might favor or harm particular candidates.

As with any other longstanding historical event, many stories and myths have grown about the primary. We explore a number of these myths — from the "independent" voter, the attentive voter, to the strategic voter — and examine the kernel of truth that has led to these frequently heard descriptions of the primary electorate. We also discuss the myth of grassroots campaigning and the chances that underfunded, outsider candidates can win the primary by focusing their time on the state. Finally, we look at the money the primary brings to the state and show that it hardly merits the envy it engenders among other states.

In recent years, polling in the primary has come under considerable scrutiny. Since most people's understanding of campaign dynamics is rooted on how a candidate fares in the polls, we believe that understanding the difficulties in conducting polls in a primary is worth exploring as a separate topic. The difficulties faced by pollsters are rooted in several critical factors in understanding primary dynamics: most voters who vote in the primary are not wedded to any one candidate, they frequently change their minds regarding who they will vote for, and they will ultimately be happy with whichever candidate wins their party's nomination and will vote for that candidate in the November general election. We encourage readers to be very cautious about what polls say about who is likely to win.

Finally, we look at 2016 and the future of the presidential nomination process and the role the New Hampshire primary is likely to play. After fending off challenges from other states for several decades, it appears that both parties have made their peace with New Hampshire as the first primary. And while nothing is certain, it appears that most other states have also accepted that it is not worth trying to bump New Hampshire from its perch. We look at the alternate plans that have been proposed for reforming the nomination process, their strengths and weaknesses, and the likelihood that any will be enacted.

Acknowledgments

As with any work of political history, we are indebted to the people who have given us their time and insights in helping us accurately describe the primary. We especially want to thank Secretary of State William Gardner; former ambassadors George Bruno, Gerald Carmen and Terry Shumaker; former attorney general Tom Rath; and former Democratic state party chair Kathy Sullivan and former Republican chair Steve Duprey, who both provided rich background on the primary and the machinations that New Hampshire has gone through to keep the primary first. We also want to thank many people who have worked in many primary campaigns for their insights into how things really work. Jamie Burnett, Dave Carney, Ned Helms, Karen Hicks, Jim Morrill, and Rich Killion have been extremely generous in sharing their experience with us. Wayne Steger of DePaul University provided us with excellent suggestions that have greatly improved this project. We especially want to thank our colleague at the University of New Hampshire, Dante Scala, for his help and support on this project. Finally, and most importantly, we want to thank our families for their forbearance and understanding during this project.

THE FIRST PRIMARY

Importance of the New Hampshire Primary

New Hampshire envy is the perception that New Hampshire,
because it holds the first primary in the nation, derives a
substantial array of political and economic benefits from that
position and plays a highly significant role in determining who
ultimately wins the major-party presidential nominations,
despite the fact that it is a small state and is, in important
ways, not particularly representative of the country as a whole.
— William G. Mayer and Andrew E. Busch,
The Front-Loading Problem in Presidential Nominations

New Hampshire Envy

In 1952, New Hampshire held its first primary in which voters could indicate their presidential preference. For the next two decades, as the results of the primary began to shape the nomination process in significant
ways, New Hampshire envy began to fester. After the major reforms to
the process took effect in 1972, which shifted the power of nomination
from party bosses to the voters, the envy blossomed into full-scale re-
sentment, as New Hampshire's increasing influence on the process at the
national level seemed way out of line with its small size.

William Mayer at Northeastern University undertook a systematic
study of the factors that predict how successful candidates are in their
quest for the presidential nomination.[1] The study is somewhat dated now,
since it was published ten years ago and thus excludes the last three elections. Nevertheless, it still provides an insight into the dynamics of the
nomination process for the previous two decades. And it confirms at least

one tenet of New Hampshire envy, that the state plays a highly significant role in determining how many delegates a candidate wins.

In fact, according to Mayer's study of the elections from 1980 through 2000, the two most important predictors of a candidate's overall success were (1) the national poll standings *before* the start of the nomination process (before the start of the Iowa caucuses), and (2) the success of a candidate's campaign in the New Hampshire primary — either a first or second place showing. His model shows that coming in first in the state increases a candidate's expected share of the total primary vote (including all states) by "a remarkable" 27 percentage points, and a second place finish in New Hampshire (in a multi-candidate race) increases the total by 17 points.[2] By contrast, Iowa's contribution to a candidate's success in the nomination process appears to be indirect at best, sometimes helping (but sometimes hurting) a candidate's success in New Hampshire, which could then influence how well the candidate does in the long run. "Of the two highly publicized events that lead off the delegate selection calendar," Mayer notes, "the New Hampshire Primary towers over the Iowa Caucuses in its impact on recent nomination races."[3]

Still, some scholars argue that New Hampshire's importance is fading as more states have moved their primaries up in the schedule, a process referred to as front-loading.[4] States that have moved closer to the front of the nomination calendar hope to increase their influence on the nomination and thereby reduce the impact of the two earliest states. Others argue that front-loading may have increased New Hampshire's importance in the process.[5]

Defenders of the primary say that its small size is a reason that New Hampshire is a good state to begin the nomination process. Candidates with little money can invest their time in grassroots campaigning, and advertising on local television and in local newspapers is within reach of small campaigns that may not be able to afford spots in the extremely expensive large media markets in bigger states. Also, high turnout seems to indicate that New Hampshire voters are more engaged in the nomination process than are voters in other states.

And political reporters like the primary as well — or certainly they like covering the small state of New Hampshire more than they like trying to cover the much more spread-out state of Iowa. Perhaps the clearest articulation of this comes from veteran columnist JulesWitcover:

> The New Hampshire primary has become as much a staple in the national political diet as national conventions, election day in November, or a president's inauguration. . . . Veteran political reporters like New Hampshire because they know all the players in presidential politics down through the years, and the state is so manageable. One can bed down in Manchester for several weeks and travel to most parts of the state and back in a day. It is like going to spring training camp for a major-league baseball player. Here is the place where rookies on the make and veterans trying to prove they have one more season in them test themselves before smaller crowds than they will encounter later down the road.[6]

Importance of the New Hampshire Primary Overrated?

Despite conventional wisdom, there is some evidence that the importance attached to the New Hampshire primary may be overblown. The very same article by William Mayer that reports the towering influence of the New Hampshire primary also contends that the nomination system has evolved into one that highly favors the early front-runners. In the first two elections following adoption of the reforms, George McGovern (1972) and Jimmy Carter (1976) were not the front-runners for the nomination, yet each won his party's nomination. And in 1980 George Bush, also not the front-runner, seemed to have the momentum to win the GOP nomination after his surprise victory over Ronald Reagan in the Iowa caucuses — but he was derailed in New Hampshire. The long-shot candidate Gary Hart in 1984 experienced the same tantalizing hope of winning the nomination after his surprise victory over front-runner Walter Mondale in the New Hampshire primary. But in the end, Mondale won. Still, these early victories and almost victories by long-shot candidates gave the impression that momentum from the New Hampshire primary was an important, and sometimes even determinative, factor in a candidate's quest for the nomination. No longer, says Mayer. "Whatever may have happened in 1972 or 1976, a very different sort of outcome has occurred in every race since then. In the last ten contested nomination races, the candidate who won was the front-runner — or at least *one* of the front-runners — before any of the delegates were selected."[7]

The implications of this development are profound. They suggest that the nomination process is mostly one of confirming what everybody (or at least a plurality) is thinking before even the first vote is cast. In that case, it no longer really matters which state goes first or second in the nomination calendar, because all of the work that is needed to win the primaries — fund-raising, establishing a competitive organization, strategic planning — has already been accomplished, and is reflected in the national polls. Thus, the presumed importance of the New Hampshire primary is really an illusion. The primary is more a reflection of the candidates' strengths more broadly than it is an opportunity for a vulnerable candidate to obtain momentum for the future.

Then came the election of 2008, which contradicts Mayer's model. The Democratic Party's dominant front-runner for all of 2007 and into 2008 was Hillary Clinton, who retained her lead even after the Iowa caucuses, which she lost to the eventual nominee, Barack Obama.[8] And the GOP front-runner for all of 2007 right up until the Iowa caucuses in 2008 was Rudy Giuliani, followed briefly by Mike Huckabee after his surprise win in Iowa, followed by the eventual nominee, John McCain.[9] Both of these nomination races reveal how important the early contests actually were. By winning Iowa, Obama did in fact gain momentum that in the long run helped him prevail. By winning in New Hampshire, Clinton staved off a complete collapse of her candidacy, which almost certainly would have occurred had she lost the primary as well as the caucuses. Similarly, McCain's "comeback" in 2008 was made possible by his victory in New Hampshire, after he had fallen to fourth place in the national polls with only 10 percent support.

The last election cycle also calls into question the prediction that the early front-runner will necessarily (or almost certainly) win the nomination. In 2011, Mitt Romney led in national polls until August, when Rick Perry surged into the lead, before Herman Cain had a temporary fling at being the leader, followed by Newt Gingrich, who was at the top of the polls just before the Iowa caucuses.[10] Romney was not the front-runner as the nomination process began, though eventually he won.

Making Sense of History: The Party Decides?

The common view of the nomination process is that the reforms of the 1970s wrested power away from the parties and gave it to voters, or if not to voters, then to the media and campaign specialists who are able to manipulate voters. In 1968, Hubert Humphrey could win the Democratic Party's nomination without ever entering a primary or caucus contest, because party leaders controlled the delegates who voted in the party convention. And the party leaders wanted Humphrey. In 1972, following the party's reforms, it was no longer possible for candidates to avoid the primaries and caucuses. Now they had to enter those contests in order to win delegates who would be committed to them at the party convention.

That the parties had thus lost power over the nomination process seemed evident. In both 1972 and 1976, the Democratic Party's nominees were not the candidates preferred by the party elite. George McGovern's candidacy led to one of the greatest landslide losses in American history. Jimmy Carter's victory led to major divisions within the party that eventually saw him lose a second term. Similarly, the Republican Party lost control of the nomination process in 1976, when Ronald Reagan challenged the incumbent GOP president, Gerald Ford, and almost won. Typically, parties do not reject their own incumbent presidents. Many argue that Ford's close loss to Carter was aided by the rancorous primary battle.

But some scholars argue that the 1970s were an aberration, a transition period when the party elite had to adjust to the new rules. Yes, temporarily, these scholars argue, the party elite did lose control, but by 1980, the parties were able to reassert their influence over the nomination process.[11] According to this view, the most consequential phase of the process occurs prior to actual voting, during the period from the time a candidate begins the campaign until the Iowa caucuses — the period of the "invisible primary." During this time, candidates vie for funds, endorsements, and activists to work on their campaigns. As Wayne Steger writes, "By rallying around a single candidate, the party establishments help that candidate become the favorite going into the presidential primaries. Through a combination of cue-giving and proxy organizational support, party elites can help a candidate gain advantages in fund-raising, media coverage, organizational support, and possibly public support in and at the polls."[12]

By the time voting begins, a consensus has usually emerged among the party elite regarding which of the candidates is the most preferred, and the subsequent voting merely ratifies the elite's choices.

According to this theory, Iowa and New Hampshire do not exert any special influence, except to the extent that these two states produce winners that conform to the wishes of the party elite. If their winners are not the chosen ones, those winners do not prevail in the long run. Evidence for this idea can be seen in every election cycle from 1980 at least through 2004:

- 1980: George H. W. Bush unexpectedly beat the GOP favorite, Ronald Reagan, in the Iowa caucuses, but Reagan recovered in New Hampshire and eventually won the nomination.
- 1984: Outsider Gary Hart upset the Democratic Party favorite, Walter Mondale, in the New Hampshire primary, but party leaders rallied around Mondale, who eventually got the nomination.
- 1988: George H. W. Bush was the GOP establishment favorite, but he lost to Robert Dole in Iowa. Once again, the favorite recovered in New Hampshire and went on to win the nomination. In the same year, Democratic Party leaders had no favorite, but the leading contenders were all acceptable, so the early contests did shape the nomination process — but only within the comfort zone of the party elite.
- 1992: Once Mario Cuomo declined to run, Bill Clinton became the anointed candidate for the Democrats. Though he lost in New Hampshire, party leaders rallied around his candidacy, and eventually he won the nomination.
- 1996: Robert Dole lost in New Hampshire to Patrick Buchanan, but the GOP was not going to allow Buchanan to be the party's nominee. Even in the conservative state of South Carolina, which should have welcomed a Buchanan candidacy, party leaders rallied to give Dole the victory he needed to get back on track.

- 2000: John McCain won handily over George W. Bush in New Hampshire, but he was a "maverick" the party leaders did not want for their nominee. The GOP establishment rallied behind Bush, helping him win the South Carolina primary and then the nomination.
- 2004: The early Democratic Party favorite was John Kerry, but after his candidacy seemed to be headed for disaster — and with outsider Howard Dean emerging as the likely winner in Iowa — party leaders called on General Wesley Clark to run. In the meantime, some party leaders helped to resuscitate Kerry's campaign in Iowa, and his victory there gave him momentum in New Hampshire, eventually leading to his nomination.

As this brief recap of the nomination contests from 1980 to 2004 indicates, either the two earliest states produced a winner whom the party wanted, or the winners in those states did not go on to win their party's nomination.

In 2008, however, according to these scholars, this theory of party control temporarily broke down with the GOP nomination of John McCain.[13] The party elite preferred Mitt Romney, but McCain's victory in the New Hampshire primary did in fact resuscitate his campaign, which was faltering badly, and gave him the momentum he needed to prevail over Romney and the Republican establishment.

It appears that the theory of party control was also challenged that year by the Democratic Party contest between Hillary Clinton and Barack Obama. Going into the Iowa caucuses, Clinton was the clear favorite among party leaders, but then — according to the authors of *The Party Decides* — Democratic Party leaders changed their minds once Barack Obama won in Iowa.[14] That was not supposed to happen. The party elite were supposed to make up their minds before the voting started and then stick with their collective decision. The authors contend, however, that it was reasonable for many party leaders to switch to Obama, once he had demonstrated that as an African American candidate he could still win in a state that included mostly white voters. After all, Democratic prospects were good for winning the presidency with either a female candidate or an African American one, and many political leaders resented Clinton for her take-no-prisoners style of political combat, while Obama had emerged as an unusually popular politician. Thus, the authors argue, it was understandable, if not predictable, that party leaders might change their minds after Iowa. And the fact that Obama overtook the position of "early favorite" after party leaders changed their minds does not undermine their basic theory of party control. Only the GOP nomination of McCain contradicts that theory.[15]

Then in 2012, the GOP party elite reasserted their control over the process with the victory of Mitt Romney, who prevailed despite not being atop the national polls by the time of the Iowa caucuses. However, he was clearly the better-funded and better-organized candidate.

Ultimately, the authors conclude that

> party insiders are the most important influence on voter decision-making in primaries. This influence is over and above their role in shaping the field of contestants during the invisible primary. A candidate's own popularity and resources also affect voter decision-making, but the preferences of party insiders matter more.

> This conclusion does not imply that the outcomes of primary elections are foreordained in some mechanical fashion. We continue to subscribe to the . . . maxim that presidential nominations are fought and won in primary and caucus elections. Our important addendum is that *the fight takes place on a playing field that tilts in the direction that party insiders want it to.*[16]

For the 2016 election cycle, there appears as of this writing (winter of 2015) to be no clear front-runner for the GOP nomination, while Hillary Clinton (should she decide to run) is the overwhelming front-runner for the Democratic nomination. Given Mayer's model and the overwhelming consensus of the party elite, it would appear that however the press might try to insist that Clinton's nomination is not a sure bet, in fact it is. The New Hampshire primary is likely merely to confirm that outcome, rather than actually contribute to it. For the front-runner-less Republicans, however, the New Hampshire primary and the Iowa caucuses are likely to have profound effects on who eventually wins the nomination. And if Clinton does not run, the two contests are likely to play significant roles in the Democratic Party's nomination process as well.

Regardless of how much the party establishments are able to "tilt the playing field" in favor of their preferred candidates, we know that candidates, political leaders, and — most importantly — the press all believe that the New Hampshire primary is monumentally important. No serious presidential candidate will skip New Hampshire in the belief that a more favorable primary later in the calendar will be more advantageous than competing in the Granite State.

This situation raises a question we do not intend to address: Given the small size and unrepresentative character of the state, *should* New Hampshire be allowed to hold the first primary? That is a question for another book or venue. Here we do not defend New Hampshire's premier position, nor do we condemn it. We recognize it as a fact of life, and that the state is doggedly determined to keep it that way. We are more interested in addressing what *is*, rather than what *should be*.

And the first question is this: How did New Hampshire get and maintain its premier position in the nomination calendar, despite widespread New Hampshire envy and almost universal opposition from other states?

2

Getting the Inside Track

While this book is primarily about the New Hampshire primary, it would be impossible to talk about New Hampshire's premier position in the nomination process without including the even earlier position in the schedule generally enjoyed by the Iowa caucuses. In fact, once Iowa wedged its way into the front, both Republican and Democratic leaders in both states often (though not always) cooperated with each other in their struggles with the Democratic National Committee (DNC) and the Republican National Committee (RNC) to maintain their premier positions.

Of course, there's nothing rational, or fair, or necessarily even beneficial about a presidential nominating process that allows two such small states to hold the first nominating contests every four years. Partisans from both states like to rationalize this controversial arrangement, arguing that candidates have to meet voters one-on-one, providing would-be presidents with insights into the American public they would not get in larger, more media-dominated states. But the actual developments by which these states first came to enjoy their leadoff positions were accidental, generated by a variety of events not at all intended at the time to educate future leaders, and they certainly were not adopted with any expectation that these states would emerge bearing the enormous influence that came with being first. But once Iowa and New Hampshire were first, and once they realized the unfair but extensive advantages that position brought to them, their leaders in both parties fought tenaciously to hold on to being the first out of the gate.

For New Hampshire, the story begins a century ago; for upstart Iowa, the story is more recent — a mere four decades ago. In both cases, the early schedules are the result of a myriad of factors, including the northern climate, historical accident, political friendships, tactics bordering on extortion, and manipulation — with simple stubbornness thrown in for good measure. National leaders from both major parties have denounced the undue influence exerted by Iowa and New Hampshire on the nominating process, and both national parties have made serious efforts to strip the two states of their premier position — but in the end, both parties gave up the fight. Still, in almost every quadrennium, one or more states will attempt to infringe on what Iowa and New Hampshire have now claimed as their "right" to be first. Often, the two states have worked as a team to defeat the challengers. In other cases, Iowa has sided with New Hampshire's opponents. In the end — that is, until now, at least — the two states have succeeded in maintaining their preferred positions.

Origin of the Iowa Presidential Caucuses

From its very beginning as a state when it joined the Union in 1846, Iowa adopted the caucus and convention process by which the political parties nominate their candidates for political office. The state has since adopted primaries for statewide elections. However, it continues to use the caucus and convention method for selecting delegates to the national party conventions, which officially nominate their presidential and vice presidential candidates. Only once did Iowa diverge from that process — in 1916, at the urging of its governor, George Clarke, who wanted Iowa to conduct a presidential primary. It did. But none of the major candidates entered the primary, turnout was low, and the financial cost of holding the primary was high. Clarke called it a "farce," and in an about-face, urged the legislature to trash the primary and return to the caucus and convention method of selecting delegates for the national party conventions. The legislature complied.[1] And that has been the process ever since.

The caucus and convention process is an extended one. It begins with precinct caucuses (meetings) throughout the state (currently Iowa has over 2,000 precincts), where party members participate in discussions about the presidential candidates and other issues and elect delegates to the county convention. Before 1972, few would-be delegates to the county conventions promised allegiance to one presidential candidate or another, but since then, the people who want to be delegates at the next level of the caucus and convention process indicate whom they prefer.

At the county conventions, a similar but more formalized process occurs, resulting in delegates that are elected to attend the congressional district conventions. There, in turn, delegates are elected to their party's state convention. Depending on the political party, presidential delegates (the people who will attend the national party convention, which officially nominates the party's presidential and vice presidential candidates) are elected either at the district conventions or at the state level. The complete selection of presidential delegates is not finalized until late in the spring of the year following the caucuses, and the results for the presidential candidates often differ considerably from what was indicated in the initial caucus meetings several months earlier. As one researcher noted after an extensive analysis of the Iowa caucuses over the years, the Iowa caucus precinct results "are neither valid nor reliable indicators of the presidential preferences of delegates elected to succeeding levels in the caucus and convention process."[2]

Until 1972, the national news media paid virtually no attention to the results of the early precinct meetings in Iowa. The process usually began in March or April, with the Democrats and Republicans adhering to different schedules. There was no way to assess the early results because there was no preference vote among the voters who attended the caucuses, and likewise there was no way to project which presidential candidates might win the most delegates in the final stage of this process, which usually ended in May.

As was the case with most caucus states prior to 1972, party leaders typically exerted tight control over the selection of presidential delegates. Often the dates and times of caucus meetings were announced suddenly, so that only the "in" group would know about them, excluding most of the rank-and-file party supporters from any meaningful participation in the process. Party leaders would attend the national party conventions with mostly uncommitted delegates in tow who would vote the way the party leaders instructed them to when candidates were nominated.

Origin of the New Hampshire Presidential Primary

The Granite State's decision to adopt a presidential primary was born out of the Progressive movement of the late nineteenth century, which, among other societal changes, led to the right of women to vote (as guaranteed by the Twentieth Amendment to the us Constitution). The movement also witnessed the spread of primary elections at all levels within many states in order to replace the power of party bosses. In New Hampshire, for example, the state adopted primaries for local and state elections starting in 1910; in 1913, it instituted a presidential primary to select delegates to attend the parties' presidential nominating conventions. Initially the new law called for the presidential primary to be held in May of each presidential election year, but in 1915, the year before the new law was to take effect, the state legislature decided it could save money if the primary were held on the same day as the traditional town meeting day — the second Tuesday in March.[3]

For over two centuries, New Hampshire's town meetings had been scheduled in mid-March[4] after the most brutal part of winter had passed but before the muddy season would make it difficult to travel from the farms surrounding the town center. And, of course, farmers couldn't take time off in the spring, summer, or fall to attend town meeting, so mid-March was the best time of the year for such activities. Thus it was that the northern clime and Yankee frugality both contributed to New Hampshire's eventual premier position in the presidential nomination process.

In 1916, however, New Hampshire's presidential primary was not the first on the electoral calendar. Indiana held its contest a week earlier, and Minnesota held its election on the same day as New Hampshire. Four years later, widespread disillusionment with the progressive electoral reforms (mostly because of abysmally low turnout) led many states to abandon the primary process, Minnesota and (as noted above) Iowa among them. Indiana retained its primary but moved it to May, leaving New Hampshire to hold the first primary of the year — a position it has maintained now for close to a century.

From 1920 until 1948, the New Hampshire primary consisted of ballots only for delegates to the party conventions. Typically, the delegates would consist of some combination of present or former elected officials, plus other prominent individuals in the state, especially those who held leadership positions in the state's party organization. Most delegates would be "uncommitted," which means that when they attended their party's convention, they would (in theory) decide *then* which presidential candidate to support. In practice, more often than not, they would be told by the leader of the state delegation which candidate to support.

Thus, even though rank-and-file voters were participating in a presidential primary, they never got an opportunity to express their views about the presidential candidates themselves. Instead, they voted merely for delegates to the party convention. During the primary campaign, some would-be delegates might advertise their support for a particular presidential candidate to boost their chances of being selected to attend the party's convention. But others were so well known that they were able to win on the basis of their own popularity.

Then, in 1952, the New Hampshire primary got a major facelift. Three years earlier, New Hampshire Speaker of the House Richard Upton noted criticisms of the primary as "too indirect to be meaningful and . . . frustrating to the average voter, who had only limited opportunity to make known his preference for the office of president." He decided the primary would be "more interesting and meaningful" to voters, resulting in greater turnout, if the names of the presidential candidates themselves were on the ballot. At his instigation, the legislature passed a law specifying that — in addition to the ballots for delegates — there would also be ballots for the presidential candidates. This arrangement was widely referred to as the "beauty contest" because the vote for the presidential candidates had no official impact. Delegates were still selected by a separate vote, so it was theoretically possible that a presidential candidate could win the beauty contest and still not win the most delegates. Some prominent delegates, well-known state leaders in their own right, might well attract more votes than other delegates supporting the candidate preferred by the voters.[5]

Still, right from the beginning, the beauty contest became the event to watch. The results reflected the direct expression of voter preferences for the presidential candidates, and they were widely reported in the news media. Political leaders and pundits generally treated the results with great seriousness, giving New Hampshire much more influence than its small size would otherwise indicate. The state itself is small, and the number of delegates it sends to either of the major party's convention is also small, since each state's delegation size is roughly proportional to population. As a consequence, New Hampshire's influence in the conventions was minimal compared to the vast majority of larger states. But, starting in 1952, the New Hampshire primary — because of its first-in-the-nation status — began to exert an influence on the presidential selection process that was many times greater than the size of its delegation.

Over the next twenty years, the New Hampshire primary remained the first delegate-selection contest in the calendar, the first "real" vote for a presidential candidate. Still, the delegate-selection process itself remained little changed. It was the party conventions that chose the candidates, and while some candidates — such as Democrat Estes Kefauver in 1952 — could arrive at their party's convention having won more delegates through the primaries than any of their competitors, they were by no means guaranteed to win the nomination. That's because less than half the delegates were chosen by primaries. Most were appointed by party bosses in the states or were selected in state conventions largely controlled by party elites (such as in Iowa). At the national party conventions, most of the delegates would vote the way they were told to by the party leaders. That allowed the leaders from the various states to confer and horse-trade in their efforts to find the strongest candidate in the general election. It mattered little what rank-and-file voters from each party across the country might think. What mattered was the collective judgment of the party bosses.

Prelude to Democratic Party Reforms

Objections to this essentially undemocratic nomination process came to a head after the Democratic Party Convention in 1968. Senator Eugene McCarthy of Minnesota, a fierce opponent of the Vietnam War, had challenged President Lyndon B. Johnson in the New Hampshire primary the previous March. Though a little-known political figure, McCarthy galvanized the antiwar movement, attracting volunteers from across the country to campaign in the Granite State. In the March 12 election, he won 42 percent of the vote, compared with 47 percent won by Johnson. In a separate ballot, McCarthy also won 20 of the 24 delegates. The results stunned most observers and prompted New York Senator Robert Kennedy to enter the presidential race just four days later. Then, on March 31, Johnson announced he would not run for reelection. Immediately thereafter, it became clear that Vice President Hubert Humphrey would also become a candidate.

Humphrey waited to make his official announcement until the deadlines for all the state primaries and caucuses had passed, thus precluding the need for him to campaign among rank-and-file voters in any state. McCarthy and Kennedy continued their competition, which culminated in the California primary on April 3. Kennedy won a narrow victory, but he was assassinated immediately after delivering his victory speech. In a raucous party convention that summer in Chicago, Humphrey — supported by the party establishment, including President Johnson — coasted to victory. Ultimately, of course, Humphrey lost to Richard Nixon in the general election, by roughly three-quarters of one percent of the vote.

Disillusioned antiwar Democrats, along with many other party leaders who felt the nomination process needed to become more democratized, supported the establishment of a special commission to propose new rules that would make the delegate-selection process more democratic. Shortly after the 1968 presidential election, the new commission was formed, officially titled the Commission on Party Structure and Delegate Selection. Initially it was chaired by Senator George McGovern and later, after he resigned to run for president, by Representative Donald Fraser — which eventually gave the commission the name by which everyone called it: the McGovern-Fraser Commission.

Party Reforms

The intent of the reforms was to increase participation of rank-and-file party members, and to insure that the full racial, ethnic, and gender diversity of party members was represented in the state delegations to the national convention. Typically, state delegations had consisted mostly of older, white males. The new rules provided guidelines — many critics thought of them as quotas — to achieve the appropriate demographic mix. To accomplish these goals, rules were established that called for more transparency in holding caucuses that would choose the national delegates. Public announcements were required, with reasonable dates and locations of meetings.

The immediate overall impact of the reforms was to change the locus of political power from the party leaders to the party voters. The voters would choose the delegates, either in primary elections or in open state caucuses and subsequent conventions. Ironically, the people who proposed the reforms expected that the net effect would be to increase the use of caucuses, giving voters more opportunity to participate in debate and discussion about the candidates. In fact, however, the net effect was to increase the number of primaries. The main reason for this increase in primaries was that the party leaders could more easily meet all the reform requirements by holding a primary than by sponsoring caucuses.

Iowa Jockeys to Be First

The reforms had little immediate direct impact on the New Hampshire primary, which continued to be scheduled on the second Tuesday of March, town meeting day. But the reforms did bring about significant changes in the Iowa caucuses, which now had to abide by a number of rules to make the process more transparent. The new rules were adopted by, and applied only to, the Democratic Party. Thus, in Iowa, the Democrats had to calculate how they could meet all of the transparency requirements and still meet a schedule that called for the final state convention to be held in mid-May (a date that was determined by the availability of a place to meet). One guideline they adopted was to give at least one month between conventions, to give party workers enough time to consolidate the results of the first meetings and prepare for the subsequent conventions. In 1972, Democrats in Iowa had five major events: the initial caucus meetings, the county conventions, the congressional district conventions, the state statutory convention, and the final state convention. Only if the initial caucuses were held in mid-January, the party officials decided, could the one-month rule work and still allow for the process to finish four months later by the mid-May deadline. Thus, the Democrats scheduled their initial caucuses on January 24, the earliest start of any state's nomination process. Yet, according to author Hugh Winebrenner, "the party leaders maintain that there was no political intent in moving the caucus date forward and confess that they were unaware that the Iowa Democratic caucuses would become the nation's first as a result of the move."[6]

But while Iowa Democrats moved their first caucus precinct meetings to late January, Iowa Republicans did not. Instead, they scheduled their caucuses on April 4. Even if the party leaders had recognized that their Democratic Party cohorts were now the nation's first contest in the nominating process, they wouldn't have thought much about it. The national media had never before paid much attention to the early caucus results, and there was no expectation that the situation would change. After all, the caucus meetings constituted just the first stage of a multistage process that would, only several months later, choose delegates to the national party conventions. Moreover, the fact was that the Iowa caucuses were not designed to produce immediate results for use by the news media, for a variety of reasons:

- There was no way to assess candidate strength among the attendees of the caucuses, because there was no preference vote.
- Even if there had been a preference vote, there was no statewide reporting system to tally such preferences.
- Most of the delegates were not committed to a presidential candidate.
- Even when delegates expressed a preference, they could change their allegiance by the time of the final convention.

- Chronically low turnout generated considerable doubt that the few people who were willing to spend hours in the caucus meetings were representative of the vast majority of voters who did not attend. Only around 7 percent of Iowa Democrats attended the caucuses in 1972.

Despite these problems, George McGovern, who had been co-chair of the McGovern-Fraser Commission that had proposed the reforms and who was now a presidential candidate, quickly recognized the potential importance of the very first contest and began organizing a campaign in the state in the summer of 1971. Later, Edmund Muskie would follow suit. In response to media interest, on election night state Democratic Party officials used results from select precincts to project how many national delegates each presidential candidate would probably receive the following May, given the support that each candidate seemed to enjoy in the caucus meetings. The projection was at best fuzzy, and at worst misleading. The *New York Times* and the *Washington Post* wrote several stories about the Iowa contest between McGovern and Muskie, though most of the national press gave little attention to the results. Still, the fact of Iowa's holding the first nominating contest was now established.

Four years later, after realizing the increased attention Democrats had received in the 1972 caucuses, Iowa Republicans decided to follow the same early schedule. Both parties set the date for their caucuses on January 19. Unlike the Democrats, however, GOP leaders initiated a poll among attendees at the precinct caucuses. It was conducted before the meetings actually took place in order to provide an early indication of the voters' preferences. In fact, it has become analogous to a primary election, in which voters go to the polls, cast their ballots, and go home. The same process occurs for the GOP caucuses: rank-and-file Republicans go to the caucus meetings, have their preferences recorded for the preference poll before the meetings during which they actually discuss the candidates and vote for delegates, and then go home. Not all voters do that, of course, but it's a testament to the importance the state Republican Party puts on its efforts to please the media that such a preelection preference poll was instituted.

In 1976, however, this was process was still new, and GOP officials were unable to organize a complete statewide tallying system for all the state's precincts — more than two thousand in total. They did "randomly" select sixty-two precincts, which called in their results on election night. In subsequent years, they expanded their tallying system to include most of the state's precincts.

The Democrats rejected doing a preference poll, arguing that their system of estimating how many national delegates each candidate would win was a more accurate indicator of candidate support. To provide those estimates, the party established a statewide system to tally delegate totals in each precinct, a system which remains in place to this day. Unlike the GOP results, however, the results from the Democratic Party caucuses are not available until much later in the evening, at the end of the meetings when votes have been cast for delegates.

On the Republican side in 1976, both President Gerald Ford and California Governor Ronald Reagan ignored the Iowa caucuses, but several of the national news media outlets did note the results (showing a narrow win for Ford). Most of the national media attention was focused instead on the results of the Democratic caucuses, which showed Jimmy Carter as the clear winner over his competitors — even though he finished nearly 10 percentage points behind "uncommitted." The next morning after his "victory," he was a guest on the three networks' morning shows, and in the following days he received five times as much post-Iowa television coverage as any other candidate.

While the GOP caucuses received relatively little attention, the exaggerated attention given to the Democratic Party results that year presaged the importance the news media would give to both parties' caucuses in the years to come. The Iowa Caucuses Media Event had arrived. New Hampshire, which had long touted its first-in-the-nation status, had no idea it was about to be upstaged.[7]

New Hampshire Stakes Its Claim to Hold the First Primary

In the immediate aftermath of the Democratic Party reforms adopted in 1971, many state party leaders across the country recognized the heightened importance of the first primary. While New Hampshire had been first, it had never had to fight for that position. But now it did — against a number of emerging rival states.

One state to take action was Nevada. Even before the McGovern-Fraser Commission had met to propose reforms, the Silver State's house and senate had passed a bill establishing its primary the same day as New Hampshire's. At the urging of the New Hampshire speaker of the house, the Granite State's Governor Walter Peterson called Nevada Governor Paul Laxalt to ask him to veto the bill. According to Peterson,[8] Laxalt apparently was sympathetic to the argument that New Hampshire intended to retain its premier position. If Nevada moved its primary up in the schedule, New Hampshire would simply move its primary a week earlier. Laxalt felt that in the end, the only result would be to create ill will with a sister state for no good reason. So he vetoed the bill.

Leaders in other states were not so accommodating. Prior to the 1972 election cycle, when the McGovern-Fraser reforms were to take effect, lawmakers in Rhode Island, Vermont, Alaska, and Florida contemplated scheduling their primaries to compete with New Hampshire's.[9] Ultimately, legislators in Vermont and Rhode Island backed off, and the governor in Alaska vetoed a bill that would have brought presidential candidates and the media to the Land of the Midnight Sun in late February — when it's more like the Land of the Midday Night. Alaska Governor William Eagan wasn't as concerned with creating ill will with a sister state as was Laxalt, but he was skeptical that the publicity surrounding the campaign at that cold, dark time of year would attract new industry and residents to his state.[10]

Florida, however, was a different case. The Sunshine State would be a glorious place for early campaigning, much warmer than New England, making it more attractive both for the candidates and for the journalists who were covering the campaigns. Indeed, Florida legislators asked, "Where do you think presidential candidates would rather be in December, January and February?" The legislators believed they could "steal the limelight from a small cold-climate state."[11]

Florida also had other more substantive attractions: It was a larger state, with many more delegates at stake. And it had a more diverse population than New Hampshire, and thus, arguably, would serve as a better microcosm of the national electorate. Moreover, the state legislature and the governor were in agreement. They enacted a law scheduling the Florida primary for the second Tuesday in March, the same day as New Hampshire's town meeting day and presidential primary.

Political leaders in New Hampshire, however, were ready for the challenge. Once the Florida law was passed, the state legislature moved town meeting day up a full week, to the first Tuesday in March, bringing with it the new date of the New Hampshire primary. It was too late in the legislative process for Florida to react.

There was also consideration in New Hampshire to move its primary ahead of the Iowa caucuses, which the Democrats in that state had scheduled for January. But the prevailing view among the Granite State leaders was to insist only on holding the first primary, not necessarily to hold the first nomination contest. As former governor Hugh Gregg and Secretary of State William Gardner noted, "The state would be in a stronger position later if it protected what it had—nothing less but nothing more."[12] Besides—the reasoning went—caucuses were different and had never received much publicity anyway, so it was unlikely that the Iowa contest would pose much of a threat to New Hampshire's premier position.

Iowa and New Hampshire Solidify Their Claims to Be First

After the 1972 election cycle, there remained serious reservations among party leaders across the country about the fairness of the delegate selection process, with some calling for a national primary as the only way to solve the question of which state would go first. But many critics of that proposal dismissed it as too expensive for most candidates, favoring only the best-known and best-financed political leaders. One suggested compromise was to hold regional primaries, and where better to start than in New England—home of the first primary? For the 1976 presidential campaign season, legislatures in all of the other five New England states considered moving their primaries to the same day as New Hampshire. In the end, only Massachusetts and Vermont actually did so. And once again, the New Hampshire state legislature quickly reacted, this time moving the primary's date to the last Tuesday in February. It uncoupled town meeting day from the primary, which meant that once again town meeting day would be held on the second Tuesday in March, as it is today. The financial savings that accrued from having both contests on the same day gave way to the determination of state leaders to protect the New Hampshire primary's first-in-the-nation status.

The state legislature also took another action that would prove crucial to saving the state's premier position. Portsmouth Representative Jim Splaine, who had sponsored previous legislation to keep the New Hampshire primary first, came up with a new idea. Rather than have the whole legislature wait to see how other states might try to one-up New Hampshire each election year, why not give blanket approval for someone — his first idea was the governor — to schedule the New Hampshire primary as needed to make sure it was first? The governor at the time, Meldrim Thomson, rejected the notion that the governor should do it. Another idea was to have a group of legislators set the date. But the governor was "adamant" that to keep politics out of the process, the authority to set the date of the primary should be assigned to the secretary of state — who, after all, was responsible more generally for the conduct of elections in the state. And so it happened. The new law required the primary to be held on "the first Tuesday in March or on the Tuesday immediately preceding the date on which any other New England state shall hold a similar election, whichever is earlier." Two years later, the legislature deleted the words "New England" to authorize the secretary of state to set the primary date before *any* other state holding a similar election.[13]

After the 1976 election, the Democratic Party took steps to compress the campaign period into a thirteen-week window, from the second Tuesday in March to the second Tuesday in June. Fearing they would lose *their* first-in-the-nation status, Iowa legislators enacted a law requiring their caucuses to be held no later than the second Monday in February, putting their contest eleven days ahead of the New Hampshire primary. Their fears, however, were not realized. The Democratic Party's rules allowed those states that had held their 1976 contests earlier than the dates set for the new window to ask for exceptions. Thus, in 1980, Iowa was allowed to hold its caucuses in January, some five weeks before the New Hampshire primary.[14] That would be the last time the two contests were separated by such a long time span. New Hampshire continued to keep its primary on the last Tuesday in February, one week before primaries in Massachusetts and Vermont. Maine also held its caucuses early, two weeks before the New Hampshire primary, and three weeks after the Iowa caucuses.

Thus, by the 1980 election cycle, Iowa and New Hampshire had successfully staked out their claims to hold the first set of caucuses and the first primary, respectively, with official endorsement from the Democratic Party and a nodding okay (no official opposition) from the Republican Party. Still, many individual states, and even officials from the two major parties, would continue to challenge the premier positions enjoyed by Iowa and New Hampshire. Maintaining their front-of-the-pack status would not be easy.

3

Keeping the Inside Track

In 1976, the New Hampshire secretary of state, Robert Stark, died. The state legislature needed to elect a replacement. The expectation was that a prominent Republican in the state house would win the election. Republicans had a clear majority in both the house and senate, and typically the vote would be along party lines. Each party would caucus to determine who its candidate would be, and then in the overall vote of the legislature, there would be a straight party vote. The Democrats would come up with a candidate, of course, but given their minority status, it was a foregone conclusion that he would lose.

However, several young Republicans in the legislature were not happy with the presumptive GOP choice, Arthur Drake, the chair of the state's House Appropriations Committee. His election by the Republican caucus was virtually assured, which led those young Republican legislators to seek a different solution. One of them was Steven Duprey, who would later serve as state party chair for the GOP and sit on the Republican National Committee. He was friends with Democrat Bill Gardner, also a young house member, who very much wanted to be elected secretary of state. Gardner promised his Republican colleagues that if elected, he would be absolutely impartial in the execution of his duties. Duprey and his party colleagues agreed to support Gardner in the final vote of the whole legislature, though in the GOP caucus, they would go along with the majority in supporting Drake to be the party's nominee. Gardner campaigned vigorously among Democrats to win his party's nomination, and he even campaigned among Republicans. By contrast, Drake essentially did nothing to further his candidacy, fully expecting that he would get the support of all Republicans in the overall vote. No one was more shocked than he when the final secret vote showed Gardner to be the winner.[1]

At the time, Gardner was just twenty-eight years old, the youngest person elected to the state's coveted office. He has now served the longest tenure of any New Hampshire secretary of state, during which time he has been reelected every two years by overwhelming majorities of the state legislature. And he is the only candidate from the minority party to be elected by the majority party. In 1985, after a particularly devastating election for the state Democrats, the GOP speaker of the house indicated she wanted to replace Gardner as secretary of state. There was bipartisan condemnation of this effort; the notion that the secretary of state's office was a partisan position was universally considered anathema. Gardner was easily reelected that year, as he has been every two years since his first victory. More important to the New Hampshire primary, he has sometimes almost single-handedly preserved the state's first-in-the-nation status. If any less skillful or determined person had been in office during some of the challenges to New Hampshire's position, it is not at all clear that New Hampshire would still enjoy the status it does.

An important point to note is that in the decades following the adoption of the party reforms in 1972, there has been a continual increase in the front-loading of primaries, with many states believing that the earlier their contests, the more likely their results will have an impact on the nomination process.[2] In this front-loading process, many states attempted to get ahead of Iowa and New Hampshire, and in one year or another, occasionally they succeeded. Still, for the most part, the two states were able to solidify their early positions in the nomination schedule, using pressure tactics that — in a different context — might be considered extortion.

1984 — The Pesky New England Neighbors

Shortly after the 1980 election, a new Commission on Presidential Nominations, chaired by North Carolina Governor James Hunt — the so-called Hunt Commission — was appointed by the Democratic National

Committee (DNC). Its main goal was to give more power to party leaders, but it was also concerned with the extended length of the nomination process. After many meetings and discussions, the final report of the Hunt Commission recommended that the thirteen-week window be enforced, but in deference to tradition, Iowa and New Hampshire could hold their contests earlier: Iowa fifteen days before the start of the window, New Hampshire seven days. This would force Iowa to hold its caucuses later in the schedule than it had been doing (there were five weeks between the Iowa caucuses and New Hampshire primary in 1980), but still allow the state to hold the first delegate-selection contest. In March 1982, the DNC adopted the recommendations, much to the relief of party officials in Iowa and New Hampshire. All seemed settled for the upcoming election cycle.[3]

Then the trouble began.

Vermont's town meeting day that year was on March 6, the same day as the New Hampshire primary. Vermont intended to hold a statewide straw poll on the presidential candidates, which New Hampshire's secretary of state interpreted as a "similar election" to the New Hampshire primary. Thus, by state law, he felt obligated to move the Granite State's primary date up one week to Tuesday, February 27. Such a move would then leave just one day between the Iowa caucuses (scheduled for Monday, February 26) and the New Hampshire primary, instead of the eight days specified by the DNC. National Democratic Party officials argued that because Vermont's straw poll did not select any delegates — that would happen on April 26, the day scheduled for the Vermont caucuses — the straw poll was *not* a "similar contest," and so the secretary of state, Bill Gardner, should not change the date of the primary.[4]

Gardner argued, however, that while the straw poll was a beauty contest for the Democrats, the Vermont Republicans were actually choosing delegates on the basis of the poll results, and therefore the Vermont straw poll was a de facto primary. And as long as Vermont insisted on this "similar contest" on March 6, New Hampshire would schedule its primary a week earlier.

To emphasize its disagreement with Gardner, the chair of the DNC's Committee on Compliance and Review, Nancy Pelosi (later to become the first female speaker of the US House of Representatives), visited New Hampshire in 1983. She went to Gardner's office and gave him a dressing down that might have terrified a nationally ambitious politico. She warned him that as a young man, he had a great future in the Democratic Party, but that his refusal to comply with the DNC rules would ruin his career. He would never get elected to anything again. Gardner was polite, as he invariably is, but after Pelosi's harangue, he insisted had no choice. The law was the law. Pelosi left Gardner's office and walked down the hallway to the office of the governor, John H. Sununu (later to serve as President George H. W. Bush's first chief of staff). She exhorted Sununu, as chief executive, to order the secretary of state to keep the date of the primary as provided in the DNC rules. Sununu replied, "That's not the way it works here." She fumed, "Well, what the hell kind of state is this anyway?"[5]

With New Hampshire's earlier date and the threat that the primary would occur only one day after the caucuses, the Iowa legislature passed its own protection law that required the Iowa caucuses to begin at least eight days prior to any other nomination event. The fear was that a one-day separation would force candidates to split their time between the two states, and that the New Hampshire primary might well draw much of the attention away from the Iowa caucuses. Moving the caucuses up by a week did not sit well with the DNC's Committee on Compliance and Review, which wanted to take disciplinary action against Iowa, as well as New Hampshire, for violating the rules. The major penalty the DNC could mete out would be to deny seating to some or all of the states' delegates at the national nominating convention. The threat of this action could, presumably, persuade presidential candidates not to participate in the states' contests, thus depriving Iowa and New Hampshire of the attention they so steadfastly sought. Iowa argued that it had been granted the right to hold its caucuses eight days before New Hampshire, so once New Hampshire moved its date forward, Iowa had the right to do so as well. Finally, a compromise was passed by the Committee on Compliance and Review that allowed Iowa to move its caucuses up a week as long as New Hampshire persisted in holding its primary a week early. If New Hampshire relented, Iowa would also.

But Gardner showed no sign of relenting. The compromise let Iowa off the hook, but it didn't help New Hampshire. Moreover, Iowa recognized that if New Hampshire were penalized for its actions, Iowa's position could be weakened as well. Thus, in 1983, according to George Bruno, then chair of New Hampshire's Democratic Party, he and his counterpart in Iowa, Dave Nagel, formed an alliance to push back against the DNC's insistence that Iowa and New Hampshire abide by the DNC's schedule. They would go around the DNC and appeal directly to the candidates themselves.[6]

That strategy came to fruition in October 1983, when party leaders in New Hampshire held a special convention at New Hampshire College in Hooksett to present all the major presidential candidates to party activists. Nagel flew in from Iowa to join Bruno and several other state party leaders to show solidarity and to engage in some not-so-subtle arm-twisting. The Maine Democratic Party chair, Barry Hobbins, joined them in an attempt to persuade Democratic leaders that his own state should be able to hold its caucuses a week before the start of the window, as it had done four years earlier.

In an interview with us, Bruno described the situation:

> As the candidates arrived at the building, we pulled them into the empty room behind the stage and said, "Look, before you go on stage, there's a little matter we'd like to discuss. We're in this dispute with the national party chair and we just want to make sure that as you present your argument to the Democratic faithful in the state, that the primary is secure and that your position is that the primary is secure. . . . We got a thousand New Hampshire Democratic Party activists out in the auditorium waiting to hear you, and I'm going to hold up this piece of paper and tell them who signed it — which candidates favor the New Hampshire primary and which candidates are dissing the New Hampshire primary."[7]

Bruno smiled as he recalled the situation during our interview. "And virtually all of them signed it. You know. Very willingly." What choice did they have?

The paper he asked them to sign was a Memorandum of Understanding, addressed to the chair of the Democratic National Party, Charles Manatt, and to the other members of the DNC. The memo affirmed each candidate's "commitment to New Hampshire's First in the Nation Presidential Primary and to the seating of the delegates chosen in that election by New Hampshire Democrats." It went on to specify the early dates for Iowa, New Hampshire, and Maine, and urged the DNC to resolve the matter expeditiously and that the proposed solution was "in the best interest of the Democratic Party."

Only Florida's Reubin Askew refused to sign. He walked into the room, listened to Bruno, and walked out. One other candidate — Bruno doesn't remember who — protested at first, saying, "Well, I don't know about this. This seems . . ." But in the end, Gary Hart, John Glenn, Ernest Hollings, George McGovern, Walter Mondale, and Alan Cranston, along with the three state party chairs, all signed the memo (Figure 1.1).

Despite this effort, it was not clear whether the Committee on Compliance and Review would continue to insist that New Hampshire be penalized at the convention. The consideration there would be twofold. First, was the state violating Rule 10A that set the time frames for holding the primary? (Clearly it was.) Second, did the state party do all it could to comply with the rule, but was thwarted by state law? State Democrats argued that they were powerless to prevent the secretary of state from setting the primary date outside the window. Their only alternative would have been to withdraw from the state-sponsored election and hold their own primary on March 6 as permitted by Rule 10A. But if that occurred, serious legal problems could arise. The state would not print the ballots, would not monitor the election, and would not certify the results. In a document outlining the legal ramifications of such an election, Gardner stated that "If the National Democratic Party were to insist that presidential primaries be held within a . . . period which would not include the time provided by New Hampshire ROTC 57:1 . . . the New Hampshire Democratic Party would immediately be immersed in a legal problem of major proportions."[8]

On November 3, 1983, state Democratic Party Chair Bruno submitted his final plan to Pelosi and the compliance committee, stating that all efforts to change Gardner's mind about setting the date of the New

MEMORANDUM OF UNDERSTANDING

October 29, 1983

Charles Manatt, Chairman
and Members of the Democratic
National Committee
1625 Massachusetts Avenue, NW
Washington, D.C. 20036

To Chairman Manatt and Members of the
Democratic National Committee:

This is to affirm our strong commitment to New Hampshire's
First in the Nation Presidential Primary and to the seating of
the delegates chosen in that election by New Hampshire Democrats.

We have no interest in, nor will we participate in, any
alternate delegate selection process for the forthcoming Democratic National Convention.

We support the compromise that has been proposed to conduct
the Iowa Caucuses on February 20th, the New Hampshire Presidential
Primary on February 28th, and the Maine Caucuses on March 4th,
1984, and believe these three states should be treated as a unit.

We urge you to resolve this matter expeditiously so that
we can get on with the business of electing a Democrat as President
of the United States and believe that our position promotes the
spirit of the Hunt Commission rules, encourages the broadest
possible voter participation and is in the best interest of the
Democratic Party.

Sincerely,

_____   _____
Gary Hart   Walter Mondale

_____   _____
John Glenn   Alan Cranston

_____   _____
Ernest Hollings   Reubin Askew

_____   _____
George McGovern   Barry Hobbins

_____   _____
David Nagle   George Bruno

Figure 3.1. Memorandum to Charles Manatt from 1984 Democratic primary candidates. *Source:* Courtesy of George Bruno.

Hampshire primary one week earlier than the Vermont primary had failed. Presumably, the state Democrats had made a good faith effort to comply with Rule 10A, which should prevent the state delegation from being penalized — unless the compliance committee expected the state Democrats to hold their own primary, with all of the legal repercussions that could arise.[9]

The New Hampshire primary took place on February 28, as scheduled by Gardner. Though it was out of compliance with Rule 10A, on May 3, 1984, the DNC officially relented and agreed to seat the Iowa and New Hampshire delegations at the national convention. It would not be in the best interests of the party, or of the party's nominee, to have an open-floor fight at the convention over which delegates should be seated.

Although the two states got their way for 1984, they knew that the fight was not over.

1988 — A "Permanent" Fix?

When Mondale lost the 1984 election, Iowa and New Hampshire lost one of their supporters, however coerced he might have been when he signed the Memorandum of Understanding in October 1983. Had he won the presidency, no doubt he would have continued to defend the premier positions that the two states had enjoyed for several election cycles. Now, Nagel and Bruno feared that other states might try to raise the issue with the DNC again. Their strategy was to help elect a new party chair, as is typically done after a presidential election, who would support the early nomination schedule that favored Iowa and New Hampshire. In the winter of 1985, they flew to Charleston, West Virginia, for a meeting of the DNC where all of the candidates for national party chair were presenting themselves. Bruno remembers that a blizzard was raging that day, and he couldn't see anything outside the small, single-engine plane as it descended to the airport. He thought to himself, "Geez, I'm risking my life to save the New Hampshire primary!" He smiled at us while recalling the memory and added quickly, "But it was worth it!"[10]

At the meeting, he and Nagel decided to approach Paul Kirk, then the party's treasurer and a strong candidate for chair. They promised him that if he would support their two states' efforts to remain first in the nomination process, they would support his candidacy and would try to persuade other state delegations to support him as well. Bruno acknowledges that he and Nagel had little clout compared with party chairs from states like New York and California, but the election for national party chair would be close and they—and whatever allies they could muster—might provide Kirk the margin of victory. Kirk agreed to the bargain. He was from Massachusetts, so the sell was probably not that difficult anyway. After he won the election, Nagel and Bruno went back to him, and he reaffirmed the agreement, telling them the party was not going to have any more fights over Iowa and New Hampshire.

But while the DNC backed off, other states took up the fight. South Dakota moved its 1988 primary to February 23, the day the DNC had scheduled for the New Hampshire primary. Minnesota moved their first caucus meetings to that same date. The Democratic Party pressured the two states to hold their contests within the thirteen-week window, but to no avail. When New Hampshire moved its contest up one week, Iowa did the same.[11]

In the end, however, Iowa and New Hampshire were not to be the first contests that year. The GOP in Michigan took the unusual step of holding a nonbinding presidential primary two years early, in August 1986, with subsequent caucus meetings on January 14, 1988—to make Michigan the first to have presidential voting results, more than three weeks ahead of Iowa. Kansas Republicans, too, decided to hold their caucuses early, to launch the presidential candidacy of their state's favored son, US Senator Bob Dole. The caucuses lasted a week, with the results announced the day before the Iowa caucuses. Even the Hawaiian Republican caucuses upstaged Iowa by four days. No Democratic contests were held before Iowa.

It appears, however, that the efforts to upstage Iowa were minimally successful. There was little media attention given to the "upstart" contests, as "the news media clearly regarded Iowa's precinct caucuses as the first real test of the 1988 nominating process."[12] Even the news media had come to defend the premier positions of Iowa and New Hampshire.

1992 — Little Change

In the previous election cycle, Michigan Republicans had started their nominating activities two years early, but in 1992 — along with Michigan

Democrats—they held their primary in mid-March. Once again, the press treated Iowa and New Hampshire as first in the starting blocks for the presidential race.

One major change adopted by the Democratic Party was to widen the delegate-selection window so that it would now start in the first week, rather than the second week, in March—thus leading to greater front-loading of contests. Thirty-one states held their contests before the end of March.[13]

1996 — Delaware, Arizona, Louisiana, Ohio, and Alaska Challenge the Status Quo

In 1995, Delaware passed a law moving the state's primary to the fourth Saturday in February, which would be just four days following the expected date of the New Hampshire primary. This posed a challenge to New Hampshire's tradition of holding its primary at least seven days before a similar contest. While he was considering his options, Secretary of State Gardner was surprised to learn of another problem: in 1992, Arizona had enacted a law for the next presidential election that would hold a presidential primary on the same day as the New Hampshire primary. It wasn't clear how Arizona could enforce this law, since New Hampshire would simply wait until Arizona had set its date and then set its own date at least a week earlier. And, indeed, perhaps recognizing the impossibility of competing with New Hampshire in such a contest, Arizona's leaders eventually expressed a willingness to follow New Hampshire by a couple of days, though not a full week. Essentially, Arizona would be competing with Delaware to become the second primary in the nomination process, while New Hampshire was insisting not only on being first but also on a week-long buffer period after its own primary.[14]

The state statute itself did not prescribe a seven-day buffer period, though Gardner and the original sponsor of the law, Jim Splaine, both insisted that had been the intent of the law. Indeed, the DNC rules that allowed New Hampshire and Iowa to hold their contests outside the window explicitly gave New Hampshire a seven-day advance start and Iowa fifteen days. Still, to make it clear that Gardner had the legal authority to insist on the week-long buffer, Splaine sponsored a bill in March 1995 to amend the original law, so that now it required the presidential primary election "to be held on the second Tuesday in March or on a date selected by the secretary of state which is 7 days or more immediately preceding the date on which any other state shall hold a similar election. . . ."[15]

In the meantime, the state's GOP chair, Steve Duprey, employed the same extortion-like tactics that his Democratic Party counterpart did in 1983 — pressuring the Republican presidential candidates to sign a statement affirming New Hampshire's premier status by not participating in any other primary that did not follow New Hampshire's contest by at least seven days. If they didn't sign, he told them, they might as well not campaign in the state. Not only would voters turn against the candidates for slighting the state's tradition, but it would be difficult to recruit state party activists who would help organize the candidates' campaigns.[16]

While the tactic produced immediate support from Senators Bob Dole and Lamar Alexander, perhaps the most important influence in getting Arizona to abandon its challenge was the fact that Arizona was subject to the 1965 Voting Rights Act. It required Arizona (and eight other states) to get federal approval for any change in their voting laws. Arizona would have to file its changes with the Department of Justice in Washington, DC, wait for approval, and then print and distribute ballots. The process would give New Hampshire plenty of time to move its primary date up by a week.[17]

Thus, Arizona repealed its law requiring its primary to be held on the same day as New Hampshire's, with the Republicans holding their primary on February 27, a week following the New Hampshire primary, and the Democrats holding their caucuses in March, within the DNC-prescribed window.

This solution meant that once again, as it did in 1992, New Hampshire could schedule its contest in the third week of February — except for the fact that Delaware's primary would follow only four, not seven, days later. There was considerable pressure from the Democratic Party, of course, not to move the New Hampshire primary any earlier. Under pressure from the state's GOP leaders, all but two of the major Republican presidential candidates had vowed not to campaign in Delaware. But Gardner was waiting to see what President Clinton would do. When Clinton finally announced he would ignore the Delaware contest and respect New Hampshire's tradition, Gardner agreed that the Delaware primary was not a "similar contest" and set the date of the New Hampshire primary on February 20. Iowa moved their caucuses eight days earlier, and the Delaware primary followed New Hampshire by just the four days.[18]

That election year saw other violations of the "rights" that Iowa and New Hampshire had unilaterally declared. The Ohio Democrats took the unusual step of holding caucuses in January, ahead of Iowa, to show their early support for President Clinton. That was the first time that any Democratic contest had preceded the Iowa caucuses. But given the lack of a viable challenger, the exercise was primarily symbolic — and intended as such. President Clinton gave a special address to the caucuses, reminding them how "Ohio is very special to me."[19]

Also, Alaska's Republicans held a nonbinding straw poll in January, as they started their caucus process, and Louisiana's Republicans held their caucuses six days before Iowa in an attempt to further the candidacy of Texas Senator Phil Gramm. But absent the participation of most of the GOP candidates, these contests received little media attention, with the Iowa caucuses still treated by the news media as the start of the nomination process.

2000 — The Delaware Challenge, Gardner under Fire from His Own Governor

The three states that held their caucuses ahead of Iowa in 1996 changed their contests in 2000 to follow both Iowa and New Hampshire.[20] The early dates had not been successful in garnering the type of media attention the states wanted, nor in influencing the nature of the nomination contest. But their failures did not deter South Carolina Republicans in 2000 from moving their primary date to compete with New Hampshire's. Since 1980, when GOP political guru Lee Atwater helped establish it, the South Carolina primary had typically been the first primary in the South. But in 1992, Georgia and Maryland went ahead of South Carolina, and in 1996, South Carolina preceded those two states by just three days. Then in 2000, when California, New York, and Ohio moved up to join Georgia, Maryland, Massachusetts, Missouri, Maine, Vermont, and Rhode Island on Super Tuesday — all of their primaries were scheduled for March 7 — South Carolina Republicans leaped forward in the schedule, distancing themselves from the Super Tuesday states and landing in front of Arizona, Michigan, and Virginia. The new date for the Palmetto State primary would be the fourth Saturday in February, just four days after New Hampshire.

The move caused considerable consternation among party officials, but it didn't bother New Hampshire's secretary of state, Bill Gardner. His mission was clear: keep the state's primary first by a margin of seven days. Since South Carolina scheduled its Republican primary on Saturday, February 19, New Hampshire would have to schedule its primary on Tuesday, February 8. This meant Iowa would have to reschedule its caucuses to January 31. No problem, as far as New Hampshire was concerned. But it did cause some disgruntlement in Iowa, which had already set its date for February 14 with the assumption that the New Hampshire primary would be held February 22, the fourth Tuesday in February, as specified by the DNC rules.

By early September 1999, however, Gardner still had not officially set February 8 as the date for the New Hampshire primary. Iowa had already set the date for its caucuses, anticipating that Gardner would eventually move the New Hampshire date up because of South Carolina. But Gardner was waiting to see what Delaware and other states would do. Though Delaware's Democrats decided to comply with DNC rules and hold caucuses in late March to be within the specified window, the state's Republicans were still set on an early primary — specifically on the same date as the New Hampshire primary, anticipated to be February 8. They recognized that in 1996 they had failed to get media attention and influence the nomination process because all of the major candidates had not campaigned in their state. This time, pursuant to a law they had passed four years earlier, they would put the names of all the candidates on the ballot, whether or not they filed to run, as long as they had received some federal matching funds. A candidate's acceptance of the funds indicated his intent to run for president, giving the party justification for putting his name on the ballot.

Much to their dismay, however, the clear front-runner for the GOP nomination, George W. Bush, refused to accept federal matching funds, which meant (according to their state law) his name could not be placed on the Delaware ballot without his permission. A primary without Bush's participation would, once again, be a non-event. Thus, Delaware Republicans were anxiously awaiting the Bush campaign's decision as to whether he would run in the Delaware primary if it were held on the same day as the New Hampshire primary. According to Tom Rath, who was on the Republican National Committee (RNC) rules committee at the time, Bush's campaign staff members were in close contact with GOP leaders in New Hampshire, and finally the campaign announced it would respect New Hampshire's first-in-the-nation tradition. If the Delaware and New Hampshire primaries were on the same date, Bush would not file for the Delaware primary.[21]

This announcement posed a problem for the Delaware GOP, which had been counting all along on the February 8 date. Because they could not get support from Democrats to run a state-supported primary, the Republicans would have to conduct the primary on their own. And from a logistical point of view, they were locked into the February 8 date. For this reason they would be quite happy if New Hampshire were to move its primary up a week, because it would mean Bush would enter the Delaware primary, giving it the full legitimacy they wanted. They were in constant contact with Gardner, indicating to him confidentially in mid-September that indeed they did intend to schedule their primary on February 8. Publically, Gardner could not reveal this information, but armed with this knowledge, on September 28, 1999, he announced the New Hampshire primary date of February 1, 2000.

The announcement stunned political leaders in New Hampshire and Iowa as well as national leaders who had scheduled debates in both states under the assumption the primary would be held on February 8. (Not to mention, it surprised hotel managers who had been planning for a later date.) The new date was particularly troublesome to Iowa, which wanted to insure that its caucuses would be held at least eight days before the New Hampshire primary. The new date would force the caucuses to be held on January 24, rather than January 31 — the date that had been announced weeks earlier.

Harsh criticism came from all directions. Several days later, New Hampshire's Governor Jeanne Shaheen called a meeting with Gardner and the state's prominent political leaders, all of whom tried to persuade the secretary of state to change the date back to the second Tuesday in February. Shaheen cited the difficulty that Iowa would have in adjusting to the new date, and she argued that national political leaders were also upset with New Hampshire. In the long run this sudden change could threaten the state's ability to get approval from the parties to hold the state's primary outside the normal thirteen-week window.

Gardner insisted to the group that by law his duty was to protect the state's primary premier status, and he believed the Delaware GOP would schedule its primary on February 8. If Iowa wanted to maintain an eight-day buffer between its caucuses and the New Hampshire primary, Gardner argued, Iowa leaders had only themselves to blame. Before scheduling their caucuses, they should have waited to see what other states would do. Iowa was not his problem. His mission was to protect the state's primary, not the Iowa caucuses.

In our interview with him, Gardner noted that most political leaders at the time seemed convinced that the Republicans in Delaware would not persist in holding a primary on February 8 because of Bush's refusal to run in the contest. And even if the GOP did persist, many leaders agreed with the sentiments expressed by Iowa Secretary of State Chet Carver, who felt Gardner should rule the GOP Delaware primary to be a "non-similar" contest as he did in 1996. After all, most of the GOP candidates said they would not campaign in the state, including the presumptive front-runner. But to Gardner, the Delaware primary was in fact similar, because it officially included all candidates but one. And to ignore it would be to set a precedent that would undermine the legitimacy of New Hampshire's claim to a seven-day buffer. In his view, he was required by law to set the date of the primary "at least seven days earlier" than any similar contest, regardless of what political leaders might want—even those in his own state. And so he did.

Still, both of New Hampshire's state party chairs criticized Gardner, as did both GOP and Democratic Party leaders in Iowa. Never before had both state's party leaders from both states denounced the secretary of state for taking steps he believed were needed to protect the state's primary. On October 1, a private meeting was held in Manchester with members of an Iowa delegation and with New Hampshire party leaders— all calling upon Gardner to relent, because of the terrible adjustment that Iowa would have to make if it were to preserve the eight-day buffer between the Iowa caucuses and the New Hampshire primary. Gardner held fast.

The next week, Governor Shaheen walked down the hall of the state house from her office to Gardner's, to plead with him to change his mind. Again, he refused. A few days later, she convened a meeting of top legislative leaders to explore the possibility of enacting a new law stripping Gardner of authority to set the date of the primary. The leaders in attendance agreed with the tactic, but an informal poll of legislators later revealed little sentiment in the house and senate for such a bill. It would not pass.

While Iowa leaders continued to criticize New Hampshire, they were in somewhat of a bind. Given the new date of the New Hampshire primary, their own state law required them to move their caucuses to January 24. But Iowa Secretary of State Chet Culver issued a statement to the press, arguing that despite the February 1 date of the New Hampshire primary, Iowa would still hold its caucuses on January 31, just one day earlier. "If the Republican National Committee and the Democratic National Committee decide not to seat delegates from New Hampshire, then we would not be in violation of the Iowa law. We could have it on the 31st."[22]

After Shaheen's last-ditch effort with legislative leaders to force a change in the February 1 date failed, opposition in New Hampshire collapsed. Instead, the state party chairs and Shaheen issued a statement acknowledging that "Secretary Gardner's decision will stand, and we must now focus our efforts on protecting our primary."[23]

And in Iowa, sentiment also began to change. Leaders there recognized that if the New Hampshire primary were to be held just one day after the Iowa caucuses, the latter would receive far less media attention than it would otherwise. Moreover, the one-day buffer would set a precedent that would undermine Iowa's "right" to the longer eight-day buffer in the future. "Once you give it up," Iowa's Dave Nagel warned his colleagues, "you'll never get it back."[24] Recognizing that their efforts to force a change in New Hampshire would not work, Iowa's leaders finally moved the date of their caucuses back one week. The horrible consequences that were predicted did not come to pass. Apparently, there was a lot of posturing by Iowa's leaders, which Iowa Governor Tom Vilsack acknowledged — indicating that his tough stance was a "bargaining ploy." But, he claimed, it was not his idea. "The governor of New Hampshire essentially wanted me to take that line in terms of her ability to talk to the legislature. I'm a team player." Shaheen's office denied the claim.[25]

In the end, both national party committees seated all the delegates from Iowa and New Hampshire. The premier status of the two states had prevailed — thanks to the stubbornness of Secretary of State William Gardner.

2004 — The Delaware Plan

Though the Delaware Republicans may have benefitted in 2000 from Gardner's decision to move the New Hampshire primary up a week, thus ensuring Bush would enter the Delaware primary, they were not satisfied with the nomination schedule. For the 2004 process, they proposed a new system of four primaries, grouped by population size. The group of smallest states would vote first in March, followed by groups of increasingly larger states voting in April, May, and June. The national GOP party chair, Bill Brock, agreed to the plan (which later became known as the Brock Plan), and presented it to the rules committee of the RNC. According to New Hampshire attorney Tom Rath, the plan did not insure that

Iowa and New Hampshire would be granted exceptions allowing them to maintain their premier positions in the nomination process. He was on the rules committee and opposed the plan, but to no avail. It was adopted and forwarded to the rules committee of the party's 2000 presidential nominating convention, only a few days away. In the end, the delegates at the convention would have to approve the plan for it to take effect the following election cycle.[26]

As Rath tells the story, there is considerable overlap between the members of the RNC rules committee and the members of the convention rules committee. As it turns out, he was on both committees. The day after the RNC rules committee had overwhelmingly approved the Brock Plan, the very same members that had strongly supported the plan now voted against it when it was officially considered by the convention rules committee. Why the turnabout? According to Rath, it was Karl Rove — acting on behalf of George W. Bush — who nixed the plan. In part, Rove could have been acting in order to preserve New Hampshire's first-in-the-nation primary, as Rath suggests, but other observers suggest Bush and Rove were concerned principally about the possible disruption of the convention over the proposal. It represented a massive intervention into the rights of states to conduct their contests as they chose, forcing the most-populated states back to June contests, and significantly affecting many states' prerogatives. Polls suggested the presidential election of 2000 would be close, and the last thing the Republicans needed as they launched their campaign was a convention in turmoil.

Whatever the motivations of Bush and Rove, the end result was the preservation of Iowa's and New Hampshire's premier positions.

Another important development was the DNC's decision to follow the example of the Republicans in allowing states to hold their contests in February — something the RNC had first allowed with the 2004 election cycle. With both parties in agreement on this point, the front-loading process would see February as the new March. When rogue states would jump into late January, Iowa and New Hampshire would get squeezed closer and closer to the beginning of the year.

2008 — The "Carve-Out" States and Great Turmoil

Just prior to the 2004 election, like they had in 1984, New Hampshire Democratic Party officials strong-armed the top candidates to affirm their support for New Hampshire continuing to serve as the first primary state. In a letter to DNC Chairman Terry McAuliffe dated January 24, 2004, Wesley Clark, Howard Dean, John Edwards, John Kerry, Dennis Kucinich, and Joe Lieberman signed to protect the positions of Iowa and New Hampshire. They had little choice, not wanting to offend voters before they headed to the polls just three days later on the 27th!

Heading into the 2008 election cycle, the DNC, according to Kathy Sullivan, then the chair of the New Hampshire Democratic Party, was on a path to moving the Nevada caucuses up in the calendar, giving it special status like that enjoyed by Iowa and New Hampshire. The DNC also had to deal with continuing pressure from South Carolina, which had long claimed its right to be the first southern primary. Different proposals being considered by the DNC had Nevada competing with Iowa to be first, or scheduling Nevada after Iowa but before New Hampshire. Another plan called for South Carolina to have its primary on the same day as New Hampshire. Sullivan recounts that attending the DNC rules committee meetings was "painful," even "brutal," since there was so little support for the special positions enjoyed by Iowa and New Hampshire. At one point, the new national party chair, Howard Dean, told Sullivan he thought he might be able to save New Hampshire, but not necessarily Iowa.[27]

The Democrats' argument for putting Nevada early in the process is that it's a strong union state. According to Sullivan, labor organizers wanted candidates to have to campaign in a state that reflected the concerns of union members. Nevada also happened to be the home state of the US Senate majority leader, Harry Reid, though Sullivan said she never heard any suggestion that Reid personally was behind the push for Nevada. Another attraction of Nevada was that it had a large proportion of Hispanic voters. Also, it was a western state, thus giving it a "three-fer" — three characteristics that could balance some of the shortcomings of Iowa and New Hampshire.

To round out the geographical component of the early contests, Democrats were amenable to South Carolina's desire to be the first southern primary. Another advantage from the Democrats' view was that the state also includes large numbers of racial minorities. Thus, the four "carve-out" states now included all four regions of the country, an attractive feature to both political parties. For the Democrats, the diversity feature of the two additional states also helped justify their inclusion. From the perspectives of Iowa and New Hampshire, this new development helped to solidify their premier positions, for now there was official acknowledgement that Iowa and New Hampshire would go first, followed by Nevada and South Carolina. That also meant there were four states that had a stake in preserving this "tradition," and the racial and geographical components mitigated the arguments against Iowa and New Hampshire.

Thus, by the fall of 2007, the DNC schedule had the Iowa caucuses going first on January 14, Nevada five days later, New Hampshire three days after that, and South Carolina on January 29 — a week after New Hampshire. No one knew whether New Hampshire's secretary of state would go along with the schedule, since he was treating any delegate-selection contest, except for Iowa's, as a "similar" event, and might thus justify moving the New Hampshire primary further up in the schedule (ahead of Nevada). But before he could officially address the issue, Florida intervened, shaking up the whole schedule.

Not content with being ignored, Florida announced its primary date would be January 29, the same day as the South Carolina primary. The Democrats in South Carolina decided against taking any retaliatory action, but the Republicans were not so accommodating. On August 9, 2007, South Carolina's GOP chair, Katon Dawson, appeared with New Hampshire Secretary of State Bill Gardner at the New Hampshire statehouse to announce that South Carolina Republicans would hold their presidential primary on January 19, 2008. The unusual step of making this announcement in New Hampshire, rather than in his own state, was to show solidarity between the two states, which — according to Dawson — were allies in protecting the "traditional" early role of both states in the nomination process. "This date will help solidify a combined 83-year history of being first in the nation and first in the south," he announced.[28] By tying in with New Hampshire, Dawson was hoping to add legitimacy to his claim.

In his interview with us, Gardner said that his appearance with Dawson did not constitute an endorsement of the South Carolina move. He was simply being a polite host. Gardner's only concern, he says, was to maintain New Hampshire's premier status, and this move by South Carolina clearly affected the date for which he would schedule the New Hampshire primary. According to New Hampshire law, South Carolina's action meant he had to move the primary up to January 8, the Tuesday in the previous week. In turn, that meant Iowa would have to move its caucuses eight days earlier — to December 31, New Year's Eve. Even worse was a threat by Michigan to move its primary to the same day as New Hampshire. Gardner made it clear that, if necessary, he would move the New Hampshire primary to before Christmas. Iowa's secretary of state indicated to Gardner confidentially that Iowa could not possibly do the same, and asked if Gardner would take such a situation — where New Hampshire would precede Iowa — as a precedent. Gardner promised he would not.[29]

Eventually, Michigan decided to schedule its primary on the Tuesday before South Carolina, but a week after New Hampshire. That left Iowa facing a bit of a dilemma. Its own law required an eight-day buffer from any other delegate-selection contest, but to hold its caucuses on New Year's Eve, or earlier during the Christmas holiday, was a nonstarter. New Year's Day was not any better, and even the day after was highly problematic. Ultimately, it appeared that Wednesday, January 3, would be the earliest the caucuses could be held. Again, Gardner indicated that he would not take the shorter buffer — just five days between the two contests instead of the eight allowed by the DNC — as a precedent for future years.

The final schedule had the Iowa caucuses on January 3; the GOP Wyoming caucuses starting on January 5; New Hampshire on January 8; the Michigan primary on January 15; and the Nevada caucuses and GOP South Carolina primary on January 19. The Wyoming results received little media attention, and that state's delegation was stripped of half its members at the national convention. The two parties also penalized the respective Michigan delegations at the national conventions. In 2012, both states would comply with their respective party's scheduling rules, leaving the carve-out states their special positions at the front of the delegate-selection process.

2012 — Reducing Front-Loading

During the long primary battle between Barack Obama and Hillary Clinton in 2008, many Democrats were concerned that the "bloodletting" would hurt the eventual nominee in the general election. Contrary to expectations, however, the long contest was eventually viewed as a positive contribution to Obama's success in the fall, because of the organizational efforts that had been made during the primary season. While John McCain had essentially won the nomination in March, by law he could not raise money for the general election until he was the official nominee — and that would not happen until September. In the meantime, Democrats were getting lots of free media attention, and in the process were using the primary and caucus state contests to organize the states for the general election.

This perception of the benefits of a long primary season apparently led GOP officials to try to lengthen the primary season. And they had cooperation from the Democratic Party, the first time that the two parties had worked together on the delegate-selection calendar. The efforts resulted in a more even distribution of events over the period from February through June.[30] Still, that did not prevent Florida from once again flouting party rules and scheduling its primary at the end of January. In turn, the four carve-out states all moved their contests up in the schedule, with Nevada Republicans voting to hold their caucuses in mid-January. That was not acceptable to New Hampshire's secretary of state, who said that if necessary he would schedule the New Hampshire primary in early December. Under pressure from the national GOP, Nevada Republicans moved their caucuses back to the beginning of February, allowing Iowa (January 3), New Hampshire (January 10) and South Carolina (January 21) to go before Florida (January 31).[31]

2016 — The Saga Continues

As of this writing, the dates for the 2016 Iowa caucuses and New Hampshire primary have not yet been officially set, although both parties have given Iowa and New Hampshire permission to go first. Iowa is savvy now, waiting until Gardner sets the date for New Hampshire before finalizing a schedule for its caucuses. And Gardner will wait until all of the other states have their schedules firmly committed before announcing his own.

Already, the Utah House of Representatives passed a bill requiring its state to hold the first primary. To give it a competitive edge over New Hampshire, which typically can wait until the last minute to make its decision, the bill provided for electronic voting. That would presumably give the state more flexibility in scheduling, since it wouldn't have to distribute ballots and deal with other last-minute logistical problems in holding an election. However, the bill died because the Utah State Senate did not vote on it. It's unclear at this time if political leaders in the state intend to refile the bill in a subsequent session. The bill's author, Representative Jon Cox, told the *Des Moines Register* that the current nomination process is unfair and creates "second class states." The only way to try to change the system, he asserted, is for a state to try to cut in line.[32]

His views are no doubt shared by many people across the country, who simply cannot understand why Iowa and New Hampshire, and now South Carolina and Nevada, should be accorded special status. As these last two chapters make clear, the "should" question cannot be answered satisfactorily. Which states should go first, or whether all should go at the same time, or whether there should be some other nominating system entirely are all complex questions on which there is little agreement. *How* it happened that Iowa and New Hampshire and Nevada and South Carolina emerged as the carve-out states, however, is a question we've hopefully answered with some degree of clarity. What the political process might produce in the next several election cycles we address in the final chapter.

History of the New Hampshire Primary prior to Party Reforms

Although the New Hampshire primary has been conducted every quadrennium for the past one hundred years, hardly anyone cares about what happened during the first third of that century. From 1916 through 1948, New Hampshire voters selected delegates who would attend their party's presidential nomination convention, but no one outside the state cared much about the results. The state's delegations to each party's convention were so small, they had hardly any significant influence on the nomination process.

Starting in 1952, when the beauty contest was added to the ballot for delegates, New Hampshire voters could directly express their preference for one candidate or another. Those results, amplified by the news media, made the primary a more interesting event to follow. Because the New Hampshire primary was the first expression of voters in the nomination process, the results took on a significance far beyond the mere numbers of voters involved. Rightly or wrongly (and we incline partly toward the latter judgment), politicians and pundits would generalize from the primary results to the wider electoral viability of candidates who participated. At first, a candidate's performance in the New Hampshire primary was treated cautiously, as perhaps a general indicator of how a candidate might be received in the larger American electorate. But eventually the dynamics of the nomination process changed, especially after the party reforms of the 1970s. Early success in the primaries and caucuses generated enthusiasm and money and additional workers, often giving the early successful candidates the resources to continue the quest.

Over the decades, the nature of the New Hampshire primary has evolved from one where well-known candidates (like Dwight D. Eisenhower and Henry Cabot Lodge) could win without ever setting foot in the state, to one where candidates (like Jimmy Carter and Ronald Reagan) had to engage in one-on-one campaigning to win, to one where candidates (like Hillary Clinton and Mitt Romney) relied more on mass rallies and television ads than on retail politicking to obtain victory. This is not to say that campaigning today for the New Hampshire primary is like campaigning in other primary states, where the candidates make brief stopovers, deliver a stock speech that indicates how much they appreciate whatever that particular state is known for and how much they would like that state's support, and then fly off to the next destination. Because New Hampshire is the second contest, and because there is a mandated week buffer around it (the Iowa caucuses typically eight days before, no other primary within a week afterward), candidates have to focus on the electorate in a way they cannot afford to do in subsequent state contests. Still, it's important to recognize how much the nature of campaigning in the state has changed over the past two-thirds of a century.

In this chapter, we review each of the New Hampshire primary contests from 1952 through 1968 — that is, the era prior to the adoption of party reforms that essentially transferred power from party bosses to the news media and the voters (and more recently, to the wealthy contributors who dominate the electoral process). We will show how the addition of the beauty contest to the delegate selection vote in 1952 affected the nomination process in significant and lasting ways. In the subsequent chapter, we'll examine how the impact of the New Hampshire primary has changed since the adoption of the Democratic Party reforms first instituted in 1972, with the primary becoming more important in the nomination process even as political forces outside the state tried to curtail its influence. The description may also give readers insight into why — despite the blatant unfairness of the process that gives such special attention to this small, mostly white, not very urbanized northern

state — there is a subtle conspiracy within the press and among democrats (note the small "d") to protect New Hampshire's premier position.[1]

1952 — New Hampshire's First Beauty Contest Makes History

The first presidential beauty contest that New Hampshire ever hosted
turned out to be a strange set of events. The Republican candidate who
won refused to campaign, relying solely on surrogates, while his major
challenger who did campaign in the state lost — in part, it appears, because of his personal campaign appearances. On the other hand, the
Democratic candidate who won really didn't want to win, and felt that in
the long run his primary victory hurt his chances to be president rather
than helped them. That was not the way the primary was supposed to
work, but as we shall see, reforms can have unintended consequences that
may thwart the best intentions of the reformers.

Republican Primary

The two major GOP candidates that year were Senator Robert Taft from
Ohio, known as Mr. Republican, and General Dwight D. Eisenhower,
who was the Supreme Allied Commander Europe for NATO at the time
his name was on the ballot. In 1950, President Harry Truman had asked
the general to give up his position as president of Columbia University,
which Eisenhower had assumed after retiring from the army, and return to active duty in order to help establish the nascent military alliance
with European countries. Many political leaders from both major parties
had approached Eisenhower over the years, requesting that he run for
president, but he was steadfast in his refusal to consider it. Truman had
made it clear even in 1945 at the Potsdam Conference that the general
could count on his support if Eisenhower wanted to run as a Democrat
in 1948. That didn't happen, of course, and Truman won an improbable
victory over New York Governor Thomas Dewey, stunning the country
(and the pollsters). By 1951, Republicans were desperate for someone to
rescue them from a twenty-year presidential drought. Taft, the presumptive front-runner, had lost the nomination to Wendell Willkie in 1940
and to Dewey in 1948. And many Republican leaders believed that the

Ohio senator, who was still staunchly isolationist, couldn't win in the postwar period, an era that demanded a more assertive US foreign policy. But Eisenhower, the war hero, would be just the ticket.

The problem was that Eisenhower did not want to run. Eventually he seemed willing to be drafted, but he did not want to campaign. He apparently had the notion that it would be ideal if both parties would nominate him and he could, as did General George Washington, be elected essentially by acclamation. That scenario could never play out in modern times, of course; moreover, as it turned out, Eisenhower would have difficulty obtaining the nomination of even *one* party, no matter how much some of its leaders wanted him to have it. The conservative wing of the GOP had its candidate in Taft, and it would do what it could to get him the victory. The moderate wing had its hopes pinned on a war hero, but moderates didn't know if their would-be candidate was even a Republican, if he would actually accept the nomination if offered, or if he could translate his war-hero popularity into actual votes for president.

After much sleuthing, party leaders were able to show that at least Eisenhower had never affiliated himself with the Democrats. He apparently had never registered to vote and had never engaged in partisan statements that would indicate his party preference. With that reassurance, they now wanted to show his electoral appeal by having his name appear on the New Hampshire primary ballot. But if they put his name on the ballot, would he repudiate it?

According to Charles Brereton[2], a breakthrough in the effort to recruit the general was apparently created by Robert Burroughs, a Manchester politico who visited Eisenhower in Europe in the summer of 1951. Burroughs found the general concerned about the 1951 cheating scandal at West Point, Eisenhower's alma mater, and used that event to stress the importance of confronting corruption in the Truman administration. Later, Eisenhower would tell Burroughs, "Those were the first reasons which were presented to me with the same purpose you had, the first ones that appealed to me at all."[3] But concerns about corruption in the Truman administration were hardly the only factor that influenced the general. He was also concerned that Taft's isolationist views were contrary to what the new postwar world needed — namely, the United States playing a more active, internationalist role. Along with many political observers of the time, he believed that after twenty years with a Democrat as president, and with President Truman being so unpopular, it was almost certain that a Republican would win the presidency in 1952. And Taft—the likely GOP nominee—was the wrong man for the job. At the end of the meeting, Eisenhower agreed to consider officially entering the primary, though he made it clear he would not actually campaign.

In early January 1952, Massachusetts Senator Henry Cabot Lodge, the man elected to be Eisenhower's campaign manager by members of the Draft Eisenhower movement, took the calculated risk of forcing the general to make a decision. Lodge announced that Eisenhower had personally assured him and others that the general was a Republican and would accept the nomination for president. This infuriated Eisenhower, who, according to one biographer,[4] almost repudiated the draft effort. The general wanted to maintain a fine distinction between being a candidate (with political implications) and being a nonpolitical public servant, who would reluctantly accept a draft if offered. The Lodge announcement apparently muddied the distinction. That Eisenhower did not officially object to the statement, however, kept the draft movement on track.

Still, it wasn't at all clear that Eisenhower would have any serious competition, which could diminish the significance of a victory. Taft had studiously avoided entering any primary during his two previous attempts at gaining the nomination, and apparently for good reason. He was widely viewed as a lousy campaigner, with a harsh speaking voice and an inability to mingle easily with strangers. On the other hand, most of the campaigning would be done by surrogates—Taft's supporters in the state—just as all of the campaigning for Eisenhower would have to be done by his supporters. Taft mulled over whether to get into the primary, on the one hand knowing his weakness as a campaigner, but on the other wanting to deliver a death blow to the burgeoning Draft Eisenhower movement. If Ike were defeated in his first electoral effort, it could completely derail his candidacy.

On the penultimate day of the filing period, Taft agreed to compete. His campaign manager called Taft's entrance into the New Hampshire primary "absolute fearlessness . . . Bob Taft has never run from a fight, and, even though he has the great disadvantage of running in a state that has been carefully selected as the first and most secure arena for General Eisenhower, he shows no hesitancy."[5]

This was great news, at least to New Hampshire, for Taft's entrance gave legitimacy to its maiden beauty contest. Here were the two major GOP candidates in a head-to-head fight for the support of actual voters (as opposed to political bosses). What could be more important? And the news was also good for the Draft Eisenhower movement, which initially expected a rather easy triumph.

As the campaign progressed, however, an Eisenhower victory appeared less certain. Taft committed himself to a personal three-day campaign effort in the state, during which he received extensive press coverage. The general's surrogates became worried, especially since earlier they had claimed that the state was "in the bag," a real no-no kind of comment that politicos today would avoid at all costs. As politicians would eventually learn, the interpretations of primary results are as much about press expectations as they are about the actual number of votes cast. Suddenly, Eisenhower's supporters were downplaying expectations, suggesting that if Ike were to win after the personal appearances by Taft, it would be a "political miracle."[6] Taft forces, of course, had already downplayed expectations when Taft entered the race by claiming the state was specially chosen because it was a "secure arena" for the general. What the Taft campaign wanted was a moral victory, winning at least some of the fourteen delegates and finishing a close second in the beauty contest.

Alas for Taft, a moral victory was not to be had. The war hero who was still defending his country on active duty in Europe and had never set foot on New Hampshire soil during the campaign won a double-digit victory in the beauty contest, 50 percent to 39 percent, and he won all fourteen delegates in a separate vote on the ballot. The presidential candidate who had broken precedent by personally campaigning in the New Hampshire primary was, according to the publisher of the *Peterborough Transcript,* his own worst enemy. "Taft's stiffness, and lack of ability to unbend was never more evident . . . it just deflated the Taft drive here."[7]

The primary victory in New Hampshire was followed a week later by a massive write-in vote for Eisenhower in the Minnesota primary, where the only listed candidate was the state's former governor, Harold Stassen. The governor won with 120,000 votes, but Eisenhower came in second with 108,000 write-in votes, no doubt in part a reflection of the post–New Hampshire publicity the general received for his victory over Taft. According to Brereton, that second good showing in Minnesota (referred to as the "Minnesota Miracle"), on the heels of his solid victory in New Hampshire, finally persuaded Eisenhower to submit his letter of resignation from his NATO post and return home to run for president.

Democratic Primary

Although there is evidence that President Truman did not intend to run for reelection in 1952, he had not yet let the public know of that intent when Tennessee Senator Estes Kefauver announced his candidacy for the Democratic Party's nomination.[8] Prior to his announcement, Kefauver had consulted with Truman, indicating that he would not run if the president were to seek reelection. But Truman said he had not made up his mind. Kefauver told the president that he would therefore seek the nomination, but hoped it would not be interpreted as an "affront."[9] The senator subsequently filed to run in the New Hampshire primary, proposing a full slate of delegates and, separately, entering his name into the primary's first beauty contest.

In the meantime, Truman was searching for a candidate other than Kefauver, offering his support (actually, his *guarantee* of the nomination, since the president controlled the party machinery) to Supreme Court Chief Justice Fred Vinson, who declined, and then to Illinois Governor Adlai Stevenson, who also declined. When Kefauver made his announcement, Truman had not yet found an acceptable candidate who was willing to run. And when asked about Kefauver's challenge during his weekly press conference at the end of January, the president was dismissive of the effort. If he decided to run for reelection, Truman said, the party would nominate him regardless of whether he had competed in any primaries. While he endorsed legislation that would establish a single national primary, he said the present system of state primaries was just "eyewash" as would be evident when the national convention was held.[10] He was right, of course, as Kefauver would in fact discover that summer at the national convention, when he arrived with more delegates won in primaries than any other candidate, but still could not get the party's nomination. But speaking the truth does not always go well with the press or the public. Truman's comment and apparent intention to remove his name from the contest created a firestorm of protest from people within the state, so much so that the president relented—sending a letter to New Hampshire Secretary of State Enoch D. Fuller, saying he had been persuaded by many Democrats nationally and in the state that his name should be left on the ballot.

Recognizing that campaigning head-to-head against the president, the leader of his own party, was somewhat of a gamble, Kefauver offered to withdraw from the New Hampshire primary if Truman would also. He made that offer to the Democratic Party's national chair, Frank McKinney, a Truman supporter. But the president's supporters, unhappy with Kefauver's challenge and eager to trounce the senator early on, rejected the compromise. Virtually everyone expected Truman to win easily. Even Kefauver expected to lose, but hoped to make the contest close in order to show that he was a viable candidate. The senator made two trips to the state in the final month of the campaign and, according to Brereton, was an especially effective campaigner. "He had a great instinct for working the ground level of politics, he ambled along countless main streets greeting shoppers and clerks, worked the assembly lines in factories, attended teas in private homes and receptions in hotel meeting rooms."[11] Truman, of course, didn't campaign personally, and his surrogates seemed unable to mount an effective effort, apparently victims of overconfidence. Only as voting day approached did some of the state leaders recognize that Kefauver might make a more impressive showing than originally anticipated. Still, the pundits and politicians all expected a Truman victory. And just as Truman's victory over Dewey in 1948 shocked the nation, Truman's solid defeat in the New Hampshire primary surprised everyone. He lost the popular vote 55 percent to 44 percent, and he failed to win even one delegate.[12]

The surprise victory, however, did not help Kefauver win the nomination. As one of his supporters noted, "He actually was quite upset the night that he was winning the primary against Truman. He didn't want to win — he wanted to make a darn good showing. But he won and when he did, that got all the pols nationwide mad at him."[13] That was a time when the power of the nomination still remained in the hands of the pols, but the power was beginning to shift from the party elite to the people (and the press). The shift would not be final for another two decades, but the New Hampshire primary had now, for the first time since its institution thirty-six years earlier, become a potent force in the nomination process.

1956 — Revitalizing Nixon's Career

The second round of New Hampshire's beauty contest was not as dramatic as the first round, but it did apparently save Richard Nixon's political career. Or maybe not. And it demonstrated once again, as it had in 1952, that winning the New Hampshire primary doesn't necessarily lead to the nomination.

Republican Primary

Most of the political drama occurred in the fall of 1955, when President Eisenhower suffered a heart attack, and it wasn't clear for several months whether he would be able to run for reelection. Over the weeks following his September attack, the president slowly recovered, and in January he convened his advisors to discuss a reelection bid. Not surprisingly, they all recommended he make the effort, a decision bolstered by a report from Eisenhower's doctors the next month that the president was fully able to perform his duties and campaign for office. In the meantime, a dump-Nixon movement had begun, with moderate or "modern Eisenhower" Republicans rejecting the brand of conservatism represented by the vice president and preferring instead a less polarizing candidate like Governor Christian Herter of Massachusetts. Nixon himself was discouraged by the attacks on him, as well as by the lack of support from the president, who had publicly advised Nixon to "chart your own course" and had privately offered Nixon a cabinet post to give him more executive experience. The pundits' pundit, Walter Lippmann, wrote a scathing commentary about the vice president, arguing that he did not represent the values that Eisenhower did. "Instead of being a national leader, he is a ruthless partisan who divides and embitters the people."[14] So dismayed was Nixon by his situation that he told his close advisors that he would make a public announcement indicating his intent to quit politics at the end of his first term as vice president.

Whether the announcement, if actually made, would have truly ended Nixon's political career is unclear, since we now know that he did in fact publicly quit politics after he lost the California gubernatorial election in 1962, and yet came back to win the presidency six years later. Still, his threat to quit caused Eisenhower supporters to intervene, fearing that the difficulty in finding a replacement acceptable to both wings of the party could be more troubling for the reelection campaign than keeping Nixon on the ticket. While still mulling over his options, Nixon was stunned to learn that in the New Hampshire Republican primary, some 23,000 voters had written in his name for vice president. In the uncontested race for president, and with his name listed on the ballot, Eisenhower had received 57,000 votes. Nixon's write-in total was an astounding figure, a solid reaffirmation of support from the rank and file, especially since it was completely spontaneous. At least, that was how it was interpreted by Nixon's supporters and by the conservative wing of the party. The next day, after being pressed for his comments about the primary and his feelings about his own vice president, Eisenhower finally made it clear that he did not intend to dump Nixon. In typical Eisenhowese, the president said, "I would be happy to be on any ticket in which I was a candidate with him."[15]

The notion that the write-in was completely spontaneous defies credulity, a skepticism reinforced by William Loeb, the late publisher of the *Manchester Union Leader.* After the results were announced, Loeb wrote in an editorial that "with no organized campaign of any kind whatsoever, this unheard-of write-in for Nixon was evidently the spontaneous expression of indignation over the apparent attempt . . . to ditch Dick Nixon from the ticket." Yet, in a story some 18 years later, Loeb acknowledged that "The [Senator Henry Styles] Bridges organization sparked a write-in vote in the New Hampshire presidential primary in March of 1956, which gave the president the up to then largest write-in vote ever achieved by anyone in New Hampshire."[16]

Whatever the genesis of the vote, it apparently was the catalyst for the president to quell rumors that he was seeking a new vice president for his second term, and it may — or may not — have saved Nixon's political career.

Democratic Primary

Once again, Tennessee Senator Estes Kefauver declared his candidacy for president and entered the New Hampshire primary. The presumptive front-runner, former Illinois Governor Adlai Stevenson, chose to skip New Hampshire, where he saw Kefauver as a solid favorite, and focus instead on the Minnesota primary a week later. A newly elected senator from Massachusetts, John F. Kennedy, offered to run in New Hampshire as a "favorite son" from New England, uniting the region behind him so he could deliver the states to Stevenson at the party's nomination convention the following summer. But fearful that Kennedy's efforts would draw too much attention to the New Hampshire primary and Kefauver's expected victory, Stevenson's advisors asked Kennedy only for an endorsement. The plan was to wage a low-key write-in campaign, perhaps obtaining a moral victory if they could win a delegate or two, and get as much as a quarter of the vote. But Kefauver stumped the state on three different occasions, his ebullient personality on full display, finally winning more than 80 percent of the vote. Stevenson got just 15 percent support, and he won no delegates. The following week, Minnesota also gave Kefauver the victory.

Finally, Stevenson realized that the road to the nomination had changed — that he had to actually stump for voters' support. In subsequent contests he proved himself more popular than the Tennessee senator, eventually winning the most delegates prior to the convention. While Kefauver's victory in New Hampshire was clearly helpful, it did not — once again — lead to the nomination. This is a point that was generally ignored by some stalwart supporters of the New Hampshire primary, whose red-herring boasts (until Clinton lost the primary in 1992, but still went on to win the general election) pointed out that no president had taken office without first winning the New Hampshire primary. Yes, that was true, but irrelevant. What is relevant is how much influence the primary had in helping candidates win the nomination, not the general election. And already, in the first two cycles of the beauty contest primary, a presidential candidate had won decisively, only to lose the nomination.

1960 — Nothing Unexpected, Mostly

In 1960, both major party candidates achieved an overwhelming victory: Nixon got 89 percent of the Republican vote, Kennedy 85 percent of the Democratic vote. Their wins were not unexpected, but each achieved what Brereton called astounding numbers, generating enthusiasm among their respective rank-and-file voters that impressed pundits and politicians outside the state. Still, the campaigns were not without notable events, which provide additional insight into the unique character of the New Hampshire primary.

Republican Primary

As the sitting vice president, Nixon was the presumptive front-runner for the GOP nomination in 1960. New York Governor Nelson Rockefeller contemplated a challenge as part of the moderate wing of the party, and although he eventually declined to declare his candidacy, the possibility of his doing so provided some behind-the-scenes melodrama for the Nixon campaign. The instigator was New Hampshire's Governor Wesley Powell, essentially a creature of William Loeb's *Manchester Union Leader* — at least that's how Loeb later seemed to describe Powell, and the description is supported by objective evidence.[17] Without Loeb's using his paper to actively campaign for Powell (as Loeb would later do for Ronald Reagan in 1980[18]), the Manchester attorney would almost certainly not have been elected governor. Believing he could take advantage of the publicity associated with the New Hampshire primary, Powell demanded to be the chairman of Nixon's state campaign, with full control over spending campaign money and other strategic decisions. Although the Nixon campaign wanted the support of the state's governor, these were unusual and, to the national campaign staff, unacceptable demands. The Nixon campaign refused. Then Powell threatened to join the Rockefeller campaign. That was a serious threat. Nixon's aides were highly concerned that Rockefeller would mount a formidable campaign effort in the state, based on his immense wealth and on his close ties to the state. Should New Hampshire's governor be part of that effort, it could seriously undermine Nixon's clear march to the nomination. Given a deadline of only several hours in which to decide, the campaign staff caved and named the governor chairman of the Nixon campaign in the state.

As it turns out, Powell got the honorary title, but without the control he had demanded. Only days later, Rockefeller announced he would not run for president, because — after conferring with party leaders across the country — "the great majority of those who will control the Republican convention stand opposed to my contest for the nomination."[19] This development vitiated Powell's threat to abandon the Nixon ship. Powell, however, had yet another trick up his sleeve to bolster his national stature.

According to Brereton, the New Hampshire governor apparently intended to gain "national prominence by engaging in some rock 'em-sock 'em smear charges [against Kennedy] in the final hours," and thus make himself an attractive candidate for vice president. With Loeb's support, a secret vice presidential write-in campaign had already been initiated on Powell's behalf, following the model that had worked for Nixon four years earlier. Perhaps to augment that effort, at his press conference on the Monday before Election Day, Powell charged Kennedy with being soft on communism. When Kennedy denounced the charge later in the day and called upon Nixon to repudiate his state chairman (which Nixon did), Powell bought time on the local television station to reiterate his accusations. He also sent a telegram to Nixon warning the vice president to "be on the attack lest the unjust attacks by Kennedy upon the Eisenhower administration leave the Republicans holding the bag."[20] On Election Day, Loeb published his editorial on the front page of his paper, supporting Powell and making his own charges that Kennedy was soft on communism and that if Kennedy were elected president, "we are just about through as a nation."[21]

Powell did in fact get a lot of publicity, though hardly the kind that he sought. On the day after the vote, for example, the *New York Herald,* a strongly Republican paper, denounced Powell's last-minute accusations, calling them "maladroit" and "irresponsible, damaging to the Republican Party," and costing Powell his "stature as a party strategist."[22]

Powell received only about 9,600 Republican write-in votes for vice president, less than half the total Nixon received four years earlier and not appreciably greater than the 6,500 write-in votes cast for United States Ambassador to the United Nations Henry Cabot Lodge (who would, in fact, become Nixon's 1960 running mate). Nixon's victory was not a surprise, but his 65,000-vote total was — it exceeded the number Eisenhower received in 1956 by more than 9,000 votes.

Democratic Primary

Four years earlier, at the 1956 Democratic National Convention, the party's presidential nominee, Adlai Stevenson, took the unusual step of throwing open the vice presidential nomination to the convention, rather than choosing a candidate himself. Both Estes Kefauver and John F. Kennedy competed, along with several other politicians. Kefauver won on the third ballot, but Kennedy actually led on the second ballot, needing only fifteen more votes to become the vice presidential nominee. Despite the failure, the effort gained Kennedy a great deal of national publicity and propelled him into the front ranks of potential Democratic candidates for 1960. But he knew that his youth and Catholic religion would be major obstacles to overcome. He needed the primaries to demonstrate his vote-getting capability. In New Hampshire, he had to get a good send-off if he were going to impress the party leaders across the country who controlled most of the delegates. The only other potential Democratic candidate likely to run in the New Hampshire primary against Kennedy was Minnesota Senator Hubert Humphrey, but even he refused to challenge the Massachusetts senator in his back yard. The lack of competition put an even bigger premium on Kennedy's efforts to get a high vote total in New Hampshire.

While a Kennedy win was clearly expected, the campaign staff went to work to maximize the vote total. First on their agenda was to eliminate the nonserious competitors, who could draw votes away from the principal candidate. That year there were three: a furniture salesman, a country music singer, and a ballpoint pen manufacturer named Paul Fisher. The Kennedy campaign challenged the ballot petitions of all three and was successful against the salesman and singer, who had nonexistent and even dead voters on their petitions. But they were unsuccessful against Fisher, who had enough valid signatures to meet the state's requirement. On the last day of the campaign, Fisher barged into a convocation being held at the University of New Hampshire, where Kennedy was the keynote speaker.[23] Fisher demanded equal time and eventually was permitted to speak before the audience. He talked about his tax proposals, but he did not criticize either his opponent or the school administrators. In the election, Fisher did in fact siphon votes away from Kennedy, but the appearance at UNH was certainly not a major factor. More important was the support he received from Loeb's *Manchester Union Leader,* which printed numerous stories and editorials unfavorable to the Massachusetts senator.

The spade work that Kennedy had done in the years leading up to his presidential bid, which included appearing in the state several times and meeting with local leaders, provided a solid base of support. His staff's careful organization during the campaign built on that base, so that when the final votes came in, Kennedy not only won (with 85.2 percent of the vote, with Fisher getting 13.5 percent), but garnered about twice as many votes (43,372) as did Kefauver (21,701) four years earlier — though Kefauver's share that year (84.6 percent) was about the same as Kennedy's. This surprisingly high vote total gave ammunition to the Kennedy campaign to support its claim that the young senator could generate enthusiasm that no other Democratic candidate could match.

Kennedy still had other primaries ahead of him — against Humphrey in Wisconsin, seen as Humphrey's back yard, and then against Humphrey again in West Virginia, where Kennedy would try to demonstrate that his Catholic religion was not an insurmountable obstacle to becoming president. But the large turnout in New Hampshire was a crucial first step, acknowledged years later by his closest advisor at the time, Bernard Boutin, who told Brereton: "If [Kennedy] hadn't done well in

New Hampshire, I think that the West Virginia victory and the victory in Wisconsin would have been impossible."[24]

1964 — Absentee Candidates Win — Once Again

In 1964, no major candidates filed for the Democratic primary, which President Lyndon Johnson nevertheless won as a write-in candidate with 95 percent of the vote. Several GOP candidates filed for their party's primary, but the landslide winner, the US ambassador to South Vietnam, Henry Cabot Lodge, did not file, did not campaign, and did not even indicate that he would return to the United States to become a candidate if he won the primary. For a state that has touted its primary as a model of retail politics — a way for the voters to get to really know the candidates and for the candidates to hear what voters are thinking — the 1964 primary was a truly sobering event.

Democratic Primary

In the months following the assassination of President Kennedy on November 22, 1963, the new president, Lyndon B. Johnson, rejected advice from his political consultants that he make a serious campaign effort in the New Hampshire primary. He felt it would be better to forego such partisan activity and instead focus on the business of being president and of helping the country to overcome the sorrow of that terrible November event. Still, it was impossible to ignore the looming presidential campaign. Many Democrats felt that the party would present the strongest ticket in the 1964 presidential election if Johnson were to select Robert Kennedy, the late president's brother and current US attorney general, as the vice presidential candidate. In 1960, the ticket had been Kennedy/Johnson. In 1964, it could be Johnson/Kennedy. But Johnson was adamantly opposed to such an arrangement. He and Bobby Kennedy had never gotten along, stemming at least from the 1960 election, when Bobby had met privately with Johnson to dissuade the Texas senator from accepting John Kennedy's offer to be vice president. Bobby's meeting angered Johnson, who called the elder Kennedy to reaffirm that the offer to be the veep was genuine. And during the next three years while he served as attorney general, Bobby was the president's closest advisor, with Johnson, the vice president, being left largely out of any meaningful role in the Kennedy administration. The last thing Johnson wanted now was for his presidency to be seen as merely an extension — and perhaps temporary at that, should Bobby decide to run for president in 1968 — of the Kennedy presidency.

In an effort to persuade Johnson to include Kennedy on the ticket, two Manchester Democrats launched a vice-presidential write-in campaign on the attorney general's behalf. The action infuriated Johnson, who saw the effort as a way to undermine his presidency. As the campaign progressed, it seemed possible that Kennedy's write-in total for vice president might well exceed Johnson's write-in total for president, which could be humiliating. It was too late for Johnson to change his mind and begin actively wooing voters in the state, but his staff did try to curtail the efforts of the Kennedy write-in campaign. And they were apparently successful. Kennedy received 25,094 votes for vice president, while Johnson netted 29,317 votes for president.[25]

The large total did not produce the positive outcome for Kennedy as had the 1956 write-in effort for Vice President Nixon. If anything, the primary increased the tensions between the two men, with LBJ constantly looking over his shoulder, afraid that the younger Kennedy had his sights on restoring Camelot. That fear was realized only four years later.

Republican Primary

After his first reelection to the New York governorship in 1962, Nelson Rockefeller contemplated running for president and was considered by many to be the front-runner for the GOP nomination. Then in May 1963, about a year after his divorce from his first wife, he got married to Margaretta "Happy" Murphy, a woman whose ex-husband, James "Robin" Slater Murphy, worked at the Rockefeller Institute and was a close friend of the governor. The romance between Rockefeller and Happy Murphy had blossomed for several years, starting when she worked as the governor's personal secretary, though the public was not generally aware of it. As *People* magazine summarized the relationship:

Their romance, played out against the broad canvas of Pocantico Hills, Seal Harbor and Manhattan, eventually became public property. On Nov. 17, 1961, Nelson and his wife, Mary Todhunter Clark, separated, later to divorce. On Apr. 1, 1963, Happy divorced Robin, signing away custody of their four children. On May 4, 1963, she and Nelson were married in Pocantico Hills. An unsympathetic public saw Rockefeller as a man who had cast aside his wife of 31 years and broken up two families in order to marry a 36-year-old woman, 18 years his junior. Happy was seen as a heartless mother.[26]

Even many GOP moderates refused to support Rockefeller after the divorce and remarriage, believing he had fatally damaged his candidacy. They began looking for another moderate to oppose Arizona Senator Barry Goldwater, known as Mr. Conservative. Undeterred, Rockefeller entered the New Hampshire primary, as did Goldwater, while moderates focused on recruiting the US ambassador to South Vietnam, Henry Cabot Lodge. The former Massachusetts senator had been instrumental in the 1952 effort to draft Eisenhower, and he had been Nixon's vice presidential candidate four years earlier. But at 61 years of age, he showed little enthusiasm for taking on a full presidential campaign, even after Eisenhower called on him to return to the United States and run.

Without explicit authorization from the ambassador, lawyer David Goldberg and businessman Paul Grindle, both from the Boston area, started a write-in campaign in New Hampshire on behalf of Lodge. Later, according to Brereton, they would admit the whole effort was a lark. They had no real expectation that Lodge would quit his post and run, and they knew that if he remained in Vietnam, there was little chance he could win the nomination. Even war hero General Eisenhower had to return from Europe to woo voters on his own behalf. But the two men wanted "something fun and exciting to do." And New Hampshire, with its lax rules about whose name could be entered on the primary ballot, was a perfect playground. The two men had previously tried to open a Lodge headquarters in Massachusetts, but the state's secretary of state closed it down immediately because the candidate had not authorized political activity on his behalf. But in New Hampshire, anyone could file as a Lodge delegate, regardless of the candidate's wishes.[27]

Still, the two supporters did not want to make a substantial effort only to have Lodge publicly disavow it right before Election Day. They needed some type of reassurance from Lodge on that point. With the support of his son, George Lodge, the two men persuaded William Treat, a GOP leader in the state, to go to Vietnam and talk personally with the ambassador. Treat agreed, and upon his return informed the trio that Lodge would not disavow any effort on his behalf, though he could not support it either. As a member of the Foreign Service, he was obligated to avoid any hint of partisan activity. If he were drafted he would serve, but he would not quit his post to campaign in the New Hampshire primary.

That was all the information the three men needed. In the next several weeks, they settled on a slate of delegates, raised money, and sent out a brochure touting Lodge's experience to almost one hundred thousand households. They also bought several time slots on the local television station to air a five-minute film that highlighted Lodge's impressive political career. So much emphasis was placed on the ambassador's close ties to President Eisenhower that the film appeared to reflect an official endorsement from the former president.

In the meantime, the Goldwater campaign was able to obtain the endorsements of most of the GOP leaders in the state, and was supported in what can only be called a vigorous campaign by the *Manchester Union Leader*. As Brereton describes the coverage: "The publicity and propaganda barrage released that year by New Hampshire's only statewide daily newspaper has rarely, if ever, been matched. Barry Goldwater was everywhere — on the front page, on the back page, and endlessly in between."[28] The editor, William Loeb, wrote numerous front-page editorials on behalf of the Arizona senator, as well as many screeds critical of Rockefeller, whom Loeb referred to as a "wife swapper" and "home wrecker"—notwithstanding the fact that Loeb himself was twice divorced.

Goldwater spent three weeks personally campaigning in the state, compared with a week by Rockefeller. Initially, Goldwater was leading comfortably in the polls, but his lead quickly dissipated. Rockefeller criticized his opponent for his "half-baked" notions about the United Nations, as well as Goldwater's comments about Social Security, taxes, invading Panama and changing his mind about debating.[29] A Harris poll in early February showed that in a two-way race between Goldwater and Rockefeller, the Arizona senator's lead had dropped from 20 points (53 percent to 33 percent) in November to just 7 points (46 percent to 39 percent) in February. More revealing, perhaps, were Harris' other hypothetical findings: in a three-way race with Goldwater, Rockefeller, and either Nixon or Lodge, the two noncandidates would beat the actual candidates by substantial margins. Nixon led with 56 percent over Goldwater's 28 percent and Rockefeller's 22 percent; while Lodge led with 48 percent to Goldwater's 36 percent and Rockefeller's 22 percent[30] Voters were torn between one candidate who seemed out of the mainstream of GOP thinking, and the other candidate, whose personal life made it unlikely he could ever be elected president.

In the final days of the campaign, the Lodge write-in campaign seemed to promise that if the voters of New Hampshire gave the ambassador their endorsement, he would return to campaign for president. One important indicator of Lodge's intent would be his decision whether to leave his name on the Oregon primary ballot or tell the Oregon secretary of state to remove it. The deadline to make that call was on the Monday before Election Day in New Hampshire. On the previous Saturday, Lodge's son, George, announced, "It is my firm belief that he will not take his name off the Oregon ballot." The Boston newspapers treated the announcement as fact, with the *Boston Globe*'s Sunday headline reading: "Lodge a Candidate: In Oregon to Stay."[31]

The last-minute publicity no doubt had a major impact on the minds of many conflicted voters. Lodge won by double-digits over his closest opponent, receiving 35 percent of the vote to Goldwater's 22 percent and Rockefeller's 21 percent. Nixon's write-in was also substantial, garnering 17 percent of the total.

But Lodge did not return to capitalize on his victory. The primary clearly hurt Rockefeller's candidacy, since he was the moderate with strong ties to the state. The New York governor did win in Oregon and came close to winning in California, but the loss in the latter state was fatal: Goldwater's victory by three percentage points (51.6 percent to 48.4

percent) gave him all the delegates in that winner-take-all contest. New Hampshire's influence was not trivial: had the two Boston politicos not decided to have fun by running a write-in campaign for a nonexistent candidate, Rockefeller might have won the New Hampshire primary and ultimately prevailed, even in California.

Little recognized at the time was the influence of the *Manchester Union Leader.* Loeb's style of journalism, a throwback to the highly partisan papers of the early nineteenth century, made the paper a potent political force in the state for decades and would, years later, provide the margin of victory for its candidates in two GOP primaries.

1968 — The Unmaking of a President and the Phoenix Rising from the Ashes

Once again an incumbent president chose to ignore the New Hampshire primary and suffered for it. And once again, the New Hampshire primary helped Richard Nixon's political career. This was the last primary before the adoption of party reforms, and it was the last time a candidate could ignore the New Hampshire primary and still reasonably expect to win the nomination.

The Democratic Primary

At the time, all evidence suggested that President Johnson intended to run for reelection, though he refused to campaign for the nomination. He would gain the nomination in the traditional way, not by entering primaries and caucuses, but by relying on state party leaders and their delegates to support him at the national convention in late summer. That was the same approach he had used in 1960, hoping that year to use his influence among party leaders to gain the nomination. He was unsuccessful, of course, but he did get second prize as the vice presidential nominee. In 1964, now the president, he justified his noncampaigning in the primaries because of the recent assassination of President Kennedy. In 1968, there was a different dynamic at play: It would have been grueling for him to run in the primaries. The country was torn apart by disagreement over the war, which drained the country's resources, diverted Johnson's attention from his Great Society goals, and produced large numbers of war casualties every week. With frequent antiwar demonstrations, Johnson was almost a prisoner in the White House. Had he tried to campaign in New Hampshire and other states, his appearances would have been dominated by the war issue. It was much easier simply to wait until the Democratic National Convention in the summer to obtain the party's nomination.

Still, the president had to decide whether to officially announce his candidacy and put his name on the ballot, or follow some other course. If Johnson didn't officially declare his intentions to seek reelection, he could have New Hampshire's Senator Thomas McIntyre run as a stand-in, with McIntyre's public declaration that he was a Johnson supporter; or the president could have his supporters launch a write-in campaign. Either of these two alternatives would not be as strong as having the president's name actually on the ballot. In the end, Johnson opted for what in hindsight was a losing strategy: Not declaring his candidacy, but allowing a write-in campaign on his behalf.

In the meantime, there emerged a national Dump Johnson movement, led by two liberal activists, Allard Lowenstein and Curtis Gans. Lowenstein had previously written a book against apartheid in South Africa, helped to mobilize white college students to volunteer for the Freedom Summer voter-registration campaign in Mississippi, and worked as a foreign policy assistant to Minnesota Senator Hubert Humphrey.[32] Lowenstein wanted Robert Kennedy to run. As the former us attorney general (having been appointed by his brother, President John F. Kennedy) and currently a us senator from New York, Bobby Kennedy was a natural choice. He had already expressed doubts about the war, even proposing in May of 1967 a three-point plan to bring it to an end.[33] But Kennedy refused to run. His direct challenge to Johnson's reelection, he felt, could divide the party and would almost certainly have been viewed as much a personal issue as a policy one, given their long-standing animosity. Besides, Kennedy could afford to wait — he was only forty-two years old and could run four years later without committing the almost unpardonable sin of challenging an incumbent president of one's own party.

Eventually, Lowenstein and Gans persuaded Minnesota Senator Eugene McCarthy to run against Johnson. Initially, however, McCarthy was reluctant to run in New Hampshire, which he perceived as too conservative and hawkish on the war. Moreover, in mid-November, before McCarthy announced his candidacy, the state Democratic Party officially endorsed Johnson for reelection.[34] The endorsement, of course, meant little, since there was no "party machine" available to help the president's campaign. Furthermore, the image at the time of a conservative New Hampshire, while correct, was irrelevant for the primary. The key question for presidential primaries is not the profile of all voters in the state, but the profile of voters who turn out in the specific party primary. Subsequent polling (see Chapter 10) suggests that the political ideology of Democratic voters in New Hampshire has generally been quite similar to the ideology of Democratic voters across the country.

After visiting the state in December, McCarthy finally agreed to make a run in New Hampshire. He officially announced his candidacy in January, and soon thereafter, antiwar activists began descending upon New Hampshire to help the McCarthy campaign. They were advised by supporters to "Get Clean for Gene"—meaning they should cut their hair and look like "normal" people rather than like the public stereotypes of ne'er-do-well hippies. Then, at the end of January, the North Vietnamese launched the Tet Offensive, a massive series of attacks in cities across South Vietnam that undermined claims made by General Westmoreland and others in the Johnson administration that the war was nearing its end. In February, thousands of antiwar activists, mostly students, poured into New Hampshire to help the McCarthy campaign. The ultimate coup, however, may have been a story that leaked over the weekend just before Election Day that Westmoreland had requested two hundred thousand more troops to fight in Vietnam. The final vote showed Johnson winning with just under 50 percent (49.6), but McCarthy garnered a shocking 42 percent—above the 40 percent threshold that Johnson's campaign team had said would be necessary for McCarthy to avoid "disgrace."[35]

Four days later, Bobby Kennedy announced that McCarthy's victory had demonstrated that the Democratic Party was indeed split. He explained his late entry: "One of the major reasons I didn't want to become involved earlier was because I thought that I might be the instrument of dividing either the country in a way that would be difficult to put back together [or] dividing the Democratic Party in a very damaging way."[36] Now that McCarthy had shown how vulnerable Johnson was, and how divided the party was, Kennedy could, in good conscience, challenge the incumbent president. That was Johnson's greatest fear and something he had long expected.[37]

The Dump Johnson movement met its goal much more quickly than anyone could have imagined. With Kennedy in the race, Johnson announced on March 31, 1968, that he was not a candidate for reelection and would not serve another term.

The final outcome, however, was not what the Dump Johnson movement wanted: Vice President Humphrey was overwhelmingly nominated as the party's presidential candidate, without having entered one primary or caucus contest, and officially supporting the president's war policy.

The Republican Primary

By the time the two major GOP candidates began their campaigns in New Hampshire, the major events that were to determine the outcome had already occurred. Despite his dramatic declaration in 1962 (after losing the California gubernatorial election) that the press would no longer have him to "kick around any more," Nixon had never really left politics. In January 1964, he made that clear. When asked on a CBS radio program whether he intended to run for president, he said: "I never wear a hat, so it must always be in the ring."[38] He didn't run, despite several hints that he was available and might enter the fray. He maintained his political contacts, however, and in 1966 stumped vigorously around the country for his fellow Republicans. That year, the GOP gained forty-seven house seats, which enhanced Nixon's stature among party leaders. By 1967, he was widely considered the front-runner for his party's presidential nomination.

The 1966 election was also a good one for George Romney, who easily won reelection for his third term as governor of Michigan. He had refrained from entering the presidential race in 1964, but with Goldwater's debacle and his own reelection, he was eager to launch his campaign for the nomination. Indeed, he was widely seen as the choice for the moderate wing of the Republic Party. Nevertheless, some supporters argued strenuously that he should not enter the New Hampshire primary, but should wait to enter the Wisconsin primary the following month. New Hampshire was seen as too conservative and too favorable toward Richard Nixon. Moreover, Bill Loeb, the outspoken publisher of the *Manchester Union Leader*, the only statewide daily newspaper, would use his paper to attack Romney in his relentless and vitriolic style. Wisconsin, a sister Midwestern state, would be a more favorable venue for the governor to begin his campaign.

But Romney didn't listen.

As it turns out, it may not have made much difference had he skipped the New Hampshire primary as suggested. Five months before Election Day, on September 4, 1967, he essentially torpedoed his own candidacy when he explained to a Detroit television newsman how he had come to oppose the Vietnam War. The reporter pointed out that after Romney's visit to Vietnam in 1965, the Michigan governor said that US involvement there was "morally right and necessary and had probably reversed a shift in the balance of power greater than if Hitler had conquered Europe." Now, two years later, Romney was arguing that the war had been a mistake from the beginning. How could the governor explain this "inconsistency"? It was then that Romney uttered the fateful words: "When I came back from Viet Nam, I'd just had the greatest brainwashing that anybody can get." He clarified that he was speaking of both the generals and the diplomats who had given him bad information. But since then, he said, he had studied the history of the conflict and had thus changed his mind, no longer believing it was necessary to get involved in Vietnam to stop communist aggression.[39]

Despite how reasonable his arguments may seem today, at the time his use of the word "brainwashing" recalled the concerns of many people about the effect that the Korean War may have exerted on the psyches of some American soldiers. The chilling film *The Manchurian Candidate* gave an artistic portrayal of a soldier who had lost control of his mental faculties and was now under the spell of a foreign agent. That a presidential candidate would suggest he had suffered such a loss of control over his own mind struck a discordant chord with the American political culture of the time. As one political scientist has since observed, "Though Romney tried in earnest to explain himself, he became the target of blistering press and partisan attacks. Romney's candidacy never recovered from the furor he created with his statement."[40] The next Harris poll showed Romney dropping 16 points.[41]

Romney's campaign in New Hampshire never gained any real traction. With three weeks before the election, after having spent considerable time and resources in the state, Romney trailed Nixon by about 60 percentage points in the polls.[42] With the advice of his campaign staff, the governor decided to quit the race, leaving Nixon with no major opponent. It's possible to give too much emphasis to the "brainwashing" gaffe for Romney's demise. His position on the Vietnam War reflected the liberal wing of the *Democratic* Party, not the sentiments of the American mainstream nor even a significant segment of his own Republican Party. It's quite likely that had he merely said to the television newsman that he was "misled" rather than "brainwashed" by the generals and diplomats, he would still have found it difficult to establish himself as a major presidential contender for the GOP nomination. Nixon had too much going for him, including his years as vice president, his yeoman-like efforts to help Republicans get elected to Congress in 1966, and of course an especially favorable launching pad in New Hampshire's first-in-the-nation primary.

History of the New Hampshire Primary Contests

ADJUSTMENT PERIOD, 1970S AND 1980S

With the Democratic Party's reforms taking effect in the 1972 election cycle, it would never again be possible for a non-incumbent presidential candidate to obtain the nomination without a vigorous campaign effort in the New Hampshire primary. Incumbent presidents running for re-election typically do not face serious competition (though Gerald Ford, Jimmy Carter and George H. W. Bush are notable exceptions). Without a serious opponent, the incumbent presidents do not have to wage as intensive a campaign as they otherwise would. But for non-incumbent candidates, winning in New Hampshire — or at least coming in second — has been crucial to obtaining the nomination.

When the reforms were first adopted, some candidates believed they could skip the New Hampshire primary and launch their campaigns in other states, where the environment might be more favorable. Thus, in 1972 and again in 1976, several potential Democratic candidates for president began their quests sometime after the New Hampshire primary, only to discover that the publicity and money generated by a good showing in the Granite State had given their competitors an advantage they could not overcome. Even as late as 1988, Al Gore decided to make his first serious campaign effort in March on Super Southern Tuesday, three weeks after the New Hampshire primary. But by then it was too late to catch up with Michael Dukakis, the winner in New Hampshire.

One net consequence of the reforms, as discussed in Chapter 3, was to create a trend toward front-loading of the primaries and caucuses. States that waited until April or later often found they had little influence on the nomination — that a party's nomination had for all practical purposes been decided by the end of March. And candidates, too, recognized the importance of the early contests, that they needed to start their campaigns right at the beginning of the primary/caucus season rather than wait until later. More specifically, history suggests that Democratic candidates need to begin their campaigns in Iowa, while in recent election cycles it seems possible — perhaps even necessary — for moderate Republican candidates to skip Iowa and begin in New Hampshire. As the early GOP presidential front-runner Rudy Giuliani discovered in 2008, launching a campaign in Florida, three weeks after the New Hampshire primary, is a fool's errand.

1972 — The Reforms Take Place

Who better to take advantage of the new reforms than the man who had chaired the committee that designed them? More than anyone, South Dakota Senator George McGovern knew that the reforms had shifted the power of nomination — from the party's national convention held in the summer preceding the election, to the caucuses and primaries that would now select the delegates. With the new reforms, party bosses could no longer appoint delegates to the convention or rig elections to favor some delegates over others. Instead, convention delegates would be chosen by voters in open elections, either in a caucus or primary election format.

The clear Democratic favorite that year was Maine Senator Edmund Muskie, mostly because of the name recognition he got from being the vice presidential nominee in 1968, running with then Vice President Hubert Humphrey. After the assassination of Bobby Kennedy, many politicos expected that his younger brother, Senator Ted Kennedy, would become a front-runner for the 1972 presidential nomination. But in July 1969, Kennedy was in a car accident on Chappaquiddick Island, which caused the death of a young woman, Mary Jo Kopechne. Kennedy did not report the incident for ten hours, leading to much suspicion about the exact circumstances surrounding her death and the nature of his relationship with Kopechne. In a televised statement, he apologized for his actions and asked his constituents whether he should continue his career. While the response to this plea was positive, and he resumed his senatorial responsibilities, the scandal essentially torpedoed his try for the nomination in 1972, leaving Muskie the front-runner, with no clear opponent in sight.[1]

A Gallup poll in January 1972 among Democrats nationally showed Muskie with 32 percent support, compared with just 3 percent for McGovern.[2] Thus, as far as the press was concerned, McGovern was not a serious contender. This perception was a boon to the senator's campaign, for it meant that any significant showing in the early contests contradicting that perception would cause the press to take notice.

McGovern announced his candidacy in January 1971, more than a year before the first nomination contests, the earliest that any major candidate had ever announced. He began organizing his campaign in Iowa and New Hampshire, recognizing the importance that an early win could have in helping to recruit campaign supporters and raise money. Muskie, too, established organizations in Iowa and New Hampshire, though other candidates — most notably Humphrey and Washington Senator Henry "Scoop" Jackson — waited until later to start their campaigns. There were hardly any salient issues that separated McGovern from Muskie at that time, at least that were highlighted during the campaign. McGovern was strongly antiwar, but by 1972, most other Democrats were also opposed to the war. McGovern also supported legalization of marijuana and limited amnesty for draft dodgers, along with abortion rights — though those issues were not stressed during the early part of the campaign. Later, in subsequent state campaigns, he was tagged for advocating "amnesty, abortion and acid." But in the New Hampshire primary, Muskie did all he could to avoid specific confrontation, refusing to debate until finally pressured into it just two days before the election. And the debate proved to be an anticlimax, having no real effect on the election.[3]

The iconic event of that primary was Muskie's rant against William Loeb, the publisher of the *Manchester Union Leader,* as Muskie stood on a flatbed truck outside the paper's offices in the midst of a light snow storm. Some journalists reported that he was crying, sobbing even, though the journalists who were closest to him during the delivery rejected that characterization.[4] He was condemning the publication of a letter sent to the *Manchester Union Leader* that claimed he had used a racial slur. As it was later discovered, the letter was a fabrication produced by Nixon's Committee to Re-elect the President. Carl Bernstein and Bob Woodward wrote about it shortly before the general election:[5]

> Law enforcement sources said that probably the best example of the sabotage was the fabrication by a White House aide — of a celebrated letter to the editor alleging that Sen. Edmund S. Muskie (D-ME) condoned a racial slur on Americans of French-Canadian descent as "Canucks."

> The letter was published in the *Manchester Union Leader* Feb 24, less than two weeks before the New Hampshire primary. It in part triggered Muskie's politically damaging "crying speech" in front of the newspaper's office.

Some members of Muskie's campaign staff argued against the senator's decision to go after Loeb, and most post hoc evaluations of the incident suggest that Muskie's candidacy was hurt by the incident. That idea is reinforced by the election results, giving Muskie 46 percent of the vote to McGovern's 37 percent. The margin was smaller than expected, and Muskie's total was below the standard set by one of his own campaign staff members, who commented just a few days before the election: "If he goes below fifty percent, I'll shoot myself."[6] (She didn't.)

Not surprisingly, McGovern did not attribute his better-than-expected showing to Muskie's crying incident. His success, he said, was due more to his extensive campaign efforts, and to being "better positioned on the issues that moved the voters: jobs, tax reform, the war, openness in government and political reform."[7] It's hard to believe that Muskie was against jobs, tax reform, openness in government, and political reform; and Muskie was clearly opposed to the war at that point. So the issues were probably of less influence than McGovern suggested.

Whatever the reasons for his good showing, McGovern was clearly the "winner," despite receiving fewer votes than Muskie. He did much better than the press expected, establishing himself as a formidable challenger to Muskie and other Democrats who would later enter the race, and his showing significantly helped his fundraising efforts. The results clearly hurt Muskie's candidacy, but for both candidates, the New Hampshire primary was merely one contest with many more to follow. In no sense can that primary be seen as decisive for either candidate. In the broader picture, however, it seems clear that McGovern would not have been the party's nominee had the old convention system of nominating candidates still been in place. The reforms led to a more democratic process, but they produced a candidate who was almost certainly not the strongest the party could offer against Nixon in the general election.

BY CONTRAST, the reforms hardly affected the GOP in 1972. Richard Nixon's re-nomination by the Republican Party was never seriously in doubt. California Congressman Paul N. "Pete" McCloskey entered the race against Nixon as an antiwar candidate, and Ohio Congressman John Ashbrook took on the president for having abandoned his conservative principles. A fourth candidate was comedian Pat Paulson, best known for his stint on television's *Laugh-In*. Nixon won easily with 68 percent of the vote to McCloskey's 20 percent, Ashbrook's 10 percent, and Paulson's paltry 1 percent.

1976 — The Halcyon Days of Retail Politicking

With Senator Ted Kennedy once again deciding against a quest for the presidency, the Democratic field was wide open, with many candidates opting to run. By contrast, just two major candidates sought the GOP nomination: President Gerald Ford, who took office after Nixon's resignation in 1974; and former California governor Ronald Reagan, a strong supporter of Barry Goldwater's failed candidacy twelve years earlier. The Democratic primary would see the one-on-one retail politicking for which New Hampshire is known, and it would turn out to be the decisive factor in producing a winner. The Republican primary, however, would find that the determinative factor in producing a winner was less the candidates' personal campaigning and more the media stories about the candidates' personal characteristics and issue positions.

THE TWO CANDIDATES who might have been the front-runners for the Democratic nomination were primarily Kennedy, and if not him, possibly Minnesota Senator Walter Mondale. After Kennedy declared his noncandidacy because of family problems, Mondale tried to raise funds for a presidential campaign, but without much success. In November 1974, he announced he would not run. "Basically," he said, "I found I did not have the overwhelming desire to be President which is essential for the kind of campaign that is required." He admitted later that after months of trying to raise money, he couldn't face another whole year "sleeping in Holiday Inns."[8] Those words came back to haunt him a bit when he later agreed to be Carter's running mate, though he had a facetious response for the press: "What I said at the time was that I did not want to spend most of my life in Holiday Inns. But I've checked and found they've all been redecorated. They're marvelous places to stay and I've thought it over and that's where I'd like to be."[9]

Whatever fire Mondale lacked to be a presidential candidate, Carter more than made up—several times over. As early as September 1972, even before George McGovern lost the election by a record margin, the one-term governor of "backwater" Georgia was planning to become the next president of the United States. It was an outrageous aspiration—that a man who was so little known nationally, had no power base, would be out of office (Georgia had a one-term limit for governor), lacked any experience in Washington, and had few political connections would seriously entertain the idea that he could become president. But Carter had the ambition. After he lost his first bid for governor in 1966, he immediately began campaigning for 1970, driving to all parts of the state. "No invitation was too small or too distant to turn down." He narrowly won the Democratic primary and then the general election. His strategy for the presidency was similar—to engage all out in one-on-one politicking, supplemented, of course, by creating an extensive get-out-the-vote organization.[10]

His politicking, however, was generally bereft of specific issue positions. The country had just gone through a decade of revelations that called into question the high level of trust the American people had in their government. Polls show a steep and (so far) permanent decline in public trust during that period,[11] a time that included President Johnson's manipulative actions that resulted in the Gulf of Tonkin Resolution, which got the country into a devastating war; the Pentagon Papers, which showed how the public had been systematically deceived about so-called progress in the war; the Watergate scandal and revelations of the Nixon administration's "dirty tricks"; the impeachment proceedings and Nixon's resignation; and the pardon that President Ford granted to Nixon barely a month later—followed by revelations that Ford had lied about whether anyone had talked with him about the pardon before he granted it. In addition to these incidents were deteriorating economic conditions (triggered by the oil embargo in the early 1970s) best described at the time by the term "stagflation." Ford's WIN button, "Whip Inflation Now," was a national joke. In that context, Carter ran as an outsider, as someone who—unlike others who had spent their careers in the federal government—could be trusted. "I'll never lie to you," Carter promised his audience. "And I'll never mislead you."[12] One of his stock openings when meeting a group of voters was to announce, "I am not a lawyer." The audience would laugh and some would applaud. Then he would say, "And I am not from Washington," to more laughter and applause.[13]

Carter's principal opponents in the New Hampshire primary were Arizona Congressman Mo Udall, former Oklahoma Senator Fred Harris, Indiana Senator Birch Bayh, and former US ambassador to France, Sargent Shriver, who had been McGovern's running mate four years earlier. All of these candidates were considered "progressive," while Carter was considered more conservative. That was, in fact, clearly the case, as understood by people who paid close attention to his record, but such differences were not stressed during the campaign. Later, Carter's ability to come down on both sides of an issue would surface as a "fuzziness" that called into question his integrity,[14] but in New Hampshire he was mostly the outsider running against a corrupt and ineffective Washington.

Nevertheless, a poll conducted by Moore's political science class at the University of New Hampshire and published in a small weekly newspaper in Boston, *The Real Paper,* showed that Carter's support was stronger among conservative than among liberal Democrats, and that Udall was slightly ahead of Carter among the latter.[15] While most voters may not have been aware of issue differences among the candidates, the most attentive voters no doubt were. And that was a problem for Udall, who was competing for the progressive vote with Bayh, Harris, and Shriver. Carter had the right end of the political spectrum to himself, since Senator Henry Jackson decided to forego New Hampshire and launch his campaign a week later in Massachusetts. Had Jackson competed with Carter in the first primary, Udall might well have emerged the victor. Or Jackson. Or . . . but history is filled with "what-ifs."

One other factor that helped Carter beat Udall is the boost he got out of winning the Iowa caucuses. He had organized a campaign in Iowa at the same time he organized one in New Hampshire, and he spent considerable time in the Hawkeye State in the year before the election. Udall decided late in the game that he would compete with Carter in Iowa, but by the time he made the effort, Carter had been there for months. The money and time Udall spent there detracted from his efforts in New Hampshire, where he had a decent chance to win. In Iowa, Carter "won" by coming in second behind "uncommitted," getting 27 percent of the vote, compared with 8 percent for Bayh, 5 percent for Harris, 3 percent for Udall, and 1 percent for Shriver. Media reporting of the results uniformly focused on Carter as the winner and therefore the front-runner going into New Hampshire. Even more devastating for Udall was the consensus that Iowa had hurt his campaign, with R. W. Apple of the *New York Times* suggesting that his campaign was of "minor-league quality."[16]

In the end, Carter's six-point victory in New Hampshire (29 percent to Udall's 23 percent) was a model of retail—though mostly issueless—politicking. Brereton best captures the candidate's efforts: "While others held to the pattern of media interviews, speeches to captive audiences and to coffees, Carter's indefatigable person-to-person, factory gate, main street efforts reached a much larger number of people. He visited, at least once and sometimes twice, every major factory near a Democratic area. . . . Carter and his family campaigned, as one Udall staffer put it, 'for a year as though it were the last six weeks of the campaign. That saturation campaigning made him impossible to beat.'"[17]

WHEN AN INCUMBENT president is challenged from within his own party, it means he is already a weak candidate. In 1976, Ford was unusually vulnerable. He was an unelected president, having been appointed to the vice presidency after Vice President Spiro Agnew resigned over bribery charges; he was widely criticized for granting a pardon to Nixon just one month after the president resigned amid impeachment proceedings in the House; he was perceived widely by the press, if not the public, as a "well-intentioned bumbler," "a nice guy who was in over his head"; and he was experiencing considerable turmoil in his administration involving both his secretary of defense and his national security advisor.[18]

Still, it seemed highly unlikely that the GOP would refuse to renominate its own incumbent president, especially by replacing him with Reagan, a man who seemed so closely identified with the extreme right wing of his party, which itself was symbolized by Barry Goldwater and his devastating loss to Lyndon Johnson in 1964. The *New York Times* senior columnist, James Reston, captured this sentiment in his article published the day after Reagan announced his candidacy on November 20, 1975: "The astonishing thing is that this amusing but frivolous Reagan fantasy is taken so seriously by the news media and particularly by the President. It makes a lot of news, but it doesn't make much sense."[19]

Yet, two Gallup polls suggested Reston and like-minded observers were mis-reading the public — or at least Republican voters. In October, before Reagan's announcement, a poll of Republicans nationally showed Ford leading Reagan by 23 percentage points; a similar poll in November, following the announcement, showed Reagan leading by 8 points — an astonishing 31-point swing in the margin between the two candidates in just one month.[20] Suddenly, the Reagan challenge was seen as real. "The President surprisingly and incongruously was cast as the underdog in the minds of many voters."[21]

The New Hampshire primary would be crucial for both candidates. If the president lost there, it would reinforce the view that as an unelected president, he was not really legitimate, and that voters, if given the choice, would select someone else. Ford's own advisors felt that if the president lost in New Hampshire, his campaign could quickly crumble. The flip side of the coin was that the early primary was a test for Reagan, too — specifically of whether his claim that Ford was not a bona fide incumbent would be validated. An early Ford win would nullify that argument, which could lead to additional Ford victories and doom Reagan's candidacy.[22]

Neither Ford nor Reagan campaigned in Iowa. That year was the first time Iowa Republicans held their caucuses before the New Hampshire primary, and it was also the first time they conducted a straw poll right before the caucuses began in order to provide the press with some sense of the results. The straw poll included 583 voters from sixty-two sample precincts out of more than two thousand. Ford "won" with a 16-vote margin, 264 to 248. The press largely ignored the results, though some news stories did note the closeness of the outcome, suggesting Ford was not necessarily a shoo-in for his party's nomination.[23]

For years in his speeches and columns, Reagan had been denouncing "big government," especially the federal government in Washington — a theme that was now at the center of his candidacy for president. One of the suggestions he made in a 1975 speech in Chicago was that the federal budget could be reduced by $90 billion if certain social programs were transferred to the states. It was a massive cut in the budget and meant that states would either have to cut programs or raise taxes, or both. At the time he gave the speech, Reagan had not yet declared his candidacy, and the implications of his proposal were largely ignored in the press. But after he announced his decision to run for president, the Ford campaign got hold of the speech and blasted Reagan for the proposal just as the former governor landed in New Hampshire for his first foray into the state. The press latched on to the issue, pointing out that 62 percent of the welfare programs in New Hampshire were federally funded. Wouldn't that mean the state would have to increase its property taxes, or institute an income or sales tax, or cut the programs? This was an especially sensitive issue in New Hampshire, since it had no statewide sales tax or general income tax (and still doesn't). The ninety billion dollar proposal was an albatross that never went away. Later, while campaigning in Florida where the primary would be held just two weeks after New Hampshire's, Reagan suggested that one way to fix the Social Security system was to have people invest in the stock market. It was just one of many suggested fixes, but the Ford campaign glommed onto that issue, suggesting that Reagan wanted to kill Social Security.[24]

Eventually, Reagan came up with stock justifications for his ideas, and the large crowds that he continued to draw in New Hampshire suggested that he was weathering the attacks on his antigovernment proposals. In the last week of the campaign, a poll by his pollster, Richard Wirthlin, showed Reagan leading Ford by 11 percentage points.[25] Hugh Gregg, Reagan's state campaign chairman, had always wanted to lower expectations, saying that if Reagan were to get even 40 percent of the vote against an incumbent president, that should be considered a victory. But the Reagan campaign was clearly excited about winning the approaching election, and — contrary to the strategy that Gregg so emphatically sought — New Hampshire Governor Meldrim Thomson told the press Reagan would get at least 55 percent of the vote.[26] Compounding the problem of setting expectations, Reagan himself left the state before Election Day, confident that he would emerge the victor.

In 1976, none of the major media organizations had yet developed their own polling apparatus, and thus had to depend on whatever polling information the campaigns would share. Dr. George Gallup refused to poll in primary states, believing they were too fluid to make accurate readings. His polls were of national samples, either of Democrats, or Republicans, or the electorate more generally. However, in late February, the UNH poll published in *The Real Paper* showed Ford leading Reagan by a couple of percentage points, but that was within the poll's margin of error, suggesting the race was a toss-up — not the clear Reagan victory that the press expected.[27]

That article, however, had little impact on the expectations of the news media or on the expectations of Reagan's own campaign staff. When Reagan lost the primary by 1.5 percentage points, it was too late to claim a moral victory, as McGovern had done in 1972 and McCarthy in 1968 — both of whom lost, but did better than expected against the presumed front-runners. In 1976, Reagan was expected to win, and he lost. The victory was a major boost for Ford, who went on to win in Florida two weeks later, the momentum from New Hampshire an important factor in that victory. Had Ford lost, it's likely the country would have seen a Carter/Reagan contest four years earlier than it actually did.

1980 — Loeb Wins One for the Gipper, and the Kennedy Bubble Bursts

It had long been expected that Ted Kennedy would one day run for president. Two of his older brothers had done so already, one assassinated after becoming president, the other while running for the office. Certainly, Teddy would keep the dream alive. Indeed, if it hadn't been for Chappaquiddick,[28] he probably would have run in 1972. But the scandal was still too fresh in the public's mind. In 1976, he had numerous family problems, he said, that demanded his attention. By the fall of 1979, however, more than a decade had passed since Chappaquiddick, which should have at least diminished the salience of the scandal — though Kennedy recognized that the questions it raised about his character would never go away completely. There were other factors this time that didn't exist earlier, most notably the pleading by many Democratic leaders across the country for him to run against President Jimmy Carter, whose presidency was seen as a disaster to the Democratic Party. The president's approval rating in the eleventh quarter of his presidency (July through October, 1979) was just 31 percent, 19 points lower than Nixon's and 27 points lower than John Kennedy's at comparable points in their presidencies.[29] Numerous Democrats across the country were dreading having to run for reelection in 1980 with Carter at the head of the ticket. Besides, the polls all indicated that Kennedy easily led Carter for the nomination and would clearly be the strongest Democrat to run in the 1980 election.[30]

After much thought and pressure from colleagues, Kennedy decided to make the run. But the timing couldn't have been worse. On November 4, 1979, just three days before he officially announced his candidacy, fifty-two Americans were taken hostage in the US embassy in Iran. Almost immediately there was a "rally 'round the flag" effect that benefitted the president. By the end of November, Gallup showed a 19-point jump in Carter's job approval rating, which continued its upward movement into December. Then, at the end of December, the Soviet Union invaded Afghanistan, Iran's neighbor, giving Carter's rating another "rally 'round the flag" boost. According to the Gallup polls, Carter's job approval was at 56 percent by the time of the Iowa caucuses, 24 points higher than it had been when Kennedy announced his candidacy.[31] Though Carter refused to campaign in either Iowa or New Hampshire, claiming his responsibilities as commander in chief precluded such mundane activities, he easily beat Kennedy in both states' contests.

Two other factors are generally thought to have contributed to Kennedy's precipitous decline. The first was an interview with CBS News reporter Roger Mudd, during which Kennedy seemed unable to articulate his ideas clearly. One reporter described the interview as "a stumbling, vacuous performance that showed Kennedy as a man with no coherent explanation for Chappaquiddick and no clear reason for seeking the presidency . . . a disaster from which the campaign never recovered."[32] The second factor was Kennedy's response in another interview a month later, when he was asked about the Shah of Iran, who had been granted asylum in the United States after the Iranian Revolution. It was this grant of asylum that had led to the Iranian hostage crisis in the first place. Instead of finessing the issue, Kennedy condemned the Shah for running "one of the most violent regimes in the history of mankind" and for stealing "umpteen billions of dollars" from the Iranian people.[33] The comments seemed to support the very justification that the Iranian hostage-takers had claimed for their actions against the United States, making Kennedy appear disloyal to the president in a time of international crisis.

After leading in New Hampshire by 30 points in the summer of 1979,[34] Kennedy lost the primary by 10 points — 47 percent to 37 percent. New Hampshire was not as much a cause of Kennedy's eventual loss of the nomination as it was a reflection of his decline and Carter's temporary rejuvenation. Afterward, one reporter wrote, "One of the longest-lived bubbles in American politics — the image of Edward Kennedy as a political superman — had been burst."[35]

SEVEN REPUBLICANS were candidates for their party's nomination in 1980, but to William Loeb, publisher of the *Manchester Union Leader,* there was only the Gipper. All the others were beyond redemption. Four years earlier, Ronald Reagan had come close to unseating an incumbent president, unexpectedly losing by less than two percentage points. Loeb had supported Reagan's candidacy, of course, but not with the energy that he had embraced other candidates and causes over the years. Jules Witcover remarked on this point, noting that "for some reason Loeb in 1976 pulled his punches."[36] Witcover suggests that the publication of Kevin Nash's *Who the Hell Is William Loeb?*[37] may have constrained Loeb's vitriol, though it's also likely that Loeb fully expected Reagan to win. The publisher, like others, had made a mistake. And in 1980, he was not going to repeat it.

That year in New Hampshire, there would be two GOP primary electorates: one that regularly read the *Manchester Union Leader,* and the other that did not. Just under half (46 percent) of GOP voters fell into that first category, leaving the rest (54 percent) not directly influenced by the paper's "virulent campaign against Bush."[38] The two electorates would turn out to have very different views of Ronald Reagan.

Though the former California governor and popular radio host was the best-known GOP candidate and was the clear front-runner for the party's nomination, Reagan had several vulnerabilities. He was sixty-nine years old and would be the oldest man in American history to be elected president if he won; he had been out of office for almost six years; he was prone to verbal gaffes; and he was reputed to have little physical energy. If a younger, appealing candidate were to win early, it could quickly derail the Reagan quest.

Initially, Loeb perceived Reagan's most serious challenger to be Illinois Representative Phil Crane, a young conservative whom Loeb himself wanted to see as Reagan's vice president.[39] But in September 1978, Crane declared his candidacy for president, which left Loeb fuming. Initially, the publisher tried to persuade the young congressman to defer to Reagan, in print calling Crane "this writer's favorite younger Republican," but when Crane persisted, Loeb went into full attack mode. In

March 1979, the paper launched a series of scathing articles about Crane's personal and professional life, charging him with (among other things) being a womanizer and a cheat. According to an unnamed Crane associate cited in the paper: "The boy scout image is a cloak of deception. For God's sake, the guy once told a friend he was committed in this life to bedding down 1,000 different women." Another unnamed associate: "He's just too good looking. The women are always throwing themselves all over him, and the party circuit was too inviting."[40] Later the paper went after his family, including a front-page story that accused his daughter of harassing two loons on Squam Lake.[41]

With Crane's candidacy in tatters, it was not clear who — if anyone — might emerge from the Iowa caucuses as Reagan's principal challenger. Loeb went after all of them, sometimes as a group, other times focusing on the individual. Former Texas governor John Connally was "Oily John: the Arab Candidate" and a "Born-Again Wheeler Dealer." Tennessee Senator Howard Baker and George Bush were dismissed as "Bakerbush," both liberals. Bush was also characterized as elitist: "The candidate of all the 'clean fingernail' Republicans, the sales-taxers and income-taxers."[42] Kansas Senator Robert Dole, the party's vice presidential nominee four years earlier, had an anemic campaign that was not worth watching, and Illinois Congressman John Anderson was too liberal to be considered a serious challenger to Reagan.

The results of the Iowa caucuses on January 21 stunned virtually everyone: George Bush edged out the overwhelming favorite Ronald Reagan by 2 percentage points, 32 percent to 30 percent.[43] The third-place finisher, Howard Baker, got just 15 percent of the vote. It was now a two-man race. Reagan had refused to participate in the *Des Moines Register* debate, and he had spent relatively few days campaigning in Iowa, a strategy based on the assumption that he could coast to the nomination. Iowans did not like that. And now, for New Hampshire, the coasting strategy would have to be abandoned.

Fortunately for Reagan, there were five weeks between the Iowa caucuses and the New Hampshire primary. Immediately, the Reagan campaign wanted to focus the contest on just him and Bush. As later noted by Gerald Carmen, head of Reagan's New Hampshire effort that winter,

"When we challenged George Bush to a debate right after Iowa, we were down twenty-two points. We were desperate for some kind of an event which would act as a catalyst to showcase President Reagan."[44] A UNH poll in the fall had shown Reagan at the head of the pack with 36 percent of the vote, 25 points ahead of Bush.[45] The new situation, with Reagan trailing by 22 points, represented a 47-point swing in public opinion, caused mostly by the results of the Iowa caucuses.

With the emergence of a single challenger to the Gipper, Loeb could now focus his efforts. Bush became the lightning rod for the paper's attacks. He was portrayed as a liberal pretending to be a conservative, as a "silk-stocking" Republican who owed his many government appointments to his connections rather than his talent, a "loser" as reflected in his separate campaigns for the House and later the Senate, a hypocrite (for many reasons), a "Bush-Leaguer" and a naïf who was soft on communism. An objective content analysis of the paper's coverage from January 1 to February 25, the day before the primary, showed the following:[46]

- Positive for Reagan: 113 stories (including 55 on the front or back page[47])
- Positive for Bush: 9 stories (including 3 on the front or back page)
- Negative for Reagan: 5 stories (including 3 on the front or back page)
- Negative for Bush: 87 stories (including 40 on the front page, 5 on the back)
- Neutral for Reagan: 127 (including 84 on the front or back page)
- Neutral for Bush: 85 stories (including 55 on the front or back page)

Some headlines that led to critical stories of Bush include: "Let's Not Be Sucker Bait"; "Only a Bush Leaguer"; "George Bush Says 'Go — Yourself'"; "Is Everybody Lying but George?"; and — perhaps as the ultimate condemnation, printed the day before the election — "'George Bush Is a Liberal.'" Headlines that were favorable to Reagan include "Ronald Reagan Lauds N.H. on Tricentennial — Cites State History in Opposing Excessive Taxation" and — perhaps as the ultimate praise — "'God Has Chosen Reagan to Lead This Country.'"

As one of us has written previously, "The figures measuring the number of positive and negative stories about Bush and Reagan reveal one of the most lopsided 'campaigns' ever conducted by the *Union Leader* for one of its candidates. Some people may disagree with the classification of one story or another as positive, negative, or neutral, but even the casual reader of the *Union Leader* in 1980, or in the year leading up to the primary, would have to conclude that the newspaper presented a strong case to vote for Reagan and against Bush."[48]

Three weeks after Iowa, a UNH poll showed Reagan still trailing Bush, but by just 5 points. Though the race was tightening, Bush still refused to participate in a one-on-one debate with Reagan. Perhaps the most notable aspect of the poll was the difference in views between readers of the *Union Leader* and nonreaders of the paper. Reagan led Bush among readers by a 31-point margin, 53 percent to 22 percent. But Bush led Reagan among nonreaders by a 32-point margin, 49 percent to 17 percent.[49]

It is tempting to think that the difference between readers and nonreaders is accounted for by ideology, that the stronger conservatives would be more likely to read the paper than the less conservative or moderate voters, which would explain why readers were more supportive than nonreaders of the Reagan candidacy. But the gap between readers and nonreaders persists even when compared by ideology. Here is a table that shows how influential the *Union Leader* was for each level of ideology:[50]

Percent Support for Ronald Reagan by Readers and Nonreaders of the *Manchester Union Leader* and by Ideology of the Voters (Compared)			
	Manchester Union Leader		
	Readers	Nonreaders	Difference
	%	%	Percentage Points
Strong conservative	84	26	58
Moderate conservative	50	13	37
Lean conservative	58	22	36
In-between	50	25	25
Liberal	41	8	33
Source: Based on UNH Poll, February 1980 (N = 379).			

Note that the largest difference is among "strong conservatives," with 84 percent of readers supporting Reagan, compared with just 26 percent of nonreaders. Clearly, the *Union Leader's* influence was especially great among voters who shared the paper's ideology. Still, the gap between readers and nonreaders persisted even among voters who were less than "strong conservatives"" — with an overall average 36-point difference between the two groups.

Without the *Union Leader's* all-out campaign against Bush, it's questionable whether the advantage Bush enjoyed after Iowa would have evaporated in the three weeks that followed. Among nonreaders at that point, after all, he still led by 31 points. In any case, as Election Day neared and the race tightened even more, Bush finally agreed to the one-on-one debate. A debate among all candidates was held on Wednesday, February 20. The two-man debate was scheduled for Saturday, February 23. The first debate produced no winners, but the second one — at least with regard to the coverage the incident received — turned out to be decisive.

The editor of the *Nashua Telegraph*, Jon Breen, intended both to sponsor and host the debate. At the last minute, the Federal Election Commission ruled that sponsoring the debate among just the two candidates would represent an illegal contribution to the candidates' campaigns. When the Bush campaign balked at sharing the expenses, Carmen paid the whole amount of $3,500 for the Reagan campaign. The Bush campaign had been notified that Reagan wanted to open the debate to the other five candidates, an option to which they had agreed; but at the debate itself, Bush deferred to Breen as to whether the others should be included. The other candidates came on stage to protest their exclusion, but Breen insisted that the debate would include only the two candidates. Reagan demanded to make a statement, but Breen tried to start the debate with the first question. When Reagan insisted again that he be allowed to make an announcement, Breen asked the sound man to turn off Reagan's microphone. But before the mic got cut off, Reagan interrupted Breen, his voice tense with anger: "I am paying for this microphone, Mr. Green."[51] Reagan looked masterful; Bush was passive. The context painted Bush as elitist and weak. It was a devastating incident just three days before the primary.

The clip was replayed numerous times over the next two days running up to the election, giving Reagan the boost he needed to win decisively, 50 percent to 23 percent. In Manchester, where the *Union Leader* naturally has its greatest penetration, Reagan won by close to an eight-to-one margin.[52] A post-election UNH poll that closely mirrored the actual results showed that in the end, Reagan won among both readers and nonreaders — 68 percent to Bush's 14 percent among readers, and 32 percent to 26 percent among nonreaders, with the rest going to other candidates.[53]

Recently, Gerald Carmen acknowledged that as head of Reagan's state campaign, he regularly fed stories to the *Union Leader*, even suggesting headlines and themes.[54] And following the primary, former congressman Pete McCloskey wrote a commiserating note to Bush, describing the paper as a "a major campaign document worth tens of thousands of dollars to the lucky beneficiary."[55] For the lucky beneficiary in 1980, it may have been worth much more: the presidency itself.

1984 — The Iowa Bump

While no major candidate challenged President Reagan in the GOP primary in 1984, eight Democrats competed in the Democratic primary. Initially, the two front-runners were former vice president Walter Mondale, and astronaut and Senator John Glenn. An Iowa poll in October 1979 confirmed the conventional wisdom, showing Mondale ahead of Glenn by 46 percent to 27 percent, with Gary Hart getting 7 percent, George McGovern 5 percent, and Jesse Jackson, Alan Cranston, Reubin Askew, and Ernest Hollings all receiving less than 5 percent each. Gallup's national results at the time also showed that the nomination was primarily a two-man contest between Mondale and Glenn.[56] Similar results were found in New Hampshire — Mondale with about 40 percent support to Glenn's 18 percent, with Hart and Jackson at about 8 percent each, and the rest scoring lower.[57]

Mondale's challenge was to overcome the bad feelings among Democrats associated with the Carter presidency and the Carter/Mondale landslide loss to Ronald Reagan four years earlier. Mondale had the name recognition, but there was evidence that in New Hampshire at least, many voters were looking for some viable alternative. Glenn could be that candidate.

While Hart and Mondale campaigned extensively in New Hampshire, Glenn did not. Nor did Glenn establish a strong grassroots campaign, relying more on media coverage and ads to convey his messages.[58] He had a similar problematic approach in Iowa.[59] He didn't seem to understand that, especially in Iowa, he needed to get out and meet voters. Communication through ads and press conferences would not suffice.

In New Hampshire, both Hart and Mondale were considered to have the most extensive organizations in the state. Nevertheless, as Election Day approached, the strength of their organizations seemed not to matter much. The extensive campaigning seemed to have made little difference in the polls, while Glenn's weaker organization and relatively meager retail politicking didn't seem to be hurting him. In the week before the Iowa caucuses, a series of ABC/*Washington Post* tracking polls showed Mondale with an average of 37 percent support, Glenn 20 percent, Hart 14 percent, and Jackson 11 percent. These figures reflected a slight decline for Mondale (–3 points) from earlier in the year, and slight gains for Glenn (+2 points), Hart (+6 points), and Jackson (+3 points).

The Iowa caucuses were a sure thing for Mondale. From the neighboring state of Minnesota, he had visited the state often and was well known, sometimes referring to himself as "Iowa's third senator."[60] He organized early and extensively in the state, and no candidate was expected to beat him there. The only question was: How well would Glenn do? The expectation was that Glenn would come in a reasonable second, and that New Hampshire could be a fairer contest between the two candidates. But it didn't turn out that way.

The candidate who spent the most money and the second greatest number of days in Iowa was California Senator Alan Cranston.[61] He was seventy years old, and he looked older. As Brereton wrote, "With his bald head . . . and gaunt appearance, he was probably the most unmarketable candidate, visually, in the television age."[62] Askew tried to run from the right, but there were few conservative Democratic activists in Iowa he could count on. Hollings and Jackson decided to concentrate their efforts in New Hampshire. McGovern was never taken seriously, given his age and his loss twelve years earlier.

That left Gary Hart as the alternative to John Glenn, should the astronaut falter. And that's what happened. With Glenn's ineffective campaign in Iowa, it was Hart who emerged the runner-up to Mondale, albeit a distant one: Mondale got 48 percent of the vote, Hart just 16 percent. Glenn came in fifth, behind McGovern and Cranston, with just over 3 percent of the vote. The poor showing essentially marked the end of the Glenn campaign. Across the country, the major newspapers focused on Glenn's poor performance. There was also little hope for Glenn in New Hampshire, where he had been trailing Mondale by double-digits since the polling started. Thus, the only remaining challenge to Mondale's nomination was . . . Gary Hart.

For the first time since the party reforms had changed the nomination process, only eight days separated the Iowa caucuses from the New Hampshire primary, and no one seemed ready for the "Iowa bump." Media polls were not around in 1980 to show the surge in support that Bush got from his win in Iowa, but now in 1984, ABC News and the *Washington Post* were initiating the first daily tracking poll ever conducted in the state. Once the Iowa results were made known, the tracking polls showed a surge in support for Hart and declines in support for Mondale and Glenn. The final tracking poll showed a 30–30 split between Mondale and Hart, and Glenn at 14 percent. But the final results gave Hart a decisive victory, 37 percent to Mondale's 28 percent, with Glenn getting just 12 percent and the other candidates coming in at 5 percent or lower. Among the top two candidates, the results represented a 32-point swing in support — from a Mondale lead of 23 points before the caucuses to a 9-point loss in the election.

Mondale's pollster, Peter Hart (no relation to Gary Hart) was analyzing his own polls and couldn't understand what was happening to cause the change. Five days after Iowa he called Moore from Washington, DC, asking if there was anything happening in the state that the national news media were not covering to help explain Mondale's erosion of support. Of course, there wasn't. Hart didn't realize at the time that this was the new reality—instead of weeks between the Iowa caucuses and the New Hampshire primary, there were only eight days, hardly enough time for the candidates to react to any surprises that might happen in Iowa. Hart's surprise second-place showing dominated media coverage and energized his otherwise middling campaign. The Mondale camp was bewildered.

The sudden reversal of fortunes generated by the Iowa results called into question the mantra that a candidate needed to engage in retail politicking in New Hampshire. Yes, in Iowa, the first contest, such activity was required, even for a well-known candidate like John Glenn. But now it would appear that it was more important to spend time and resources in Iowa than to organize and campaign in New Hampshire. After all, little had changed in New Hampshire from December through the end of February. Then suddenly, the Iowa caucuses upended the whole race. But the Hart staff in New Hampshire contended that the months of organizing and campaigning in the state had made it possible for Hart to take advantage of the Iowa bump.[63] As Jeanne Shaheen explained: "We knocked on about 80,000 doors and we'd handed all this literature to people, yet there were a couple of questions on people's minds. One was we couldn't win." But after Hart came in second in Iowa, doing much better than expected, "it made him suddenly this national figure and he became a personality to them."[64]

The lesson learned from the 1984 primary was this: the Iowa caucuses can exert a major influence on the New Hampshire primary.

Another lesson learned from the 1984 primary: Because there are few policy differences among most candidates in a party primary, voters can quickly change their minds about which candidate to choose. Major media events can easily lead to last minute reversals in voter preferences.

These lessons would be relearned four years later.

1988—The Iowa Screen

By the last week preceding the New Hampshire primary campaign, just days after the Iowa caucuses, the field of Democratic candidates had been narrowed to just three contenders. At least one in the loser group, Al Gore, didn't see his situation that way, expecting to make his show on

Super Tuesday the following month. In fact, he had done the inexcusable — inexcusable, at least, if he'd were to have a ghost of a chance of doing well in Iowa — by excoriating the nomination process that allowed Iowa to hold the first contest. And he did this in Iowa. At the annual Jefferson-Jackson dinner in Des Moines, to boot. There he caustically attacked "a nomination process that gives one state the loudest voice and then produces candidates who cannot even carry that state." He was, of course, referring to the Hawkeye State, which had not voted for a Democratic president since LBJ in 1964.[65] Criticizing Iowans for their caucuses, just days before the election, gave him what might charitably be called a negative boost. He ended up with one hundredth of one percent of the vote.[66] And he would eventually learn that skipping Iowa and making a half-hearted effort in New Hampshire was not a strategy for success.

At the beginning of the election cycle, the clear front-runner among Democrats in Iowa, New Hampshire, and the country overall was Gary Hart, a reflection of the strong campaign he had waged in 1984 against Walter Mondale. But in May 1987, Hart was caught spending the weekend with a woman, Donna Rice, who later admitted that she and Hart had previously gone on a trip aboard the yacht *Monkey Business.* That incident, amid other similar womanizing accusations, forced Hart to drop out of the race just days later. His reentry the following December was a nonstarter, especially after new accusations of campaign spending violations were reported.[67] Other candidates who did not survive Iowa included Delaware Senator Joe Biden, who was caught plagiarizing a speech from Neil Kinnock, a British Labor leader. This in turn led to discoveries of other situations in which he had lifted quotations from politicians without attribution, an incident in law school where he submitted part of a paper with apparently several plagiarized pages, and finally a confrontation with a heckler when Biden overstated his academic achievements.[68] There was also former Arizona governor Bruce Babbitt, who bombed in Iowa, a relatively conservative candidate appealing to a mostly liberal electorate. Jesse Jackson had his moments in the early polls because of his high name recognition and because most of the other candidates were not well known, but at the end he fared poorly in Iowa and subsequently lost his slight traction in New Hampshire. Colorado

Representative Patricia Schroeder made a brief effort at running for president in 1987, but bowed out by the fall of that year.

That left three candidates—Missouri Congressman and House Majority Leader Richard Gephardt, Illinois Senator Paul Simon, and Massachusetts Governor Michael Dukakis. After Hart's demise, Dukakis was the clear favorite in his neighboring state of New Hampshire, but in the first contest of the nomination process, he was competing against two candidates who lived in states that were neighbors to Iowa. Nationally, no candidates (other than Hart) polled well, because none were widely known. But Dukakis was exceptionally successful in the "invisible" primary—raising funds for his campaign. In the first quarter, he drew in more than four times as much money as did either Gephardt or Simon. And he continued to out-raise his competitors in the following months.[69] This success gave him credibility among politicos and the press, though it didn't mean much to the Iowa voters.

Dukakis was also hurt in Iowa because it was revealed that his campaign manager, John Sasso, had been the person who had brought Biden's plagiarism of Kinnock's speech to the press' attention. Sasso had done it surreptitiously, trying to hide from both Dukakis and the press more generally the role he had played in the incident. Even when rumors circulated (erroneously) that it was the Gephardt campaign that had ratted out Biden, Sasso didn't step forward to take responsibility. When Dukakis publicly condemned the action, Sasso finally admitted to Dukakis what he had done, resulting eventually in his dismissal and abject apologies by Dukakis to both the Biden and Gephardt campaigns.

Gephardt won the Iowa caucuses vote with 31 percent, while Simon came in second at 27 percent and Dukakis third at 22 percent.

Given the 1984 experience, when Hart's surprise second-place showing boosted his standing in New Hampshire, one might have expected Gephardt to get the same Iowa bump. And he did. Polls before the caucuses showed Dukakis the clear front-runner in the Granite State, with 35 percent to 45 percent in the polls, with Jesse Jackson typically in second or among the also-rans. After the caucuses, both Gephardt and Simon surged into second and third place, respectively, but as the week progressed, they were unable to catch up to Dukakis. There are two possible explanations for this failure — Dukakis's strength among his neighbors, and the slugfest between Gephardt and Simon.

Dukakis's strength came from several sources. He had been governor of neighboring Massachusetts for over a decade (though not continuously), and had been covered mostly positively in the Boston press. Boston news stations all reach a good portion of the southern part of New Hampshire, so in effect, many residents in southern New Hampshire saw as much or more about Massachusetts politics as they did about events in their own state. Dukakis was also a frequent visitor to the state, less than an hour's drive from Boston, for receptions and dinners with supporters.[70] He had also been supportive in the (failed) campaign in the 1970s to prevent a nuclear power plant from being built in Seabrook, a town bordering Massachusetts. As governor, Dukakis had delayed the licensing process for Seabrook by refusing to submit the emergency evacuation plans of nearby Massachusetts towns. This, of course, endeared him to a significant segment of the liberal New Hampshire Democrats.[71]

The second reason Iowa didn't give Gephardt as big a boost as he anticipated is that the Missouri congressman was competing with a fellow Midwesterner to be the alternative to Dukakis. Germond and Witcover speculate that it would have been better for Gephardt if Dukakis had come in second in Iowa, thus squeezing out Simon and making the New Hampshire contest one between Gephardt and Dukakis. But after coming in second, Simon would not be denied and immediately attacked Gephardt, not Dukakis — which forced Gephardt to defend and counterattack. The net result was that the last week before Election Day of the New Hampshire primary consisted mostly of a political brawl between the second and third place candidates, leaving Dukakis relatively unscathed. He won by a 16-point margin, 36 percent to Gephardt's 20 percent, followed closely by Simon at 17 percent, Jackson at 8 percent, Gore 7 percent, Babbitt 5 percent, and Hart 4 percent.[72]

WHILE GEPHARDT didn't get the Iowa bump he expected in the Democratic primary, Robert Dole did get a good boost in the GOP primary. After coming in a surprising first place in Iowa with 37 percent of the vote, followed not by George Bush but by television evangelist Pat Robertson at 25 percent, and then Bush at 18 percent, Dole's polling numbers soared. Before Iowa, Bush had been up by 20 points; two days after the caucuses, the race was dead even.[73] By the end of the week, Dole was up by 6 points.[74] This bump was not unexpected, but Dole's win in Iowa was somewhat surprising, and Bush's third place finish behind Robertson was stunning. And Bush knew that he had precious little time to stop Dole's soaring numbers before the primary would effectively be over for him.

There were other GOP candidates screened out by Iowa. Former Delaware governor Pierre S. "Pete" du Pont never seemed to connect with the voters, nor did former secretary of state Alexander Haig both of whom fared poorly in Iowa. Former New York congressman Jack Kemp experienced a mini-surge in the New Hampshire standings before the Iowa caucuses after running a TV ad that criticized both Bush and Dole for their stands on Social Security, but a fourth-place showing in Iowa was his death knell.[75] Despite coming in second in Iowa, Robertson was never taken seriously in New Hampshire, where the number of fundamentalist Christian voters is considerably smaller than in Iowa.[76]

The key to Bush's comeback victory in New Hampshire appears to be the campaign's decision to go after Dole for "straddling" on the issue of raising taxes. Dole's key advisor in New Hampshire, Tom Rath, had previously warned Dole that the most potent attack Bush could make against him could be on taxes, given the sensitivity of that issue in a state where there was no statewide sales or income tax. Dole, however, was unwilling to take "the pledge," a staple of state politics injected into the national campaign, which required complete opposition to any form of increased or new taxes. Bush was more than willing to take the pledge. He stamped that image firmly in the public's mind with his speech later that summer at the Republican National Convention, when he uttered the fateful words: "Read my lips: No new taxes!" Dole may have been right to refrain from making a promise he felt he couldn't keep, but not doing so provided Bush the opening he needed. A "straddle" television ad against Dole on three issues, one of which was taxes, ran over the weekend. "Bob Dole straddles, and he just won't promise not to raise taxes.

And you know what that means." The spot was, in the views of Germond and Witcover, "a classic case of seizing on an opening and, with just the right amount of distortion, exploiting it." Dole had no response ads on air. It was too late.

In a political environment where two candidates are seen as virtually identical in their issue positions, voters can easily switch from one candidate to another. That happens again and again in primaries, especially early ones when the candidates' themes are just being formulated. Bush emerged the victor, with 38 percent to Dole's 29 percent, followed by Kemp with 13 percent, du Pont 11 percent, and Robertson 9 percent. As Germond and Witcover observed, "What was most striking about the Bush campaign for political resurrection was how insubstantial it really was — a quintessential example of the shallowness of the politics of 1988."[77]

Bush would discover four years later that his promise on taxes, while helpful in getting him elected in 1988, would contribute to his undoing in 1992.

The 1990s and Beyond

By the 1990s, after five election cycles under the reforms adopted in 1972 (along with the reforms of the reforms), the Democratic Party had accommodated itself to the new reality of the nomination process. It was more difficult now for insurgent candidates to upset the apple cart, as George McGovern and Jimmy Carter had done in 1972 and 1976, respectively, and Gary Hart had almost done in 1984 (winning the New Hampshire primary, but ultimately losing to Walter Mondale in the overall contest for the nomination). The accommodation was in part a reflection of the changes in the nature of the campaigning in both Iowa and New Hampshire. Initially, the image of candidates engaging in retail politics, meeting voters one-on-one, or at least in small groups, giving everyone present an opportunity to question the candidate, was largely an accurate reflection of much of the process in Iowa and New Hampshire (at least for non-incumbents). Candidates like McGovern and Carter and Hart could start their campaigns with little money and use their early victories to raise money for subsequent contests. But by the 1990s, the retail politicking that the two states like so much to emphasize was complemented by old-fashioned wholesale politicking. Extensive television ads, large public gatherings for candidates to address hundreds and even thousands of voters at one time, mass mailings, and automated phone messages had all emerged as crucial campaign tactics that overshadowed, if not (in some cases) replaced entirely, the romanticized image of the candidate meeting voters in a more personal setting.

In addition, the news media had adapted, covering the run-up to the nomination process by focusing on national polls of potential voters, as well as on various activities of the candidates, in what is now widely referred to as the "invisible primary." During this period, candidates raise funds, recruit staff in the primary and caucus states, obtain endorsements, give thoughtful speeches, and in general try to portray themselves as presidential material. By the time of the Iowa caucuses and New Hampshire primary, reporters have already formed opinions about the viability of the various candidates based on their performances during the invisible primary — which ones are in the first tier and deserve continuous coverage; which are in the second tier and deserve occasional coverage, with perhaps one reporter assigned to multiple candidates; and which candidates can for all practicable purposes be ignored.

Adaptation by the Republican Party to the new nomination process was less dramatic than it was for the Democrats in those five election cycles. Both Richard Nixon (1972) and Ronald Reagan (1984) were not seriously challenged for reelection, and the GOP establishment candidate prevailed both in 1976 (when Ford beat Reagan) and in 1988 (when Vice President George Bush beat Iowa caucus winner Robert Dole). Bush had learned from the Democrats in 1984, and from his own experience in 1980, how significant the Iowa bump could be, so he was able to prevent Dole's surge after Iowa from being decisive. Only in 1980 was the new process a bit unsettling for the Republican Party, when its clear frontrunner came in second in Iowa (Bush beating Reagan), temporarily upending the contest in New Hampshire. Already by that time, wholesale politicking was an integral part of Reagan's ultimate victory.

The 1990s do not signify a quantum break from the 1970s and 1980s, but rather the continuation of a gradual increase in wholesale politicking in Iowa and New Hampshire, and the increasing influence of the national news media's coverage of the contests. Another significant change during this latter period was the emerging influence of GOP evangelical Christian voters in Iowa — much more so than in New Hampshire. The first indication of this change was Pat Robertson's second-place showing in Iowa in 1988 ahead of Vice President Bush, though in New Hampshire, Robertson came in last among five candidates. That disconnect between Iowa and New Hampshire has become much more obvious in recent election cycles. While Mike Huckabee (2008) and Rick Santorum

(2012) both won the Iowa caucuses[1] with much of their support coming from evangelical voters, neither was even a serious competitor in New Hampshire. This marked incongruity between GOP voters in Iowa and New Hampshire was a break from election cycles past, when the Iowa winner benefitted from the victory and ended up no worse than second in New Hampshire.

On the Democratic side, however, the ideological leanings of voters in Iowa and New Hampshire are similar, though that doesn't mean the same candidate will always emerge victorious in both contests — as Obama discovered in 2008.

1992 — "The Comeback Kid" and the Protest Vote

For the first time in twenty years, the New Hampshire primary was the first significant nominating contest of the election cycle. No Republican challenged President Bush in the Iowa caucuses, prompting the state's GOP to cancel its caucus contests. Commentator Pat Buchanan would, however, launch his insurgent candidacy in New Hampshire. The Iowa Democratic Party's caucuses were held as usual, but the results were discounted, because of the overwhelming advantage enjoyed by Senator Tom Harkin, who was from the state. All the other Democratic candidates decided not to waste their time and money competing with the hometown boy. With no significant competition, Harkin easily won the contest on February 10, receiving 76 percent of the vote, followed by "uncommitted" with 12 percent. But the press paid no attention. Much more interesting news had just broken about Bill Clinton; and Harkin, who was fourth in the New Hampshire polls before the caucuses, ended up fourth on Election Day.

In 1991, when most potential candidates were considering whether to run, President George Bush appeared unbeatable for reelection. In a quick six-week war (mid-January to the end of February), US-led coalition forces had ousted Iraqi troops from Kuwait, which Iraq had first occupied the previous August. At the conclusion of the hostilities, Bush's overall approval rating soared to 89 percent, the highest level ever measured by Gallup at that time.[2] In the five-month period from April through

August, when most candidates were mulling over a run for the presidency, Bush's approval rating remained at 70 percent or better. Numerous Democratic leaders made their decisions during this period not to run, no doubt influenced at least in part by the president's positive poll numbers—including Al Gore and Richard Gephardt, who had both run four years earlier; and other luminaries such as Senators Jay Rockefeller of West Virginia, Bill Bradley of New Jersey, Sam Nunn of Georgia, George Mitchell of Maine (the Senate Majority Leader), and Lloyd Bentsen of Texas (the vice presidential candidate in 1988). By the time New York Governor Andrew Cuomo finally decided not to run in mid-December, Bush's approval rating had dropped to the low 50s, but still the governor could not be persuaded to make the effort.[3]

In the meantime, six Democrats took advantage of the disinterest of their better-known colleagues to declare their intentions: Harkin, Governor Bill Clinton of Arkansas, Senator Bob Kerrey of Nebraska, former Massachusetts senator Paul Tsongas, Virginia Governor Doug Wilder, and former California governor Edmund G. "Jerry" Brown. Reporters considered Harkin, Clinton, and Kerrey to be the top tier, while Tsongas, Wilder, and Brown were second tier.[4] But whatever the media's ratings, they appeared not to make much difference to New Hampshire voters. Tsongas started campaigning early in New Hampshire, focusing on the economy and how he proposed to improve it. He had a plan, a written plan, eighty-six pages long, which voters could physically obtain. Soon, Clinton was also campaigning about how to fix the economy, also touting a specific plan, a written plan, which voters could physically obtain. This intense focus on how to improve the economy played well in New Hampshire, whose economic conditions were among the worst in the country.[5] The fact that both candidates had specific plans, rather than simply broad generalities, made their campaigns stand out from the rest.

In contrast, the rest of the candidates seemed much less attuned to the voters' needs. Harkin touted himself as the "only real Democrat," but seemed not to have much more to offer. Kerrey focused on health care, believing it would be the magic bullet issue to give him traction with voters. That issue had played well in Pennsylvania the previous November, when Harris Wofford won the special election to the US Senate by running on his support for national health insurance.[6] But in New Hampshire, voters' concerns were broader, and it was a long time before Kerrey came to this realization. Brown was never taken seriously in New Hampshire. After running two times previously and having been out of office since 1983, he hardly seemed like a viable candidate, though later in the year, after all the other candidates had dropped out of the race, he would be Clinton's last viable challenger. And Wilder, a one-term governor from Virginia who had few resources and little time to campaign, and who was moreover an African American candidate positioning himself as a conservative, never really addressed the economic issues facing the state. Besides, no one believed that an African American could win the nomination, much less the presidency.

By mid-January, Clinton was the New Hampshire front-runner, followed fairly closely by Tsongas. The former Massachusetts senator, however, faced several challenges: Few people thought the Democratic Party would nominate yet another "liberal Greek from Massachusetts," given Michael Dukakis's ignominious defeat four years earlier. And there was continued doubt regarding Tsongas's health. After one term as senator, he had retired in 1985 because of lymphoma, and though his doctors said he had fully recovered, there never could be certainty about the remission of cancer. Tsongas was also a less-than-charismatic speaker — he was clearly no match for Clinton, who was a master at speaking and responding to audience questions. And Tsongas was taking some unpopular positions in his self-proclaimed "truth-telling" to the voters, opposing a middle-class tax cut and supporting nuclear power, among other positions not generally appealing to many of the Democratic voters who would decide the nomination. While it appeared in mid-January that Clinton would mostly likely win in New Hampshire and that Tsongas's failure to win in his neighboring state would derail his campaign, there was much excitement left in the month before Election Day that upended these calculations.

First came charges of womanizing, triggered on January 16 by a tabloid story claiming that Clinton had had long-term sexual relationships with several women, including Gennifer Flowers. Denials and new accusations followed, but the issue seemed to be defused when Bill and Hillary

Clinton appeared on CBS's *60 Minutes* in a segment that aired after the Super Bowl. Despite further charges by Flowers after the appearance, a poll sponsored by WMUR (a local television station) and conducted by the University of New Hampshire Survey Center found no erosion of support for Clinton. The electorate, it seemed, was not about to have its focus shifted from the economy to unproven charges of personal failings.

Three weeks later, on Thursday, February 6, came a *Wall Street Journal* article quoting a retired army recruiter who claimed that in 1969, Clinton had avoided the draft by signing up for the ROTC program, but then "was able to manipulate things so he didn't have to go in."[7] Once again, Clinton was on the defensive, denying that he had manipulated anything and arguing that the very same army recruiter quoted in the *Wall Street Journal* story had always told reporters that Clinton had not violated any laws. Coincidentally, the very next day, Gallup released a new poll (taken before the *Wall Street Journal* story) that showed Clinton leading Tsongas by 37 percent to 24 percent. The timing made it appear as though New Hampshire voters were taking the new charges in stride, as they had the womanizing charges. But the WMUR/UNH poll released on Saturday, taken after the draft-dodging charges became public, found a sudden drop in Clinton's numbers — from a 5-point lead to an 9-point deficit, Tsongas now leading 28 percent to 19 percent.[8] Over the weekend, the talk shows all focused on the results of that poll and what it portended for the primary and the nomination contest. A follow-up Gallup poll released on Tuesday confirmed Tsongas's lead, this one showing him ahead of Clinton by 33 percent to 26 percent.[9]

On the Monday following Clinton's fall in the polls, Harkin won the Iowa caucuses. His victory caused hardly a ripple in the media feeding frenzy that had engulfed the Arkansas governor. With only a week until the New Hampshire vote, Clinton went on *Nightline* to explain what actions he had taken as a student that eventually resulted in his not being drafted. He also commented on an antiwar letter he wrote at the time, which had just resurfaced in the media. He told Ted Koppel that he had obtained a deferment from the draft lottery so he could finish his studies in Cambridge, and he had promised to return and join the ROTC while he went to law school. But once he returned, he changed his mind about joining the ROTC and instead immediately put his name in for the lottery, expecting to be drafted and sent to Vietnam. Instead, he got a high number, which meant he wouldn't be called. "That's what the records reflect," he said. "A Republican member of my draft board has given an affidavit in the last couple of days saying that I got no special treatment and nothing in the letter changes that, although it's a true reflection of the deep and conflicted feelings of a just-turned-twenty-three-year-old young man."[10]

In the end, Tsongas came in first with 33 percent of the vote, but Clinton had staved off disaster, coming in second with 25 percent. Kerrey and Harkin trailed by double-digits, 11 percent and 10 percent, respectively, with Brown coming in at eight percent. The write-in for Cuomo gave him 4 percent, while Ralph Nader got 2 percent write-in votes. By then, Wilder had dropped out.

"Winners" in the early contests are not necessarily those who get the most votes. Tsongas was the highest vote-getter, but few political leaders or pundits thought his campaign would persist much past New England. On election night, at the suggestion of Joe Grandmaison, Clinton's New Hampshire campaign chairman, Clinton appeared early before his supporters to preempt any conclusions that pundits and reporters might make about his "loss." Instead, he declared that after this trial by fire, he was "The Comeback Kid."[11] That was the narrative that carried the day. He received the second highest number of votes, but to the media, he was the winner.

THE REPUBLICAN PRIMARY, which pitted President George Bush against a television news commentator and newspaper columnist who had never been elected to any political office, produced a classic protest vote. No serious political observer thought Pat Buchanan could possibly win the nomination, but he was the lightning rod for much of the anger that New Hampshire Republicans felt about the sorry state of the economy. New Hampshire had produced a protest vote in 1968, with Gene McCarthy taking on President Johnson. While many at the time interpreted the 42 percent vote for McCarthy as antiwar, a post-election poll showed that many voters supporting McCarthy were not necessarily against the war, and some even supported it. Whatever McCarthy might personally have stood for, he was the vehicle for all voters who wanted to express dissatisfaction with the Johnson administration.

A quarter of a century later, a similar dynamic was occurring—though the major antagonist was not antiwar, but anti-tax, and anti-civil rights bill, and antispending. Buchanan was outraged (confrontational outrage over one issue or another was his primary shtick, and he was often viewed as racist and anti-Semitic in his use of intemperate language[12]), this time about Bush's signing the Civil Rights Act of 1991. It was the "triggering event" for Buchanan that impelled him to enter the primary, finally announcing his candidacy on December 10, just two and a half months before Election Day.[13] He had been thinking about the challenge earlier but had refrained after Bush's approval ratings soared in the wake of the successful Gulf War. By December, the president's rating had declined to just over 50 percent, but Buchanan's anger with Bush for caving into the Democrats on raising taxes had not. Throughout his 1988 campaign, Bush had pledged not to raise taxes, a promise that was instrumental in his victory over Dole in the New Hampshire primary[14] and one that was repeated at the Republican National Convention where Bush declared to thunderous applause: "Read my lips: No new taxes!" It was that particular part of Bush's acceptance speech that the Buchanan campaign folded into an anti-Bush ad, which—according to one journalist's notable understatement—"blanketed the state, and [its] constant repetition, by some accounts, has begun to irritate some voters."[15]

Unlike the McCarthy challenge twenty-four years earlier, this one was subject to the scrutiny of several polls, which confirmed the protest character of Buchanan's support. A WMUR/UNH poll in early February found that half of his supporters admitted their support was mainly to send a message to Bush, while just 29 percent said they thought Buchanan was actually the better candidate.[16] By contrast, 93 percent of Bush supporters favored him because they thought he would make the best president.[17] Moreover, the poll also showed that only 18 percent said Bush had betrayed the public trust, while 62 percent said Bush was forced to raise taxes because of the Democrats. Another poll for the *Boston Herald* and

WCVB-TV found only 3 percent of Buchanan's supporters saying Bush's broken tax pledge was why they were voting for Buchanan.[18] While Buchanan believed his supporters agreed with him about the broken tax pledge, excess spending, and Bush's support for the Civil Rights Act of 1991, the polls revealed a more complex picture. People had their own reasons for voting for Buchanan. Bush's campaign chairman, Bob Teeter — who was also a widely respected pollster — ordered his own poll, which came to a similar conclusion. There was "a great deal of Republican disaffection over the economy and a potential for a big protest vote against Bush."[19]

The actual magnitude of the protest vote was far smaller than what the press made it seem at the time. Bush won by 16 percentage points, 53 percent to 37 percent. But the final exit poll results, released long before the votes had been officially counted, showed a much closer race, 48 percent to 42 percent. The numbers were shocking to the Bush campaign, to Buchanan, and to the press. The dominant question on the news that night was: How could the president have fared so poorly? By the time the official figures were released, the pack media had committed itself to the story line of a stunning setback for the president. As Mary Matalin recalled, "We'd won and everyone said we lost."[20] This was yet another New Hampshire primary in which the media's interpretation of results trumped reality.

1996 — A Big Win . . . for the *Manchester Union Leader*

Earlier we described how, in 1980, the *Manchester Union Leader* waged a furious campaign on behalf of Ronald Reagan, helping to keep his poll numbers from tanking after his loss to George Bush in the Iowa caucuses.[21] With a continued close contest, Bush was cajoled into accepting a one-on-one debate with Reagan, but then Reagan turned the tables on Bush, secretly inviting the other candidates to join the debate and giving the impression that it was Bush's fault for their exclusion. Clearly, Bush didn't handle the situation well, and the dramatic scene that followed was the key to Reagan's decisive victory several days later. In this way, the *Union Leader*'s influence did not appear to be the key to Reagan's victory; most people believed it was the Nashua debate that did Bush in, not the newspaper.

In 1996, however, the impact of the *Union Leader* was direct and decisive. Without the newspaper's editorial support and biased coverage in its news columns, Bob Dole would almost certainly have won the primary, and it's very likely that Lamar Alexander would have come in second — producing a very different political context from the one that actually occurred.

Several Republicans declared their candidacies for president in 1995, but by the time of the New Hampshire primary, only four were taken seriously: the front-runner, Senate Majority Leader Bob Dole, who had given Vice President George Bush a scare eight years earlier when Dole won the Iowa caucuses; *über*-wealthy publisher Steve Forbes; former Tennessee governor and education secretary in the Bush administration Lamar Alexander; and Bush's nemesis from four years earlier, journalist and television commentator Pat Buchanan. Initially, Forbes was perceived as the major threat to Dole, because of Forbes's immense wealth and because of his proposal for a simple flat tax that would replace the current complicated income tax system. The Dole campaign believed such a proposal would appeal to the anti-tax New Hampshire electorate. Alexander hoped to be seen as the younger Dole, a moderate but still a Washington outsider who would bring fresh ideas to the capital. Dole, on the other hand, portrayed himself as a tested leader who could get things done in Washington. And Buchanan was once again railing against high taxes, excessive government spending, and the need to reform trade policies in order "to put Americans first."[22]

As noted earlier, Buchanan had the enthusiastic support of the *Manchester Union Leader,* which provided a major boost to his campaign. William Loeb had died in 1981, and the paper was not as vitriolic in 1996 as it had been in 1980 in its support of Ronald Reagan. Nevertheless, it was clearly a crucial part of Buchanan's campaign. Still, the expectation was that Dole would prevail in the primary and go on to win the nomination. Clearly, Buchanan could never win the nomination, nor could Forbes, if the GOP had any hopes of competing against President Clinton in the fall. That left only Alexander and Dole, a match-up that Alexander desperately wanted. But he was not getting the traction he needed, either in Iowa or New Hampshire. In its final poll before the Iowa caucuses, Gallup showed Dole and Forbes in a tie in New Hampshire, each with 25 percent support, followed by Buchanan (20 percent) and Alexander (12 percent).[23]

The results of the Iowa caucuses were felt immediately in New Hampshire. Dole won as expected, but the surprise second-place winner was Buchanan, who trailed Dole by just 3 percentage points — Dole getting 23 percent of the vote, Buchanan 20 percent. In third place was Alexander at 17 percent, while Forbes came in at a disappointing 10 percent, after spending nearly $14 million in the state from the period of December 1995 to January 1996.[24] Within the next two days, Forbes's standings in New Hampshire collapsed while Buchanan's numbers jumped several percentage points, Dole saw a small uptick in his numbers before they began falling, and Alexander experienced a surge that made him competitive with the two front-runners. The final days saw the candidates attack each other in ads, and the last debate was filled with "bitter accusations hurled between the candidates as the race in New Hampshire quickly turned into a demolition derby."[25]

In the midst of the melee was the *Union Leader*. The nature of the paper's coverage was subjected to systematic, objective examination by Stephen Farnsworth and Robert Lichter,[26] who looked at all the paper's news stories and editorials from January 25 through February 19, 1996. Excluding comments about the horse-race aspects of the campaign, the article reports that there were two hundred editorials mentioning Buchanan and 157 mentioning Dole on what the authors call "substantive evaluations" that "relate to a candidate's capacity to be president and include discussions of character, policy issues, and previous job performance."[27] Overall, Buchanan received eighty-eight positive editorials, eight times as many as Dole received (eleven), twenty-two times as many as Alexander (four) and nearly fifteen times as many as Forbes (six).

With respect to the "objective" substantive news coverage of the two candidates, Dole was mentioned in about two and a half times as many stories as Buchanan (283 vs. 107), no doubt a reflection of Dole's front-runner status. But almost two-thirds of Buchanan's stories were positive about him, while just over half the stories about Dole were negative. Forbes was mentioned in the most substantive stories (341), with more than three quarters of them negative.

The authors found strong correlations between ongoing coverage about the candidates and their standings in the tracking polls. But the authors were limited in their analysis because they could not classify voters into readers and nonreaders of the *Union Leader,* since the tracking polls they used did not include that information. However, the CNN/*USA Today*/Gallup tracking poll did include that information, and it shows quite different dynamics between the two groups of voters. Among readers, Dole and Buchanan were both in the 35 percent to 40 percent range of support just before the Iowa caucuses, but immediately thereafter, Dole's poll ratings plummeted to the 20 percent level where they remained until the election. Alexander's poll standing surged from less than 5 percent up to the 20 percent level, where it remained. Forbes showed little change over the week following the Iowa caucuses, remaining at about 10 percent (Figure 6.1).

By contrast, among nonreaders, Dole was the overwhelming front-runner just before the caucuses, with about 35 percent of the vote, compared with Forbes and Buchanan at just under 20 percent each, and Alexander at 10 percent. Over the course of the final week before the New Hampshire primary, Buchanan got a small boost, but Alexander jumped up 14 points to 24 percent, then leveled out a few percentage points lower, then dropped 10 points, then recovered about 5 of them. In the end, Dole won by just over 4 points, and Alexander came in second, with Buchanan a very close third (Figure 6.2).

What these figures confirm is that the *Union Leader* was the crucial determinant in Buchanan's victory. Without the paper, Dole would almost certainly have won by at least 4 points, and it seems likely that Alexander would have come in second, with Buchanan coming in a close third. The overall impact of the *Union Leader* remains essentially undiminished even when we control for ideology. Instead of Dole winning by 4.5 percentage points, the data suggest, he would have won by 4.0 percentage points.

Figure 6.1. CNN/*USA Today*/Gallup Poll standings of GOP candidates during last week of New Hampshire primary campaign among readers of *Manchester Union Leader* (percent support for each candidate).

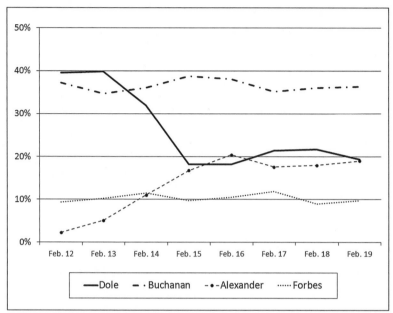

Source: CNN/*USA Today*/Gallup Poll.

These data probably underestimate the influence of the paper, because it is the dominant print news source in the state (the only daily statewide paper) and often sets the tone and the agenda for other news sources. So even nonreaders may have been consuming news that was shaped by the *Union Leader*'s bias in favor of Buchanan.

Buchanan's upset victory by just one percentage point shook up the GOP establishment. A CNN news release captured the angst: "Conservative commentator Pat Buchanan's stunning victory tonight over embattled front-runner Sen. Robert Dole (R-Kan.) throws the Republican race for the nomination into a tumult and ensures that the campaign will get bloodier as the battle for the heart and soul of the GOP intensifies. . . . The surprising result is a wake-up call for Republican party elders."[28] As it

Figure 6.2. CNN/*USA Today*/Gallup Poll standings of GOP candidates during last week of New Hampshire primary campaign among nonreaders of *Manchester Union Leader* (percent support for each candidate).

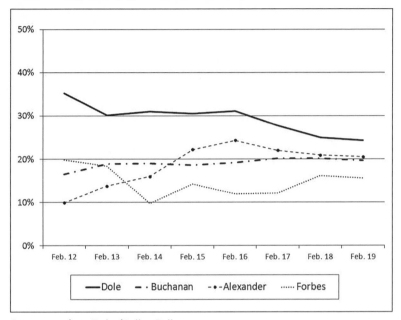

Source: CNN/*USA Today*/Gallup Poll.

turns out, Buchanan was unable to win any more contests. Only in New Hampshire, with the support of the *Union Leader,* was he the victor.

2000 — Last Gasp for the Outsider?

The 2000 New Hampshire primary kicked off with the country in good shape — the United States was at peace, the economy was still enjoying the late 1990s tech boom, and the federal government was running a budget surplus. A Gallup poll in early 1999 reported that 70 percent of Americans were satisfied with the direction of the country and only 28 percent were dissatisfied. The issues in the presidential campaign were consequently much less divisive than would be seen in future primaries; the top concerns were education and the conflict in Kosovo.[29] The names of the top candidates were familiar from the 1990s: Vice President Al

Gore sought to continue the Clinton legacy, while George W. Bush and Elizabeth Dole, son and wife of the last two Republican candidates, led the Republican field.

After the debacle of the 1996 nomination campaign, Republicans wanted to be sure that a protest candidate like Pat Buchanan could not damage the mainstream candidate again. To do this, the party lined up behind Texas Governor George W. Bush. Bush had the advantage of very high name recognition, although many may have mistaken him for his father. He had worked very hard in the late 1990s to secure support from Republicans across the country, especially from those who raised money. The Bush campaign raised a then record $7.6 million within four weeks after he announced the formation of his exploratory committee, and by January 2000, his campaign had raised more than $67 million, more than the combined total raised by Bill Clinton and Bob Dole for the 1996 election.[30] The fundraising was a key part of Bush's strategy to appear the inevitable nominee. As Dan Balz reported in the *Washington Post*: "Whether his candidacy is a speculative bubble or the opening phase of a long, steady march to the White House can't be known at this point. But his strategy for winning the GOP nomination at least appears designed to create an aura of invincibility around his candidacy. Bush and his advisers cannot quite believe what they're seeing, from the rush of money into his campaign in the last few weeks to the earlier consolidation of the party establishment that not even his father enjoyed in his first campaign. Even Republican strategists predict rougher days ahead."[31]

IN NEW HAMPSHIRE, Bush was the early front-runner as well. A CNN/WMUR/UNH poll in May 1999 found that Bush had the early lead in the Granite State, with 37 percent saying that Bush was their first choice and another 19 percent saying he was their second choice. And the strategy to make Bush look inevitable was working, as 81 percent of likely voters in the same poll said they thought Bush was the candidate most likely to win the primary.[32]

Bush ran as a moderate Republican in 2000, calling himself a "compassionate conservative" to position himself to the left of more conservative candidates like Steve Forbes, Pat Buchanan, Lamar Alexander, and Dan Quayle. His campaign steered clear of divisive social issues, instead focusing on tax cuts and improving education.

But while the Bush campaign was a well-oiled machine, George Bush the candidate was less than impressive. His first visit to New Hampshire as a candidate didn't occur until June, and his inability to articulate his position on a variety of issues fed the impression that he was not yet ready for the big stage. This perception was also fueled by his campaign's decision to skip the first two debates in New Hampshire, which reinforced the suspicion that he had little command of the issues and resulted in heavy criticism by the press and his fellow candidates.[33] While Bush was still ahead in New Hampshire polls in the late fall, the sense of inevitability had been damaged.

The other early front-runner was Elizabeth Dole, president of the American Red Cross and former secretary of transportation during the Reagan administration. Dole, like Bush, had name recognition; after all, there had been a Bush or a Dole on every GOP presidential ticket since 1976. In a January CNN poll, Dole led the field in New Hampshire with 27 percent to Bush's 23 percent.[34] But while she was popular, her campaign slid as interest in Bush increased. By May, she trailed Bush, although she was the second most popular candidate — 16 percent of likely voters said that Dole was their first choice and another 26 percent said she was their second choice. Unlike Bush, Dole was unable to raise money and dropped out of the race in October, long before the primary. During the third quarter of 1999, the Dole campaign had raised a total of only $4.8 million and had less than $1 million cash on hand. While the once-promising Dole campaign collapsed primarily due to lack of funds, she was also a poor campaigner — good at giving speeches, but often unable to make connections with voters and appearing stiff and brittle before crowds.[35] Dole ultimately endorsed Bush, in January 2000.

The anti-Bush candidate was Arizona Senator John McCain, who ran as a reformer in the mold of Teddy Roosevelt. Like another Arizona candidate, Barry Goldwater, he was not afraid to speak out against the party establishment. McCain was also known for his military background: His father had been an admiral and McCain had been a Navy pilot in

Vietnam. Moreover, his plane had been shot down over North Vietnam, and he spent more than five years as a prisoner of war in the infamous "Hanoi Hilton." His military service stood in contrast to that of George Bush, who had also been a pilot—but in the National Guard; he never saw action in Vietnam.

McCain was familiar to many Americans from his regular appearances on television news programs. He was a press favorite for his willingness to talk to reporters and for his inclination to take "maverick" positions on many issues. This was exemplified by his support for campaign finance reform. This position put him out of step with many Republicans and distinguished him from Bush, whom McCain criticized for the enormous sums his campaign had raised. McCain held a joint event with Democratic candidate Bill Bradley to highlight their support for reforming campaigns, burnishing their reputations as reformers willing to work across party lines.[36] Bush had hoped that he would be the candidate for moderate Republicans, leaving the more conservative candidates to split that voting bloc. But McCain outflanked Bush to his left, forcing Bush to fight in the crowded contest for conservative voters.

But because he did not have the resources that Bush wielded (McCain only raised about $14 million in 1999), his campaign had to be more thoughtful about how and where they would invest their capital. The campaign decided to forego Iowa and concentrate on New Hampshire, where McCain felt he could make his limited resources last and where he could engage voters directly. Part of his strategy was to capitalize on his good relations with the press to get free, or "earned," media coverage.

McCain also felt that he needed to target the more independent voters that New Hampshire was famous for, which would also enhance his credentials among the press. As his campaign bus (dubbed the Straight Talk Express) crisscrossed the state, he would spend hours talking with reporters, making their jobs easier—and certainly not boring. He also made himself available to questions from the public, holding more than one hundred "town hall" appearances across the state. He was known to relish hostile questions from the audience, often engaging critical questioners in extended repartee, savoring the political combat.

The other major Republican candidate who stuck it out until Election

Day was Steve Forbes, reprising his 1996 campaign. Forbes had hoped that his tax reform message would resonate in a country that had seen budget surpluses for the past two years, the first since 1969.[37] Forbes had spent heavily on ads in 1996 and promised to do the same in 2000, but he was again unable to capitalize on his wealth, never really catching on among voters.

Conservative activists Alan Keyes and Gary Bauer ran on socially conservative messages, but their antiabortion, religiously themed campaigns never caught on in New Hampshire, where Republican primary voters were much more pro-choice and less religious than other early states like Iowa and South Carolina (see Chapter 8).

Several other Republicans tested the waters in New Hampshire but withdrew before the primary. These included former Ohio congressman John Kasich, New Hampshire Senator Bob Smith, former vice president Dan Quayle, 1996 New Hampshire primary winner Pat Buchanan, and Utah senator Orrin Hatch.

By the late fall, the race had become a two-man contest between Bush and McCain. McCain's grassroots campaigning, and more importantly the media coverage he got, led more Republicans to consider that he had a chance. McCain's decision to skip Iowa also paid off, leaving him an open field during much of January, while Bush, Forbes, and the other candidates spent time and money in Iowa. Bush won Iowa, but by a smaller margin than many expected, getting only 41 percent of the vote, 10 percentage points ahead of Forbes (31 percent) while Keyes came in third with 14 percent. The sense that Bush was the inevitable candidate had been eroded, giving voters in New Hampshire more reason to look at McCain.

The Fox/WMUR/UNH tracking poll taken the week between Iowa and New Hampshire showed slight movement — Bush slipping from 37 percent to 34 percent and McCain growing from 38 percent to 41 percent. Most of the final polls showed McCain leading but predicted a relatively close finish. McCain ended up proving pollsters wrong, trouncing Bush by 19 percentage points (49 percent to 30 percent) with Forbes a distant third with 13 percent. The Bush campaign groused that McCain's win was because of independents, not "real Republicans" who voted in the

GOP primary. But exit polls showed that McCain won among registered Republicans by an eight percentage point margin (44 percent to 36 percent). The magnitude of McCain's win was due to undeclared voters, who enabled him to clobber Bush by 42 percentage points (61 percent to 19 percent).

2000 was one of the few times that the early front-runner did not win the New Hampshire primary, and it would not happen again in either 2008 or 2012.

THE DEMOCRATIC BATTLE in 2000 wasn't expected to be of much interest, certainly when compared to the Republican contest. President Clinton was finishing his second term with high approval ratings and his vice president, Al Gore, had secured the support of most national party insiders, who hoped Gore would win a third consecutive Democratic term for the first time since the FDR and Truman administrations.

Gore was backed by New Hampshire Governor Jeanne Shaheen and her husband, Bill, who was a key player in Democratic Party politics in the state. Observers believed Gore had the financial and organizational advantages to win comfortably in New Hampshire and to easily secure the nomination. And it was evident that most major Democrats agreed with this assessment, as only one other Democrat challenged Gore, former New Jersey senator Bill Bradley.

But Gore did not live up to the top billing in the early months of 1999. First of all, his fundraising, while large by prior standards, paled compared to Bush's. By the end of June 1999, Gore had raised only $18 million, half of Bush's $37 million. More importantly, Bradley was not far behind Gore, raising $12 million by the end of June. The third quarter was even worse for Gore; he raised only $6.5 million while Bradley raised $6.7 million. By September, Gore had only $10 million cash on hand, the same as Bradley. The fundraising woes caused Gore to cut his staff and relocate his campaign headquarters from Washington to Nashville, Tennessee, in order to save money, and to get him closer to voters.[38]

A big cloud over the campaign was how to deal with President Clinton. While Clinton enjoyed high job approval numbers, the Monica Lewinsky scandal and subsequent impeachment made him a potential liability on the campaign trail. Gore sought to distance himself from Clinton, the person, while still hoping to get credit for the strong Clinton economy. And Clinton didn't help Gore any when he was quoted in the *New York Times* saying that he (Clinton) was concerned about the sluggish start to the campaign and revealing that he had coached Gore in how to loosen up on the campaign trail. Clinton reportedly was happy that Gore had hired Tony Coelho to help straighten things out.[39]

Not only was Gore stumbling when it came to raising money, his staff were feuding over the direction of the campaign. The campaign was top-heavy, adding more and more advisors early as it failed to gain traction with voters. Former Clinton staffer Carter Eskew was brought in by Gore's new campaign chairman, Tony Coelho;[40] but by October, Coelho was in trouble, accused of mishandling taxpayer funds, again raising unflattering comparisons to the Clinton era.[41] The concerns about "Clinton fatigue" were again plaguing the campaign, leading Gore to criticize Clinton's behavior in an October debate at Dartmouth College, saying, "I understand the disappointment and anger you felt toward President Clinton. I feel it myself. I also feel that the American people want to move on and turn the page and focus on the future, not the past."[42] And the money woes continued, forcing Gore to schedule more official vice presidential events to coincide with campaign events and fundraisers, so that taxpayers would pick up travel costs.[43]

Gore continued to have problems connecting with voters. Some of this was due to his being the vice president, requiring greater security than most candidates. Secret Service and rope lines kept him physically away from voters at his events. By October, he was reinventing himself, sporting khakis, sweaters, and shirts in earth tones, instead of the typical Washington dark suit.[44] This was part of a strategy to make him more attractive to women, who were being wooed not only by Bradley, but by Bush. October brought a further shake-up in the Gore campaign. Donna Brazille, a former Dukakis campaign staffer, was added as Gore's new campaign manager to bring tighter organization to the campaign.[45] Gore continued to be uncomfortable in front of voters, and some of his comments on the campaign trail, while not quite gaffes or untruths, fit into the media template that Gore was a pompous technocrat.

Bill Bradley was seen as both smart and as a man's man. He was a Princeton graduate and a Rhodes Scholar, but most people knew him from his ten years playing for the New York Knicks in the NBA. He then was elected to three terms to the US Senate from New Jersey, earning a reputation as policy wonk, best known for his work on the 1986 tax reform bill. While Gore ran as the mainstream candidate, Bradley ran as the liberal alternative to Gore. This dynamic was familiar in Democratic nomination battles, with the likes of Carter and Kennedy (1980) and Mondale and Hart (1984) taking the respective roles as mainstream and liberal candidates.

Bradley started out as a long shot. A May CNN/WMUR/UNH poll showed him trailing Gore 68 percent to 23 percent.[46] But by September, the gap had closed so that Bradley trailed by only 46 percent to 41 percent.[47] Despite being known as somewhat aloof, Bradley proved to be good on the stump, perhaps because of his years in the spotlight while in the NBA, or because he was the underdog with nothing to lose. Whatever the case, his campaign gained momentum throughout the fall as Gore stumbled. As he gained on Gore, Bradley's fundraising picked up so that by December, he was leading Gore in both money and New Hampshire support.[48]

Bradley had originally planned a halfhearted campaign in Iowa, but Gore's stumbles gave him an opening in the Hawkeye State. By October, he trailed Gore by only 3 percentage points.[49] But as Bradley rose in both states, the pressure on him increased, and it was Gore who loosened up. In the final weeks of the campaign, Gore finally connected with voters. He ditched the Secret Service and the campaign schedule, staying at events until every question had been answered. Gore ended up winning Iowa convincingly, getting 53 percent of the vote to Bradley's 35 percent. And it was Gore's good fortune that the press focused on the Republican race in the week between Iowa and New Hampshire. Both McCain and Bradley hoped to get the support of undeclared voters in New Hampshire, who have the option of voting in either party's primary. Unfortunately for Bradley, just 40 percent of the undeclared voters opted to vote in the Democratic primary, with the other 60 percent choosing the Republican primary.

Had more undeclared voters chosen to vote in the Democratic primary, Bradley may have had a chance of winning. As it was, Bradley beat Gore by 52 percent to 47 percent among undeclared voters in the Democratic primary, while Gore won 58 percent of registered Democrats to 42 percent for Bradley. In the end, Gore won New Hampshire by 50 percent to 46 percent. Had the Gore-Bradley race gotten more attention, Bradley may have won. Bradley did not win a primary in 2000, New Hampshire being his high-water mark. He dropped out of the race in March and endorsed Gore.

2004 — Rise of the Progressives

Democrats entered the 2004 campaign season frustrated; the 2000 election had left a bitter taste in their mouths. Party activists not only thought that Al Gore should have been president, they felt that the Bush presidency was illegitimate. But Bush was popular in the wake of 9/11 and the war in Afghanistan, and the Democratic Party was divided about how to beat him. Should they nominate a candidate with a military background who could stand up to Bush as a potential commander in chief? Or should they choose a more progressive candidate, someone who was not tarnished by a vote for the Iraq war? Party insiders were more comfortable with a mainstream candidate with a resume to match Bush, while party progressives were looking for a "purer" candidate. This is a dynamic that Democrats had faced time and again since 1968. Importantly, 2000 candidate Al Gore announced in December 2003 that he would not be seeking the presidency, leaving the field open.

The mainstream of the party favored Massachusetts Senator John Kerry, who had several advantages in New Hampshire. First, he was from Massachusetts, winning reelection three times since being elected to the Senate in 1984. New England candidates had won the Democratic primary several times before — Muskie (1972), Dukakis (1988), and Tsongas (1992). All had a high familiarity factor because of their home states' proximity to New Hampshire. The visibility of Kerry's campaigns on Boston television and in Boston newspapers made him well known in the Granite State. Kerry also had seen action in Vietnam and received three Purple Hearts as well as a Silver Star. Many Democrats felt that Kerry's combat experience contrasted favorably with Bush's stateside service. Kerry was also seen as a foreign policy expert, having served on the Senate Committee on Foreign Relations since 1987. But Kerry was also attractive to many progressive Democrats. After returning from Vietnam, he famously testified before Congress about us atrocities during the war. His antiwar bona fides were enhanced because he had been there. An early UNH poll in January 2003 found that 39 percent of likely Democratic primary voters favored Kerry. He also had the highest net favorability rating of any early candidate, +65 percent.[50] Kerry's senior advisor was New Hampshire veteran Sue Casey, who had worked on Kennedy's 1980 run and had partnered with Jeanne Shaheen to engineer Gary Hart's 1984 win.[51] Ned Helms, a veteran of the Carter and Hart campaigns, was his state chair.

But Kerry's one major weakness was that he had voted to authorize us military action in Iraq in October 2002 while also voting *not* to authorize funding for the war. This, to antiwar Democrats, smelled of politics, not commitment to an antiwar position. They hungered for someone who was willing to stand more boldly for progressive priorities, and they found him in Vermont governor Howard Dean. Dean was not as well known as Kerry, as most New Hampshire residents were Boston-focused, while only folks living near the Vermont border would have been familiar with Dean's campaigns in the Green Mountain state. But Vermont, like New Hampshire, has a two-year term for governor, and Dean had been elected five times to that post, giving him considerable campaign experience. And as governor of a progressive state (Vermont had regularly elected Bernie Sanders, the former Socialist mayor of Burlington, as their congressman and now senator), Dean could point to putting his progressive principles into practice. Dean was clearly in sync with New Hampshire voters as he drew increasingly larger crowds in the summer and fall. By mid-December, a WMUR/WCVB/ UNH poll found that 34 percent of Democratic primary voters said Dean's positions on the issues were closest to their own; the next closest candidate was Kerry, with only 15 percent.[52] Dean surpassed Kerry in polls by October, and by mid-December Dean held a nearly 30-point lead over Kerry (46 percent to 17 percent).[53] The same poll showed that 77 percent of likely Democratic primary voters thought that Dean would win the primary. Dean's success in New Hampshire led his campaign to think that if they could win Iowa, they would have a lock on the nomination. Dean shifted much of his campaign attention to the Hawkeye State, assuming that New Hampshire was already in the win column.

A third New England candidate, Connecticut Senator Joe Lieberman, jumped into the race in January 2003. Lieberman had been Gore's running mate in 2000 and so had widespread name recognition. Lieberman was widely seen as a moderate Democrat, known for working with Republicans, especially John McCain, in the US Senate. But his bipartisanship, and his support for US intervention in the Middle East, did not help him in the very different electoral environment of 2004, when Democrats were in no mood to cooperate with Republicans, especially on intervention in the Middle East. Lieberman's net favorability ratings dropped over the summer, from a high of +53 percent in February to only +14 percent by November, an indication that he was out of step with the mood of the electorate. Lieberman was also not doing well in Iowa and decided that concentrating in New Hampshire was his best shot at getting the nomination. He announced that November would be "Joevember" and that he was building "Joementum."

The only major Democratic candidate without a political background was retired four-star general Wesley Clark. Clark had been NATO's Supreme Allied Commander Europe (a post once held by Dwight Eisenhower), but despite this experience, he was unable to give a coherent position on the war in Iraq. He was sharply attacked by his fellow Democrats for shifting his position, which led many observers to think he wasn't ready for the nomination.[54] Clark, like Lieberman, decided to skip the Iowa caucuses to concentrate on New Hampshire, but for Clark, it looked — for a time — like a good choice. Clark's poll numbers were not great, but he was in third place behind Dean and Kerry by mid-December in the UNH poll. Other polls in January showed that support for him was increasing while Kerry, Edwards, and Dean slugged it out in Iowa.

John Edwards ran in 2004 as a young, populist, southern, moderate

Democrat, much in the mold of Bill Clinton. Edwards had been elected to the US Senate in 1998 from North Carolina and had his sights set on the presidency soon afterwards, reaching out to party insiders in Iowa and New Hampshire as far back as 2000. Edwards would campaign on a populist platform, best characterized by the "Two Americas" speech he gave at the 2004 Democratic convention. Edwards spent more time campaigning in Iowa and South Carolina than in New Hampshire, recognizing that Kerry and Dean, both New Englanders, had the advantage in the Granite State.

Former Missouri congressman and 1988 candidate Dick Gephardt campaigned on a platform similar to Edwards, emphasizing his blue-collar roots as the son of a milkman in St. Louis. Gephardt did have an organization in New Hampshire (chaired by Obama's 2008 co-chair Jim Demers), but he concentrated his campaign on Iowa, Missouri's neighbor to the north. Gephardt's campaign failed to gain any traction in New Hampshire.

Several other candidates lent flavor to the 2004 campaign. Progressive congressman and former mayor of Cleveland, Ohio, Dennis Kucinich ran to keep progressive issues in the debate. Similarly, former Illinois senator Carol Moseley Braun and activist Al Sharpton were in the mix, but each only made occasional visits to New Hampshire, primarily for debates. Kucinich, Moseley Braun, and Sharpton were asked by ABC newsman Ted Koppel in a December debate at UNH: "This question is to Ambassador Braun, Rev. Sharpton, Congressman Kucinich. You don't have any money, at least not much. Rev. Sharpton has almost none. You don't have very much, Ambassador Braun. The question is, will there come a point when polls, money and then ultimately the actual votes that will take place here, in places like New Hampshire, the caucuses in Iowa, will there come a point when we can expect one or more of the three of you to drop out? Or are you in this as sort of a vanity candidacy?"[55]

Kucinich in particular fought back, but it was clear that the media had dismissed the campaigns of these three candidates.

THE FOCUS ON IOWA in 2004 was quite different from what had been seen in recent cycles. Al Gore had won Iowa handily in 2000, getting

63 percent of the vote over Bill Bradley, who had largely conceded the state to Gore. And the 1992 caucus had favorite son Tom Harkin, who won an essentially uncontested race. But in 2004, Gephardt, Edwards, Dean, and Kerry all bet on winning Iowa, but each had a different reason for doing so. Gephardt felt he had an advantage with the unions that dominate the caucuses; Edwards believed his populist message would resonate better there than in New Hampshire; Dean felt that he had locked up New Hampshire and an Iowa win would give him the nomination; and Kerry, surprisingly, went to Iowa because he believed New Hampshire was lost.

In late fall, the Dean campaign looked ready to roll to an easy win in New Hampshire. The Kerry campaign was going nowhere. It was so low on cash that Kerry took out a mortgage on his Boston home for funds, and he fired his two campaign managers, Mary Beth Cahill and James Jordan. The campaign decided to go all in on Iowa and hope that they could make it a two-man race heading to New Hampshire. Kerry campaigned intensively and spent more time in Iowa in December and January than any other candidate. Kerry also benefitted from a nasty media war between Dean and Edwards in Iowa, making Kerry look like the good guy who was able to rise above the fray. Kerry's shift to Iowa worked out better than they could have hoped — he actually won Iowa convincingly, getting 38 percent of the vote to Edwards's 32 percent. Dean, the one-time front-runner in Iowa, finished a distant third with only 18 percent.[56] Gephardt finished fourth and dropped out of the race, eventually throwing his support to Kerry.

The campaigns now turned to New Hampshire, but Iowa had largely set the table. Dean's collapse in Iowa was mirrored in New Hampshire. Internal numbers from the Fox/WMUR/UNH tracking poll showed the impact that Kerry's Iowa win had on the New Hampshire race. Polling done before the caucus results were announced showed Dean with a 34 percent to 23 percent lead over Kerry. Post Iowa, Kerry led Dean 36 percent to 17 percent — Dean from 11 points up to 19 points down in a single day! Despite having an extensive campaign organization in New Hampshire, Dean was unable to recover from the body blow his campaign took in Iowa. While it is debatable whether his famous scream caused his post-Iowa crash, his loss in a race that he had been expected to win shattered his image as the expected winner.

Dean managed to claw back some support, but Kerry won the January 27 vote with 38 percent, followed by Dean with 26 percent, Clark and Edwards with 12 percent each, and Lieberman with 9 percent. A hint as to why voters turned on Dean can be found in the Fox/WMUR/UNH poll—39 percent of Democratic voters said that Dean was the most inconsistent candidate. Kerry was a distant second in this dubious measure with 11 percent.[57]

Despite considerable ups and downs during the campaign, John Kerry, the early front-runner and candidate from neighboring Massachusetts, won handily, defeating another New Englander, Howard Dean. The important difference was that Iowa had a greater impact on the New Hampshire Democratic primary than it had since the 1984 race. Candidates spent more time campaigning in Iowa than they had in the past, and because the Iowa results had a significant effect on the eventual New Hampshire result, candidates looking to secure the Democratic nomination in 2008 took note. And progressives in the Democratic Party did not have to look far to find the man to carry the progressive banner in 2008.

2008 — The Biggest Ever?

The 2008 presidential election would be the primary's biggest year ever. It was the first time since 1952 that neither a sitting president nor vice president was actively running, leaving both parties with wide-open fields. Consequently, both parties drew a large number of high-quality candidates. Both parties believed they could win the presidency. Democrats hoped to capitalize on anger from the ongoing war in Iraq, anger that had led to their taking control of the House and Senate in 2006. Republicans were optimistic as they had won the last two elections and believed that the electoral vote map favored them.

The campaign calendar made 2008 unique in that a front-loading push by Florida bumped the New Hampshire primary up to January 8 and the Iowa caucuses up to January 3, leaving only 5 days between the two early states. All of the major candidates, except for McCain and Giuliani, put extra emphasis on Iowa, counting on momentum from a win there to carry them through New Hampshire. However, neither of the Iowa winners ended up winning the Granite State.

With a majority of Americans thinking the country was headed in the wrong direction, Democrats felt they could reclaim the White House after eight years of Bush. Among Democrats, the early front-runner was New York Senator Hillary Clinton, the first former First Lady to run for office. She had led in UNH polls since February 2005, leading even 2004 nominee John Kerry. While several women had run for president in the past — Margaret Chase Smith (1964), Shirley Chisholm (1972), and Carol Moseley Braun (2004) — only Elizabeth Dole (2000) was considered to have had a real chance of winning the nomination.

Clinton had the support of most of the Democratic Party, especially the support of her husband, Bill, who used his considerable political skills in aiding her campaign with strategy and fundraising. Clinton especially hoped to capitalize on Bill's popularity in New Hampshire, the state that had revived his 1992 campaign. She also had the support of the Shaheens. Senator Jeanne Shaheen was an early backer, and her husband, Bill, was named the co-chair of the New Hampshire campaign. Clinton's strategy was to run the classic front-runner campaign, emphasizing her inevitability as the nominee.

John Edwards, the Democratic vice presidential candidate in 2004, was the second candidate to jump into the campaign. He had done well in New Hampshire when he ran for president in 2004, finishing fourth with 12 percent of the vote. In 2005, almost immediately after the 2004 election, Edwards had let it be known that he was going to run again, and he was able to raise considerable funds for his campaign. Edwards was doing well in New Hampshire polls, getting about 20 percent support — until Barack Obama entered the campaign. Edwards's strategy was to focus on economic issues, particularly the difficulties that poor Americans were facing. He kicked off his campaign in hurricane-ravaged New Orleans to emphasize what he metaphorically described as the Bush administration's treatment of the poor. But Edwards felt his strength was in the states that bookend the New Hampshire primary — Iowa and South Carolina — and he concentrated most of his effort in those states. Eyebrows were raised, though, when his 2004 campaign chair, local politico Jim Demers, dropped Edwards to serve as co-chair of the Obama campaign.

Barack Obama was a relative latecomer to the race, although his name had been circulated widely in progressive circles since his keynote address at the 2004 Democratic National Convention. He ran on an antiwar ticket, stressing again and again that he was the only major Democrat who had not voted to send troops to Iraq. While his legislative accomplishments were slim, his campaign cultivated an aura of intelligence and competence that enabled him to attract voters who were less progressive. Obama also understood the early-state strategy and felt he had an advantage in Iowa as it neighbored his state of Illinois. Moreover, Iowa Democrats had a reputation as peaceniks, the kind of voters who would be attracted by his anti-Iraq war position. However, he was determined to build a formidable campaign in New Hampshire as well.

Among the other candidates who ran were Delaware Senator Joe Biden, Connecticut Senator Chris Dodd, Former New Mexico governor Bill Richardson, Iowa Governor Tom Vilsack, and perennial progressive candidate Dennis Kucinich, congressman from Ohio. None of these candidates had much chance of winning, given the firepower of the top three candidates, but running for president has often paid off in other ways. From the 2008 second-tier candidates, Biden went on to be vice president, Vilsack became secretary of agriculture, and Bill Richardson was nominated to be secretary of commerce.

Both Obama and Clinton touted their organizational skills. Clinton hired some of the best campaign organizers from both New Hampshire and across the country, and her campaign built perhaps the most sophisticated voter identification and targeting system the state had seen. Karen Hicks, a veteran of earlier New Hampshire campaigns with Jeanne Shaheen (and including a stint as Howard Dean's campaign manager in 2004), was in charge of voter turnout efforts. But the Obama campaign team included advisors from his Illinois Senate campaign who were known for their work in campaign and community organization, so neither campaign enjoyed a significant advantage in this area.

When the campaign in New Hampshire began in earnest, it was characterized by large-scale rallies typically not seen until the final weeks of the campaign. The retail politics that New Hampshire was famous for would be a challenge for both Clinton and Obama. As Terry Shumaker, an early Bill Clinton backer from New Hampshire and one of Hillary Clinton's trusted New Hampshire advisors, asked, "How does a rock star do retail?"[58] Clinton's first major event was a rally at Concord High School on February 10, 2007. Billed as a "Conversation with Granite Staters," it was actually a rally with nearly one thousand people jammed into the high school gymnasium and featured closed circuit television for overflow crowds in other rooms. To remind local Democrats about her connection to the presidency, she made sure to mention Bill Clinton, and made sure that message made it into the papers.[59]

After announcing his candidacy to more than fifteen thousand people in Springfield, Illinois, Obama's first visit to New Hampshire included a town hall-style meeting with a crowd of more than three thousand packed into Lundholm Field House at the University of New Hampshire. His speech was reminiscent of his keynote address at the 2004 Democratic National Convention, introducing the lofty themes he would continue to use throughout his campaign. Because both the Obama and Clinton campaigns would require enormous resources, both candidates spent considerable time outside of New Hampshire raising money. And because Iowa was becoming critically important to the three top candidates, more time was spent there than in past years. This reduced the opportunity for retail politicking in New Hampshire by both Obama and Clinton, forcing them onto larger stages.

Clinton had held a formidable lead in New Hampshire polls throughout 2006 and 2007, but Obama began to gather momentum in the fall. Heading into the new year, Clinton still held a slim 4-point lead over Obama in a CNN/WMUR/UNH poll released on January 2. Clinton held the lead among registered Democrats (37 percent to 29 percent), but Obama maintained a narrow edge among Undeclared voters. Both Obama and

Edwards counted on winning Iowa and making the New Hampshire a two-person race against Clinton.

Iowa was Clinton's worst nightmare. Not only did Obama carry the Hawkeye State with 38 percent of the vote, but Edwards finished second (29.7 percent), with Clinton coming in a close third (29.4 percent). The question for the Clinton camp was whether all of the organizational work they had put into New Hampshire would hold up, especially since there were only five days to right the ship. Polls did not look good for Clinton; Obama got a solid bounce in New Hampshire with his Iowa win, moving up 10 percentage points in the UNH poll to a 39 percent to 30 percent lead over Clinton. In fact, every final poll predicted that Obama would win by an average of seven percentage points. As expected, Edwards, the third wheel, was not much of a factor in New Hampshire as he got no bounce out of his second-place finish. The race was clearly between Obama and Clinton.

But Clinton ended up narrowly winning (34.8 percent to 32.5 percent), leaving pollsters scrambling to explain what happened. The simple explanation is that when polls wrapped up Sunday night, the campaign wasn't over. Exit polls showed that 38 percent of Democratic voters said they had made up their minds in the last three days of the campaign, and 17 percent had made up their mind on Election Day. The Clinton campaign simply outhustled the Obama campaign over the final days, and she was helped by two heavily covered events. First, in a Saturday night ABC/WMUR debate, Edwards and Obama seemed to gang up on Clinton. When she was asked a question about her likeability, she seemed to be genuinely hurt. And when Obama retorted "you're likeable enough, Hillary," it was the boys picking on the girl. On Sunday morning, Clinton was filmed becoming emotional at a Portsmouth coffee shop, and footage of this was run over and over on television. These two events seemed to humanize Clinton. Finally, the Clinton campaign, seeing that they had everything on the line, went into overdrive in the closing days, holding events and greeting voters right up until the polls closed. The Obama campaign, by contrast, coasted in the final days. All this was enough to pull out a victory for Clinton (see Chapter 10 for more detail on this race and about the difficulties of polling in the New Hampshire primary).

So, once again, many of the myths about New Hampshire were proven wrong. The early front-runner won, defeating the "outsider" candidate. Retail politics played little part in the campaign as both candidates relied on large rallies instead of house parties or town hall events. The candidates fought to a stalemate in money spent, neither having a significant advantage, and the polls were wrong. All in all, a typical New Hampshire election!

WHILE THE Clinton/Obama battle rolled through New Hampshire, the Republican campaign seemed a sideshow, despite the heavyweight candidates that were in the running. At the forefront was Arizona Senator John McCain, who been the runner-up to George W. Bush in 2000; former New York City mayor and 9/11 hero Rudy Giuliani; former Massachusetts governor Mitt Romney; former Tennessee senator and television star Fred Thompson; and Texas congressman and one-time Libertarian party presidential candidate Ron Paul. A number of lesser-known Republicans rounded out the field: former Arkansas governor Mike Huckabee, former Wisconsin governor Tommy Thompson, former New Mexico governor Gary Gilmore, Kansas Senator Sam Brownback, and Congressmen Tom Tancredo from Colorado and Duncan Hunter from California. Several other Republicans had made early visits to New Hampshire to test the waters, but decided that the timing was not right; these included New York Governor George Pataki and former Nebraska senator Chuck Hagel. This surprised no one as their poll numbers throughout 2005 and 2006 were barely above zero.

McCain had several distinct advantages over his rivals. First of all, he had won in New Hampshire in the 2000 primary, handily defeating George W. Bush. McCain's 2000 run made him one of the best-known candidates among the Republican field; what's more, he was perceived as a moderate Republican, perfect for New Hampshire's moderate Republican electorate. Second, many Republicans who were disappointed by the Bush administration's war in Iraq were certainly thinking what might have happened had McCain, a candidate with greater foreign policy experience, won the 2000 nomination. Third, he was the early front-runner by a significant margin. As far back as February 2005, 40 percent of likely Republican primary voters said in the WMUR/UNH poll that they would vote for McCain.

Rudy Giuliani was in second place in the early UNH poll. He had won plaudits for his handling of the September 11 terrorist attacks in New York, and his campaign hoped that his reputation of being tough on terrorism as well as his management of New York City would make him an attractive candidate. He also was a moderate on social issues: he was pro-choice on abortion and he favored civil unions, but he opposed gay marriage. These positions put him in the center of the New Hampshire Republican electorate, which largely does not hold socially conservative positions on these issues.

Mitt Romney was also an early entry into the race. He hoped that his business background with Bain Capital, his rescue of the Salt Lake City Winter Olympic Games, and the fact that he kept a vacation home on Lake Winnipesaukee, would pull moderate Republicans his way. He had been elected governor of heavily Democratic Massachusetts in 2002 and had worked with Democrats in the state to pass a health care reform bill that later became the model for President Obama's controversial reform. Romney looked the part of a president — tall, dark haired, with a broad smile and large, attractive family. Romney also had great personal wealth and business connections, which made him a well-funded candidate. He had the support of longtime New Hampshire Republican advisor Tom Rath, who had advised the 1996 Alexander campaign as well as the Bush campaign in 2000. Romney had also been chair of the Republican Governors Association, a position that gave him reason to travel to early primary states and to meet and build alliances with Republicans from around the country.

Fred Thompson got into the campaign rather late, but he was well known from his role as District Attorney Arthur Branch on the popular television show *Law and Order*. He had been a senator from Tennessee and was seen as a strong, articulate social conservative in a field in which the top three candidates were battling for the moderate wing of the GOP.

McCain was the early front-runner both in New Hampshire and national polls, and he campaigned like one. After all, he had finished a close second to George W. Bush in 2000, and Republicans had a history of choosing the runner-up from the previous nomination battle. And since he had won big in New Hampshire in 2000, he felt the Granite State would be a springboard to the nomination, or at least a firewall if he did poorly in Iowa. He hired some of the best political talent in the GOP and began running a national campaign that focused on his inevitability as the eventual nominee. But his support for immigration reform and the war in Iraq cost him support, as did a minor controversy about his missing votes in the Senate, many while campaigning for President.

But by the time he announced his candidacy on a gray April day at Portsmouth's Prescott Park, across the river from the Portsmouth Naval Shipyard, McCain's campaign was already showing signs of trouble. And by mid-summer, his campaign had all but collapsed. Poll numbers had dropped, fundraising plummeted, staff left, and McCain headed to New Hampshire carrying his own bags into Manchester airport. He abandoned running a national campaign and dusted off his 2000 strategy of focusing on New Hampshire.

While McCain stumbled, Mitt Romney charged into New Hampshire. Despite being governor of neighboring Massachusetts, Romney was not as popular among Republicans as either McCain or Giuliani. His campaign worked to overcome this by running ads on WMUR starting in February 2007, and they continued to run them until the election. All told, Romney spent almost $7 million on television ads during the primary. As McCain dropped and Romney rose in the polls, the Romney campaign changed their strategy. Instead of running a New Hampshire-focused campaign, they dove into Iowa. Romney won the Ames Republican straw poll in July and hoped this would presage a victory in the caucuses. Winning Iowa, they believed, would lead to a certain win in New Hampshire and the nomination.

Rudy Giuliani's campaign developed an unusual strategy for winning the nomination that was at odds with winning campaign strategies since the 1970s. Instead of trying to win in Iowa or New Hampshire, or even in South Carolina, the Giuliani campaign bet that they could win in Florida, three weeks after the New Hampshire primary. Despite pleas from his New Hampshire chair Wayne Semprini, Giuliani made few visits and spent little money in New Hampshire.[60] When Giuliani finally made a push in November, his poll numbers had begun to slide — he fell into third place behind Romney and McCain in a mid-November CNN/ WMUR/UNH poll.[61] The $3 million they had spent on TV and radio ads in November was largely seen as wasted.[62]

McCain revived his campaign in New Hampshire, and he started to creep up in state polls in the fall, largely at the expense of Giuliani. His fundraising picked up, too, and by October he was running ads again. McCain also secured the endorsement of multiple newspapers, including the *Boston Globe,* the *Portsmouth Herald,* and perhaps most importantly, the *Manchester Union Leader.*[63] The *Union Leader* endorsement was particularly important to McCain as he hoped it would help him among more conservative Republicans who were turned off by Romney and Giuliani.

Among other Republicans, Fred Thompson may have run the worst campaign in the history of the New Hampshire primary. He ambled into New Hampshire on September 8, 2007, and his initial speech was at best uninspiring. His halfhearted campaigning in New Hampshire was reflected in polls — by November he was in low single digits in UNH polls. Reading the writing on the wall, his campaign packed up and left New Hampshire in early December, announcing that they would not campaign in New Hampshire but would concentrate on South Carolina instead.[64]

Ron Paul was able to energize younger libertarian voters in the Granite State, but his campaign never seemed to capitalize on this energy. His poll numbers topped out just below 10 percent, and he was even excluded from the final Fox news debate two days before the election.

As the campaign entered the final weeks, McCain continued to rise in polls, surpassing Romney in early 2008. While Romney was in Iowa, McCain stayed in New Hampshire, and the Iowa caucuses results had little impact on his campaign. Iowa did have a big impact on the Romney and Huckabee campaigns, however. Despite investing considerable time and money in Iowa, Romney ended up finishing second, 9 percentage points behind social conservative Mike Huckabee. Romney, who hoped that a win in Iowa would put him over the top in New Hampshire, peaked at 29 percent in the UNH poll before the Iowa caucuses, and he trailed McCain by 5 percentage points in the final UNH poll. Meanwhile, Huckabee capitalized on his Iowa performance, emerging as the leading socially conservative candidate. McCain was not hurt by not contesting Iowa. His campaign actually received a boost as Romney's Iowa loss made him look weaker when compared with McCain.

The days between Iowa and New Hampshire were anticlimactic on the Republican side as it was overshadowed by the Democratic race. McCain won with 37 percent of the vote, followed by Romney at 32 percent and Huckabee with 11 percent. Giuliani's strategy of skipping New Hampshire backfired; his once-promising campaign ended with only 8.5 percent of the New Hampshire vote, barely edging out Ron Paul (7.7 percent). McCain, Romney, and Huckabee jousted in subsequent states, but McCain's win in New Hampshire put him over the top his second time around. McCain's wins in 2000 and 2008 made him the only non-incumbent candidate in the modern era to win the New Hampshire primary twice.

2012–Mitt 2.0

Mitt Romney entered the 2012 New Hampshire Republican primary as the prohibitive front-runner. He had finished in second place behind John McCain in the 2008 nomination battle, and Republicans had historically nominated the next person in line. Like Reagan following Ford, Bush following Reagan, Dole following Bush, and McCain following (the second) Bush, Romney knew it was his turn. Romney also had the most money, had secured the most endorsements, and arguably had the best combination of business and political credentials of the Republican field. He also knew the state. Not only had he campaigned in 2008, he had been governor of neighboring Massachusetts and also had a summer home in New Hampshire. Whatever happened in Iowa, he felt he could count on New Hampshire as his firewall. It turned out that he would need New Hampshire, as he only tied former Pennsylvania senator Rick Santorum in the Iowa caucuses. Romney had to win New Hampshire to give his campaign the momentum it needed to secure the GOP nomination.

The Romney campaign had assessed the order of the states in the nomination process — particularly the early states — and had calculated that their best chance to win a convincing victory and to build momentum was New Hampshire. The Iowa caucus and South Carolina primary electorates were historically very conservative and, more importantly, predominantly evangelical Christian — a difficult hurdle for a Mormon like Romney to overcome. But a big win in New Hampshire's primary, Romney's team calculated, would provide momentum for Romney to weather the less friendly South Carolina primary and eliminate any other moderate competitors, leaving the remaining conservative candidates to duke it out for the conservative South Carolina vote. The Romney team was very familiar with this strategy. In 2008, their campaign had been derailed by a resurgent John McCain, who narrowly defeated Romney by 5 percentage points. That was enough to propel McCain to the nomination despite being short of cash. Romney was determined not to lose again.

As far back as early 2009, Romney had been the clear front-runner in New Hampshire polls, and he remained the favorite throughout the campaign.[65] But Romney had also led in New Hampshire as late as November 2007, only to be overtaken by McCain in the final month of the campaign. Mindful that New Hampshire was a place where outsider candidates had won in the past (even though the most recent real outsider to win was Pat Buchanan in 1996), Romney's team certainly knew that a win could not be taken for granted. To guard against a replay of 2008, Romney started early. In late 2008, he directed money from his political action committee to support staff and campaign infrastructure for a 2012 run. He also channeled funds to candidates running for state office, including candidates in New Hampshire, whose support he would need in 2012.[66] He took advantage of the Supreme Court's decision in *Citizens United v. Federal Election Commission* to create a Super PAC to help independently support his campaign. To underline the importance of New Hampshire to his nomination strategy, Romney announced the formation of his campaign exploratory committee, the first step to begin raising funds for a campaign, in a videotaped speech before students at the University of New Hampshire.[67]

Romney made extensive use of the political contacts he had made during his 2008 primary bid to secure the endorsements of New Hampshire Republican leaders, from all wings of the party.[68] And while many political observers say that endorsements don't vote, a growing body of research has shown that endorsements are a clear indication of the breadth of support within one's party and is related to the chances of winning the nomination.[69]

Romney officially kicked off his presidential campaign at the farm of Doug Scamman, a former speaker of the New Hampshire House of Representatives and an important 2000 Bush supporter, on June 1, 2011.[70] Romney needed the support of the many traditionally moderate, northeastern Republicans who came to Scamman farm that June afternoon. Only six months before, Republicans had regained the state senate and house of representatives after four years of Democratic control, with the help of energized Tea Party Republicans who were suspicious of Romney and other moderate Republicans. Not coincidentally, 2008 vice presidential candidate Sarah Palin, darling of Tea Party Republicans, held a rally that same afternoon in neighboring Hampton, New Hampshire, to underscore Tea Party anger with so-called RINO ("Republican in name only") Republicans.

Romney hoped to minimize opposition among all Republicans, but especially among the more conservative New Hampshire activists who might oppose him. One way of doing this was to give what seemed like small, but in fact were rather significant, campaign contributions to Granite State Republicans, including $1,000 to each Republican running for state senate in 2010. This strategy of winning friends and disarming potential enemies seemed to have worked as Romney mostly avoided the intra-party ideological splits he faced in more conservative states.[71]

He campaigned often in New Hampshire but not as often as in 2008 and not as often as some of his opponents. He was, however, the best-funded Republican and arguably had the best campaign organization as well as the support of the business wing of the Republican Party nationally. When communicating to New Hampshire Republicans, he would speak at large events, like the one at the Scamman farm, as well as through advertising. This gave Romney a bigger bang for his significant bucks and, more importantly, it helped him maximize his most precious resource, his time. As the front-runner and heir apparent after his close call in 2008, he would be expected to campaign in other early states, especially Iowa, so he could not spend as much time in New Hampshire as some other candidates. He also needed to spend a great deal of time raising the money necessary for upcoming nomination elections as well as the November general election.

Former Utah governor Jon Huntsman, another moderate Republican, was determined to win in New Hampshire by going after the famous "independent" New Hampshire voters; those officially registered Undeclared, who could vote in either the Republican or Democratic primary. And as President Obama was unopposed on the Democratic side, Huntsman believed he could attract both moderate Republicans as well as those undeclared voters who leaned Democrat. He had been President Obama's ambassador to China, an appointment that he felt would make him attractive to Democrats, or at least to show he was the most independent in the Republican field.

With this strategy, Huntsman hoped to recapture the success of John McCain's two New Hampshire victories as an independent, or maverick. McCain had won by staking out a position to the left of the Republican field, emphasizing his independent credentials, and getting strong support from undeclared voters. Like McCain, Huntsman positioned himself as an independent Republican, introducing himself to New Hampshire voters three weeks after Romney at an event in Exeter, New Hampshire, on June 21. This event featured a video of Huntsman riding his motorcycle across the Utah desert and showing his early years playing in a rock band, images that helped establish him as a different Republican. Like McCain, Huntsman met voters at house parties and town hall meetings, listening and answering questions in the hope of winning their support rather than relying on advertising. The story of New Hampshire electing outsiders who campaigned hard for each vote, like McCain in 2000 and 2012, but also Jimmy Carter in 1972 and Eugene McCarthy in 1968, had convinced Huntsman he had a chance to topple Romney in New Hampshire. That Huntsman's strategy mirrored McCain's was not coincidental; he had hired John Weaver as a senior strategist, the man who planned McCain's 2000 and 2012 campaigns.

Ron Paul most definitely did not represent the center of the Republican Party, but he also hoped to win because of the independent, libertarian-minded voters he believed made up much of the Republican electorate. The success of the Tea Party in 2010, fueled in New Hampshire by libertarians and recent migrants from the Free State Project, made Paul optimistic that 2012 would be better for him than 2008, when he finished fifth. Paul also had an extensive fund-raising effort making his campaign more credible than it had been in 2008, and he had support from a large cadre of young volunteers.

Several socially conservative candidates campaigned in New Hampshire as well, most notably former Pennsylvania senator Rick Santorum and former speaker of the house Newt Gingrich. Both candidates downplayed their chances of winning New Hampshire, but each was determined to do well enough to stay in the campaign until South Carolina, where social conservative voters dominated the Republican electorate.

Despite a tie with Rick Santorum in Iowa (eventually, it was determined that Santorum won by 34 votes), Romney went on to easily win New Hampshire, getting 39 percent of the vote. Tea Party favorite Ron Paul got 23 percent, and Jon Huntsman was a distant third with 17 percent. Social conservatives Santorum and Gingrich tied for fourth place with 9 percent each. Romney won despite an energized Tea Party contingent (Paul's supporters) and despite Huntsman holding more campaign events. Instead, the front-runner Romney, as is typically the case, won the New Hampshire primary and eventually the Republican nomination.

The tiny state of New Hampshire, with its moderate-to-liberal, mostly nonreligious Republicans, largely determined that Romney would become the Republican nominee. And 2008 was not unique for Republican candidates: Ronald Reagan (1980), George H. W. Bush (1988), and John McCain (2008), all lost convincingly in Iowa but then won in New Hampshire, propelling them to the nomination. Since the modern primary began in 1972, only Bob Dole (1996) and George W. Bush (2000) were able to secure the Republican nomination despite losing New Hampshire. As the Republican electorates in the two earliest states move further apart ideologically, look for candidates to pick and choose where to go in order to maximize their resources. However, a candidate that truly appeals to all segments of the party will need to run in both states to prove the breadth of his or her support.

The Democratic dynamic is not much different between Iowa and New Hampshire. Apart from natural loyalties to candidates from their own region (either the Midwest or New England), the voters in each state have generally similar views. The big difference between these two states is the method of voting — a low-turnout caucus versus a high-turnout primary.

A Demographic and Political Profile of New Hampshire

Perhaps the most frequently heard criticism of New Hampshire's position as the first primary is that it does not represent the country demographically, economically, or politically. This critique comes from both sides of the political spectrum. As Fox News anchor Uma Pemmaraju succinctly put it, "[New Hampshire has] got a population of a little over a million and the voters tend to be primarily white . . . and it's one of the least populated states in the country."[1] Democratic Senator Carl Levin from Michigan concurs: "I see an absurdity in a system where candidates make dozens of visits to New Hampshire and understand their issues so thoroughly." Levin has been pushing for a change for nearly two decades. "We have a lot of issues that are important to us. We're a Great Lakes state, we have water issues, garbage being dumped in Michigan. . . . We're more diverse than New Hampshire."[2] Just how different is the Granite State from the rest of the country? And how does any distinctiveness of New Hampshire's electorate impact the kind of candidates who can win the New Hampshire primary? To answer these questions, we need to take a close look at the demographics of New Hampshire to see how different the state is from other states, and then examine whether the differences actually influence the kind of candidates that can do well in the primary.

A Demographic Profile of New Hampshire

Carl Levin and Uma Pemmaraju are among many who have complained that the state is too small, too white, too rural, and too rich compared with the rest of the country to merit its premier position in the primary process. The implication is that issues important to voters in other parts of the country, especially issues that are important to voters in states with large urban centers, are ignored by candidates when they campaign in New Hampshire.

The state is indeed small by any measure. It is the fifth smallest state in area, slightly larger than New Jersey and slightly smaller than Vermont. It is the eighth smallest state in population with 1.3 million people in 2010, approximately 0.4 percent of the US population. This makes it slightly less populated than neighboring Maine and slightly more populated than Rhode Island. New Hampshire is certainly not an urban state (60 percent of New Hampshire residents lived in urban areas in 2010, compared to 81 percent of the country as a whole), but, despite its bucolic image, it is certainly not rural either: New Hampshire's population density in 2010 was 147 people per square mile, which is much more heavily populated than the United States as a whole (87.4 people per square mile). In fact, New Hampshire ranks in the middle of US states as the 23rd most densely populated (Table 7.1).

Most of New Hampshire's population lives in a triangle from Nashua to Concord to Portsmouth, in the southeast portion of the state. Its six northern and western counties — Coos, Grafton, Carroll, Belknap, Sullivan, and Cheshire — comprise only 26 percent of the state's population. There are two significant cities in New Hampshire, both of which are quite small by national standards. Manchester, with a population of 110,000 in 2010, has been the largest city in the state since the 1800s, but is only the 290th largest city in the country. The Amoskeag Manufacturing Company mill buildings, once the largest manufacturing space in the world, line the banks of the Merrimack River. These mills, which once made everything from clothing and shoes to locomotives, are now filled with offices, shops, and high-tech companies.[3]

Table 7.1. Population Size and Growth: New Hampshire and US

	US Pop.	NH Pop.	US Pop. Growth	NH Pop. Growth	US Pop. Density (sq. mi.)	NH Pop. Density (sq. mi.)	NH Density Rank	US % Urban	NH % Urban
1910	92,228,531	430,572	21.0%	4.6%	26.0	48.1	20	45.6	51.8
1920	106,021,568	443,083	15.0%	2.9%	29.9	49.5	22	51.2	56.5
1930	123,202,660	465,293	16.2%	5.0%	34.7	52.0	25	56.1	58.7
1940	132,165,129	491,524	7.3%	5.6%	37.2	54.9	25	56.5	57.6
1950	151,325,798	533,242	14.5%	8.5%	42.6	59.6	26	64.0	57.5
1960	179,323,175	606,921	18.5%	13.8%	50.6	67.8	27	69.9	58.3
1970	203,211,926	737,681	13.3%	21.5%	57.5	82.4	23	73.6	56.4
1980	226,545,805	920,610	11.5%	24.8%	64.1	102.8	22	73.7	52.2
1990	248,709,873	1,109,252	9.8%	20.5%	70.4	123.9	20	75.2	51.0
2000	281,421,906	1,235,786	13.2%	11.4%	79.7	138.0	22	79.2	59.2
2010	308,745,538	1,316,470	9.7%	6.5%	87.4	147.0	23	80.7	60.3

Source: US Census Bureau.

Further south on the Merrimack River and on the Massachusetts border is Nashua (2010 population: 88,000), the 330th largest city in the United States. It too prospered during the 1800s and early 1900s as a manufacturing center, driven by the Nashua Manufacturing Company. And like Manchester, Nashua saw jobs move south after World War I. It boomed again during the 1970s and 1980s as companies such as Digital Equipment and Sanders Associates fueled the first tech boom in greater Boston. Evidence of the old and new manufacturing activity in Nashua can be seen in the old Nashua Manufacturing Company plant, which now houses BAE Systems Electronics and Integrated Solutions, the company that purchased Sanders in 2000. BAE is now the state's largest manufacturing employer, producing advanced electronics for the aerospace and defense industries.

The next three largest cities are the capital, Concord (population: 45,000) in Merrimack County, and the former mill towns of Rochester (population: 38,000) and Dover (population: 28,000), both in Strafford County. Both of these towns were once thriving manufacturing centers, but like Manchester and Nashua, the brick-and-stone mill buildings, formerly filled with machines driven by water power from the Merrimack, Salmon Falls, and Cocheco rivers, now house a variety of commercial, office, and residential spaces.

Portsmouth (population: 21,000) represents an unusual community in that it is relatively small, even by New Hampshire standards, but it is economically significant in that it is central to two military bases: Pease Air National Guard Base and the Portsmouth Naval Shipyard just across the river in Kittery, Maine. The Portsmouth Naval Shipyard is the oldest operating yard in the US Navy. It was established in 1800 and currently refits and modernizes Los Angeles-class nuclear attack submarines. At its peak in World War II, it employed more than twenty thousand people, and it currently employs about three thousand, many of whom live in New Hampshire. Pease was a Strategic Air Command (SAC) base during the Cold War, but it was closed in 1990. The New Hampshire Air National Guard currently maintains a refueling wing at Pease, but most of the former base is now a corporate office park with more than 245 companies employing more than seven thousand people. Because of these two important economic engines, the New Hampshire Seacoast, centered in Portsmouth, is one of the most important economic regions in the state.

While New Hampshire is not an urban state, it certainly cannot be characterized as a state filled with rural hunters decked out in black-and-red wool plaid, as Lamar Alexander famously found out in 1996. But it is also not the manufacturing powerhouse it once was. An accurate description of New Hampshire is that it is a suburban state, largely tied to the greater Boston economy, following Boston sports and watching Boston television — although it does boast one TV station of its own, WMUR, which covers most of the state.

Migration

New Hampshire is unique in the Northeast in that it is the only state that has experienced significant population growth in recent decades. While it slowed late in the 2000s when the stalled housing market prevented people from selling their homes and moving north, population in New Hampshire still grew at a much more rapid clip than in any of the neighboring states.

Migration into New Hampshire that has kept the state growing at a faster pace than its New England neighbors is due to several factors. Some of these were identified in a survey conducted for the *Boston Globe* in 2006, which found that the top three reasons people moved from Massachusetts to New Hampshire were the more affordable cost of housing, lower taxes, and the political environment.[4] Inexpensive housing, as well as inexpensive land available for housing, has been a driver of suburbanization across the country, and this has also been true for Boston. An average house in the northern Boston suburbs typically costs at least $100,000 more than a similarly sized house in southern New Hampshire, and commuting from New Hampshire does not take appreciably longer. As the Greater Boston suburbs have sprawled — particularly with the development of manufacturing companies, technology outfits, and retail stores on the Route 128 and I-495 corridors north and west of Boston — the need to have an easy commute into the heart of Boston has become less important. Concurrent residential development occurred west of Boston and also over the border into southern New Hampshire.

Rockingham County in the southeastern corner of New Hampshire saw its population nearly triple between 1960 and 2010, from 99,029 people to 295,223. The median price of a detached home in Rockingham County in 2009 was $372,305, the highest in any New Hampshire county, but considerably less than $482,856 in neighboring Essex County, Massachusetts.[5] Low-cost housing has provided a major financial incentive to live in the Granite State.

A second important factor in New Hampshire's growth, also identified in the *Globe* survey, is that it has never had a "broad-based" tax, that is, either an income or general sales tax. Lower taxes make New Hampshire, for many, a much more attractive place to live than other New England states. This is particularly true for small business owners and consultants who report their business income with their personal income taxes. New Hampshire residents pay no broad-based sales or income tax, compared to a 5.3 percent income tax and a 6.25 percent general sales tax Massachusetts residents pay.

But the lack of a sales or income tax means that most New Hampshire residents pay high property taxes. In 2009, the Tax Foundation found that New Hampshire residents paid $5,244 per year in property taxes on a home of median value ($316,200), the fourth-highest property taxes in the country. Despite high property taxes, New Hampshire has consistently ranked near the bottom of the list of states in terms of the total state and local taxes paid by residents. In 2009, the Tax Foundation ranked New Hampshire 44th out of 50 states in the overall amount paid in state and local taxes, and it has been among the ten lowest-taxed states as measured by the Tax Foundation since the 1970s.[6]

A third important factor in New Hampshire's growth is that it is consistently rated as one of the best places in the country to live. It has a beautiful natural environment with the White Mountains, hundreds of lakes, and a short seacoast with popular beaches. Morgan Quinto Press regularly ranks New Hampshire as one the best states in the country to live, and CQ Press regularly names New Hampshire the most livable state. And ten times between 2002 and 2012, the Annie E. Casey Foundation rated New Hampshire as the best state in which to raise children (it came in second place in 2007). Low crime, good schools, a vibrant economy, and an attractive environment are all cited as advantages for New Hampshire.

New Hampshire's population has grown largely through domestic migration from other states — primarily Massachusetts, Maine, other New England states, and other states in the Northeast. The result is that only 43 percent of New Hampshire residents were born in the Granite State.

Race

New Hampshire has been characterized as a "white" state by critics of the New Hampshire primary, a state that does not have to deal with many of the problems facing minorities that other states routinely confront. New Hampshire is indeed one of the least diverse states in the country, with 95 percent of the adult population identified as white in the 2005–2009 American Community Survey (Table 7.2). New Hampshire has the third-highest percentage of whites of any state in the country, behind only its northern New England neighbors Maine and Vermont. The minority population of New Hampshire is also not typical of minorities in other states. The largest minority group in New Hampshire is Asians, who make up 1.9 percent of the population, followed by African Americans (1.1 percent). And unlike the largest minorities in most states, New Hampshire's largest minority group, Asians, have higher levels of education than the overall population.[7] Hispanics or Latinos (of any race) make up 2.6 percent of the state population, but are growing at a faster rate than other minority groups, increasing by 79 percent between 2000 and 2010. Minority populations are greatest in Nashua and Manchester, but there are significant pockets in other smaller cities and towns.

Although it is small, the minority population in New Hampshire has been growing in recent years, growing more by migration and by natural increase than has the white population. But it will be decades before the minority population of New Hampshire increases to the levels in most other states. New Hampshire is not representative of the diversity in other parts of the country or even of either of the major political parties. Both of the political parties, especially the Democratic Party, have much higher minority representation among their voters elsewhere in the country.

Table 7.2. Racial Makeup: New Hampshire and US

	US	NH
Race		
White	74.5%	94.8%
African American	12.4%	1.1%
Asian	4.4%	1.9%
Other	6.5%	0.9%
Two or more races	2.2%	1.2%
Hispanic or Latino (of any race)	15.1%	2.6%
Foreign-born	12.4%	5.2%

Source: American Community Survey, 2005–2009 estimates, US Census Bureau.

Age

New Hampshire, like other states in the Northeast, is older than the rest of the nation. The median age in New Hampshire is 39.6 years old and has been increasing in recent years as the baby boomers age. But this does not mean that New Hampshire is full of old people who might strain its social safety net. In fact, only 12.8 percent of its population is 65 or older, about the same as the nation as a whole (Table 7.3). This compares very favorably with other New England states. For example, neighboring Maine has a median age of 41.4, with 15 percent of its population 65 or older.[8]

New Hampshire does an excellent job attracting people from surrounding states who are in their 30s and 40s, many of whom have children. This is the primary reason that the median age in New Hampshire is quite high, yet it manages to remain an economically robust state as people between 30 and 60 are in their prime earning years, are at optimal ages for starting new businesses, and are buying products for their homes and for their children.

New Hampshire residents are also a tad more likely to be married than are people across the country, reflecting the higher percentage of people in their child-rearing years and the higher levels of education and income of Granite State households.

Table 7.3. Age and Marital Status: New Hampshire and US

	US	NH
Age		
Median age	36.5	39.6
Under 5	6.9%	5.8%
18 and older	75.4%	77.3%
65 and older	12.6%	12.8%
Marital status (15 and older)		
Never married	30.8%	28.2%
Married	50.3%	53.5%
Divorced or separated	12.6%	12.5%
Widowed	6.3%	5.8%

Source: American Community Survey, 2005–2009 estimates, US Census Bureau.

Education and Income

New Hampshire has a much more highly educated population than the country as a whole, and this translates directly into higher levels of income. Nearly one-third of New Hampshire adults (25 and older) have at least a four-year college degree, with one in eight having an advanced degree, trailing only Massachusetts and Connecticut on this measure. High levels of education typically result in higher incomes, and the median household income in New Hampshire is $63,000, almost $12,000 higher than median household income nationally (Table 7.4).

Because of this high level of income, it might be argued that New Hampshire residents do not understand the hardships endured by people in poverty in other parts of the country. In particular, New Hampshire does not have any large cities and does not experience the magnitude of urban poverty that other states do. The poverty rate in New Hampshire has been the lowest in the country for several years. In 2011, the poverty rate for New Hampshire was 7.7 percent, while the national rate was nearly twice as high (13.5 percent). However, the northern parts of the state as well as older mill towns have significant pockets of poverty.

Table 7.4. Educational Attainment: New Hampshire and US

	US	NH
Education (25 and older)		
Less than high school	15.5%	9.5%
High school graduate	29.3%	30.2%
Some college	20.3%	18.7%
Associate's degree	7.4%	9.2%
Bachelor's degree	17.4%	20.9%
Advanced / Professional degree	10.1%	11.5%
Unemployment Rate (June 2011)	8.2%	5.1%
Employment (16 and older)		
Private	78.1%	78.9%
Government	14.9%	13.2%
Self-employed	7.0%	7.8%
Income		
Median household income	$51,425	$63,033
Median family income	$62,363	$75,552
Percent below poverty level	13.5%	7.7%
Home Ownership		
Own home	66.9%	73.0%
Rent	33.1%	27.0%

Source: American Community Survey, 2005–2009 estimates, US Census Bureau.

Religion

Religion has been a major factor in politics and elections for much of the United States' history. Roman Catholic immigrants, especially Irish and Italian, made up a key component of the FDR coalition and are still major components of the Democratic Party in many northeastern states.[9] The shift of white evangelical Protestants from the Democratic to the Republican Party across much of the country has been an important factor in the rebirth of the GOP since the 1980s. And while they represent a much smaller voting bloc, Jewish voters remain a central pillar of the modern Democratic Party.

When asked their religious preference in 2012, 36 percent of New Hampshire adults identified as Protestant, 34 percent as Catholic, 1 percent said they were Jewish, and 5 percent said they were of some other religion.[10] Almost one-quarter (22 percent) of New Hampshire adults said they have no religion (and another 3 percent refused to answer or were not sure).[11] This is significantly different from the United States as a whole. According to a 2007 Pew Forum on Religion and Public Life study, 51 percent of Americans identified as Protestant, 24 percent as Catholic, 2 percent as Jewish, 7 percent as some other religion, and 16 percent did not identify with any religion.[12]

Political scientists and sociologists have noted that measures of "religiosity"— that is, how important religion is in a person's life or how often they pray or attend church — are more important to politics than religious affiliation. According to a Gallup study in 2009, New Hampshire ranked second lowest in the country on the importance of religion in its residents' lives.[13] While 65 percent of Americans said that religion is an important part of their daily lives, only 46 percent of New Hampshire residents said it was. New Hampshire residents are also not regular churchgoers: only 27 percent say they go at least once a week, 10 percent a few times a month, 28 percent a few times a year, and 34 percent say they never attend church services.[14] A 2010 Gallup survey found that 43 percent of adults nationwide attended religious services at least once a week.[15] Religion may not be something that is important for many Granite Staters, but it still is a key predictor of how people vote and what issues are important to them. According to a 2008 UNH poll, 57 percent of voters who said they attend church services at least once a week said they would vote for John McCain, while 73 percent of voters who said they never attend church said they would vote for Barack Obama.[16]

In conclusion, New Hampshire is a highly educated, upper-middle-class, low-poverty, white, suburban state with a lower-than-average religious population. It stands out from the rest of the country in all of these categories. Critics of New Hampshire's first-in-the-nation status often point to one or more of these factors as disqualifications for its disproportionate impact on the nomination contest. But while New Hampshire may have a demographic profile that places it outside the national average, this does not mean that its political profile is out of step with either of the major parties or the country as a whole. As Northeastern University political science professor Bill Mayer puts it, "The question of New Hampshire's representativeness is often raised — and very rarely answered in the proper way.... The key question in a primary ... is whether the state Democratic (or Republican) party, whatever its size, is representative of the national Democratic (or Republican) party."[17]

Political Profile of New Hampshire

Prior to the modern New Hampshire primary, New Hampshire's impact on national politics was modest at best. Only one president, Franklin Pierce (elected in 1852), hails from the Granite State and New Hampshire was largely overshadowed by other states in national politics before the modern nomination process. But it is, importantly, one of several states that boast to be the home of the Republican Party. A meeting of local antislavery politicians met on October 12, 1853, at Major Blake's Hotel in Exeter, where former congressman Amos Tuck proposed that several parties combine to run under the Republican Party banner.[18] The Republican Party has had a tremendous impact on state politics ever since, and New Hampshire remained one of the most Republican states in the country until the 1990s. During the 20th century, it cast its electoral votes for Democratic candidates only eight times, while Republican candidates won in the other seventeen elections. Since the Civil War, New Hampshire has elected only three Democrats to the us Senate, seventeen Democrats to Congress, and seven Democrats to the governor's mansion. Republicans have held the majority in the state house of representatives and the state senate for all but a handful of years since the Civil War.

Realignment in New Hampshire

While New Hampshire has been a solidly Republicans state for most of the past century, in recent years the GOP has lost its dominance. Democrat Bill Clinton narrowly won New Hampshire in 1992 and again in 1996, and Democrat Jeanne Shaheen won the governorship three times

(1996, 1998, and 2000). Also, Democrats briefly gained control of the state senate for four years (1998–2002). In 2004, Democrat John Lynch was elected for the first of his record four terms as governor, and in 2006, Democrats won both US Congressional seats and majorities in both the state house and senate for the first time since 1872. It seemed as though New Hampshire had joined the other five New England states as firmly in the Democratic column. Big Democratic wins in 2008 (president, governor, both congressional seats and control of the state house and senate) seemed to confirm this.

Political scientists have long recognized that partisanship is slow to change and that political domination by one party switches to the other party in one of two general ways. The first is the rise of an important new issue that splits the parties and leads to either the creation of a new party or a shuffling of groups that back the existing parties, typically culminating in a "critical election" in which electoral control is secured.[19] The classic example of this type of realignment is the rise of the national Republican Party over the issue of slavery in the 1850s. The Republican Party harnessed the political energy of abolitionists in both the Democratic Party and the Whig Party, leading to the demise of the latter and eventually to the final resolution of the slavery issue with the Civil War. The Republican Party ended a thirty-year period of dominance by the Democratic Party and brought about more than sixty years of largely Republican dominance of national politics. The second most frequently cited example of this type of realignment is the landslide victory of 1932 for FDR and Democrats across the country. Republicans were seen as either being responsible for, or at least having failed to end, the Depression, and America turned to Democrats to fix things. Democrats then largely controlled national politics until the 1980s and 1990s.

But there is a third, more gradual type of realignment, first discussed by V. O. Key, called a "secular realignment."[20] This occurs not necessarily because of a political issue like slavery or the Depression, but because of longer-term changes in the electorate itself. This has happened most recently with the slow conversion of the old Confederacy from Democratic to Republican control. The southern realignment resulted in part from a migration of northern companies and people after World War II, and in part from the dying-off of the older generations of southerners mostly tied to the old Democratic Party of slavery and segregation. The political conversion of the South began in the 1960s with the election of a few Republican senators, such as John Tower (Texas), but it wasn't completed until thirty years later with the 1994 Republican landslide.[21] A similar secular realignment occurred in the northeastern states. This region, once the backbone of the Republican Party, began slowly voting more Democratic beginning in the 1960s and now, with the notable exception of New Hampshire, is perhaps the most reliably Democratic part of the country. Looking specifically at New England, Rhode Island began voting consistently Democratic in the 1930s, Massachusetts in the 1960s, Vermont and Connecticut in the 1970s, and Maine in the 1980s. Connecticut and Vermont's conversions were largely driven by people who moved out of New York City to suburbs in Connecticut and those who sought a rural lifestyle in Vermont.

New Hampshire has been undergoing a similar secular realignment in recent decades, as the Republicans who have dominated state politics since the Civil War have died or moved to the South and have been replaced by migrants from other Democratic northeastern states, who were much less likely to be Republicans than the people they have replaced. Migrants to New Hampshire did not change their political allegiance when they moved to the Granite State; instead, they began changing the political landscape of the state itself. A study by Kenneth Johnson, Dante Scala and Andrew Smith looked at the impact of new voters on the New Hampshire electorate over a rather short time period, 2000–2008. They found that despite overall population growth of only 90,000 people during this period, 321,000 people actually moved to New Hampshire during those eight years, while 292,000 people moved out of the state. This is a tremendous turnover of people. Adding in young adults who were not old enough to vote in 2000, about one-third of the 2008 New Hampshire electorate consisted of different people from the 2000 electorate — 21 percent were people who moved to New Hampshire and 11 percent were newly eligible voters. These new voters were significantly more likely to identify as Democrats than were established voters. More than half of new migrants (52 percent) and young voters (53 percent) identified as Democrats, while only 43 percent of established voters did.[22]

The realignment that has been underway for the past two decades seemed to have reached the tipping point with big Democratic wins in 2006 and 2008, but Republicans rebounded strongly in 2010, taking back both of New Hampshire's Congressional seats, holding a US Senate seat, and winning veto-proof majorities in the state house and senate. Some argue that New Hampshire has returned to its Republican past after a brief flirtation with the Democrats, but the primary reason for these swings in partisan control in the Granite State is that there is now rough parity between Democrats and Republicans. This is also the reason that New Hampshire has been seen as a battleground state in presidential elections since the 1990s. It would be easy, but misleading, to conclude that New Hampshire voters are swinging wildly from Democrat to Republican from election to election. A more accurate description is that New Hampshire is equally balanced between Republicans and Democrats, making differential turnout a key factor in determining electoral outcomes. This can be seen by political party identification measured over the past ten years in the Granite State Poll. Democrats and Republicans have hovered at 40 percent each of the adult population, fluctuating somewhat with national political winds. Democratic identification increased from 2005 to 2008, as the wars in Iraq and Afghanistan became more and more unpopular and President Bush's job approval ratings plummeted. But as the economy failed to rebound during the first three years of the Obama administration, Republican identification has risen to its pre-Bush levels. The overall trend from these data is that New Hampshire has grown slightly more Democratic in the past decade — Democratic identification has increased by approximately 5 percentage points and Republican identification has dropped by approximately 5 percentage points, while the percentage of political independents has remained unchanged (Figure 7.1).

Although party identification has trended somewhat in favor of Democrats, party registration has shown a marked increase in the percentage

Figure 7.1. Party identification in New Hampshire, 1999–2014.

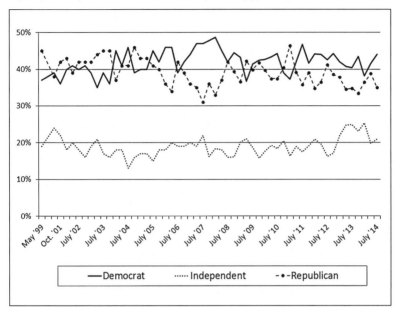

Source: UNH Survey Center Polls.

of New Hampshire registered voters registering "Undeclared," a legal status frequently and erroneously referred to as "independent." Under New Hampshire law, citizens can register to vote as members of the Republican Party or the Democratic Party, or they can register "Undeclared," which means they do not want to publicly declare allegiance to either of the major parties. (For a short time in the 1990s, it was possible to register as a Libertarian, but the fortunes of the Libertarian party have declined, and it no longer qualifies as an official party under state law.) Republican registration has steadily declined since the early 1990s, from 39 percent of registered voters to 33 percent after the 2012 GOP primary. Democratic registration declined in the 1990s, rebounded in the late 2000s, and currently stands at 29 percent. The percentage of voters registered "Undeclared" increased rapidly during the 1990s, peaking at 44 percent in 2006 and declining slightly to 42 percent in 2014 (Figure 7.2).

Figure 7.2. Party registration in New Hampshire, 1980–2014.

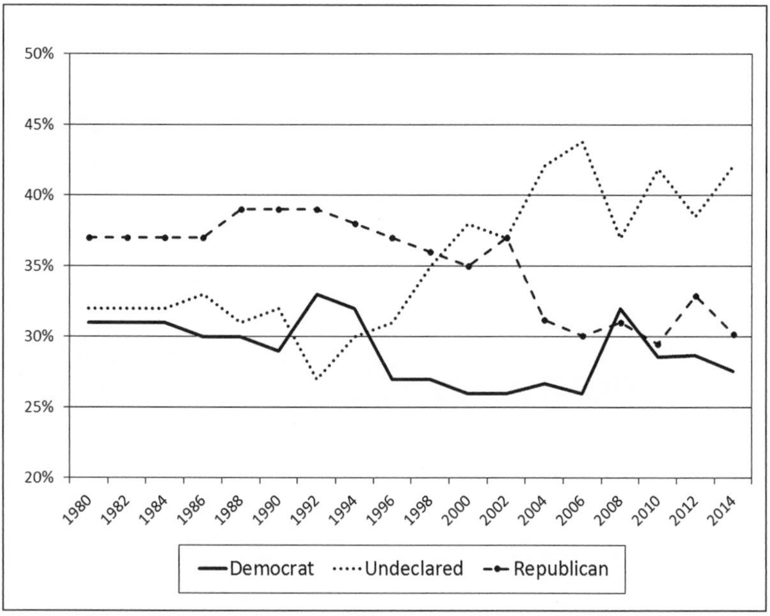

Source: New Hampshire Secretary of State.

The major reason for the increase in Undeclared voters during the 1990s and 2000s is not that New Hampshire has become less partisan in recent decades, but that there were legal changes that made it easier for people to both register and remain Undeclared. Among the important legal changes was allowing people to register to vote on Election Day, which meant that such voters did not have to declare their party registration in advance.[23] The default registration is "Undeclared" — so as long as they do not vote in a primary, they automatically remain registered as Undeclared.

Even more important was the passage of legislation that dropped the requirement that Undeclared voters must declare the primary they will vote in at least sixty days before that primary election; instead, it permits them to choose a party at the polls on Election Day.[24] This law also allows Undeclared voters who have just voted in a primary to change their status back to Undeclared before leaving their polling place. In essence, such Undeclared voters are only "members" of a party during the time they are handed a ballot and vote.

Figure 7.3. Political ideology of New Hampshire adults, 1999–2014.

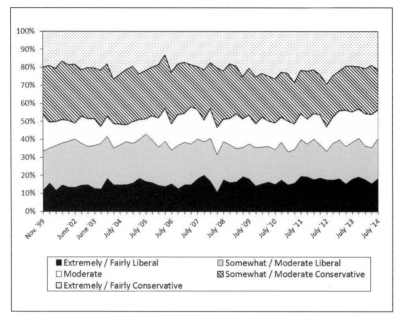

Source: UNH Survey Center Polls.

Conflating Undeclared voters with truly independent voters is a common and misleading mistake made by media covering the New Hampshire primary. This will be discussed in much greater detail in Chapter 9.

Political Ideology of New Hampshire

Behind party registration and party identification lies the concept of political ideology. Many researchers have commented on the increased polarization of the American electorate, which has resulted in a moderate to liberal Democratic Party and a moderate to conservative Republican Party.[25] Specifically, there are few conservative Democrats or liberal Republicans left, either as elected officials or in the electorate. This pattern of partisan polarization has also occurred in New Hampshire. But before we get into the details, let's look at the political ideology of the entire state. Figure 7.3 shows that despite dramatic shifts in political control, overall there has been little change in the political ideology of the people of New Hampshire in the past twelve years. In November 1999, 46

Figure 7.4. Political ideology of New Hampshire Republicans, 1999–2014.

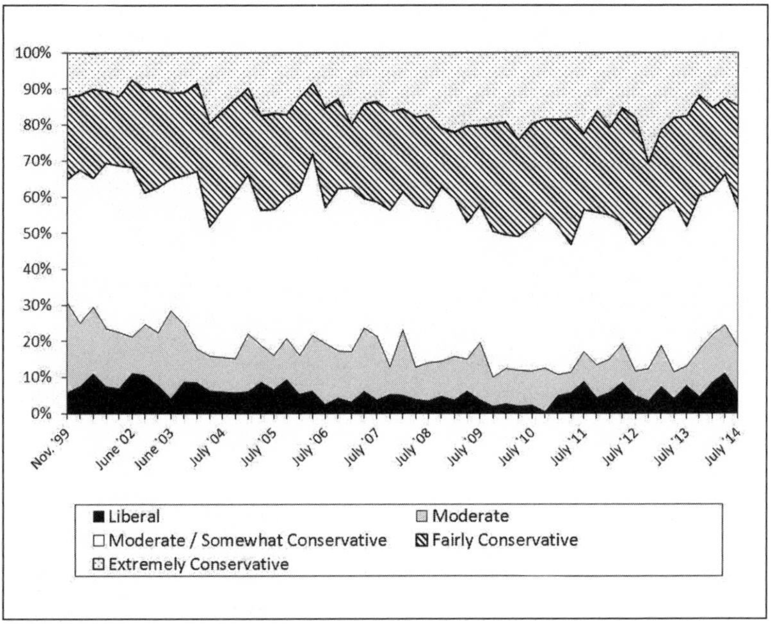

Source: UNH Survey Center Polls.

percent of New Hampshire adults identified as conservative, 20 percent as moderates, and 34 percent as liberals. In 2012 the state is only slightly more conservative — 53 percent now consider themselves conservative, 14 percent moderate, and 33 percent liberal. But there have been some fluctuations over the years, owing both to the vagaries of public opinion polling as well as to short-term politics. If we had looked at the halfway point in this data series (2006), we would have concluded that the state had become slightly more liberal: Only 46 percent identified as conservative, 16 percent as moderate, and 38 percent as liberal.

Looking specifically at self-identified Republicans, we see evidence of ideological polarization over the past decade. In late 1999, 69 percent of New Hampshire Republicans identified themselves as some shade of conservative (with 12 percent saying they were extremely conservative), 25 percent as moderates, and only 6 percent as any kind of liberal (Figure 7.4). But by 2012, 88 percent of New Hampshire Republicans identified

Figure 7.5. Political ideology of New Hampshire Democrats, 1999–2014.

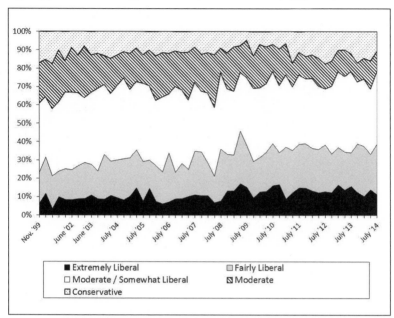

Source: UNH Survey Center Polls.

themselves as conservative (18 percent as very conservative), only 7 percent as moderates, and 5 percent as liberals. Republicans in New Hampshire have become somewhat more conservative, as measured by this poll question, than they were a decade ago. But self-identified moderate and liberal Republicans are making something of a comeback over the past year.

There has also been polarization among New Hampshire Democrats, but not quite as strong as among Republicans. In 1999, 61 percent of self-identified Democrats said they were liberal (13 percent said they were extremely liberal), 22 percent said they were moderates, and 17 percent were conservatives (Figure 7.5). By 2012, 69 percent of Democrats said they were liberal, an 8-percentage-point increase (13 percent extremely liberal); only 14 percent said they were moderates; and 18 percent said they were some stripe of conservative. But again, the long-term trend hides some rather large changes over time. In late 2006, only 19 percent

Figure 7.6: Political ideology of New Hampshire independents: 1999–2014.

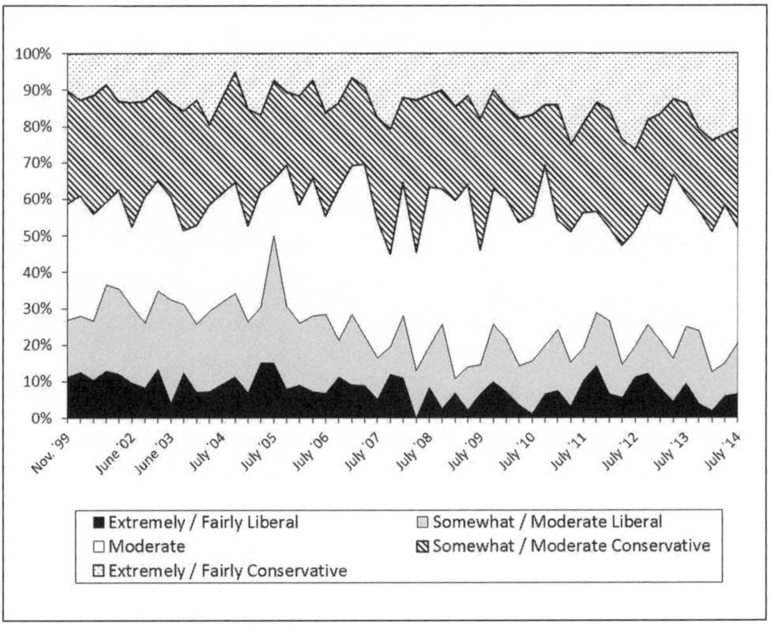

Source: UNH Survey Center Polls.

of Democrats said they were moderate and 11 percent said they were conservative, in line with the anti-Republican, anticonservative tenor of the
2006 elections.

When we turn our attention to self-identified political independents
(as opposed to people who are registered to vote as "Undeclared"), we
see considerable short-term variation, but not much long-term change.
New Hampshire independents tend to reflect national political trends,
becoming more liberal in the mid-2000s as unpopularity with President
Bush increased, and more conservative as the economic downturn of
2008 continued. In late 1999, 11 percent of New Hampshire independents
said they were either extremely or fairly liberal, 16 percent were somewhat or moderately liberal, 32 percent were true moderates, 31 percent
were somewhat or moderately conservative, and 10 percent said they
were fairly or extremely conservative (Figure 7.6). By 2012, 11 percent of
New Hampshire independents said they were either extremely or fairly

liberal, 8 percent were somewhat or moderately liberal, 32 percent were true moderates, 22 percent were somewhat or moderately conservative, and 26 percent said they were fairly or extremely conservative.

In conclusion, political parties in New Hampshire have become somewhat more ideological, much as the nation has, in the past thirteen years. New Hampshire Republicans have become more somewhat more conservative and to a lesser degree, so have New Hampshire independents. Democrats have become somewhat more liberal during the same period. But this measure, although useful in tracking broad changes over time, doesn't help us understand how Republican and Democratic primary voters think about the issues of the day.

LOOKING AHEAD TO 2016, any political change in New Hampshire will be minor. Typically, people do not change their partisanship in their lifetimes, although the intensity of their partisanship may wax and wane because of economic booms and busts or because of problems in foreign affairs. We can expect that the kind of candidates that were attractive in 2008 and 2012 should be attractive in 2016 and the kind of candidates who were not attractive, particularly social conservatives, are not likely to get much traction in 2016.

Who Votes?

THE NEW HAMPSHIRE PRIMARY ELECTORATE

As a general rule, primary voters tend to be more partisan and more ideologically extreme than nonvoters. This is generally true in the New Hampshire presidential primary, although to a much lower degree than in other states because turnout in New Hampshire is so much higher. Turnout in the New Hampshire primary has often been greater than 40 percent of the voting age population — and often higher than some states have in their general elections for president. Table 8.1 shows the ten states with the highest turnout rates in the past four primary cycles. New Hampshire tops the list in every election with the exception of the 2004 Democratic primary, when California turnout was one percentage point higher.

Turnout in the New Hampshire primary has fluctuated in recent cycles depending on whether both primaries are contested or not. As Table 8.2 shows, turnout is significantly higher in years when both primaries are contested, as each party's voters have a meaningful reason to want to get to the polls and have been subject to a real campaign for their vote. The 2008 primary generated tremendous interest because both parties fielded several well-known and well-funded candidates. This resulted in record turnout, both in the number of people who voted in the primary (529,711) and in the percentage of registered voters who voted (59.7 percent).

Undeclared Voters

The New Hampshire primary is a semiclosed primary. Registered Republicans and Democrats can vote only in their own party's primary,

Table 8.1. Ten States with Highest Primary Turnout (plus Iowa), 2000–2012, Percentage Voting of Eligible Population

2000		2004		2008		2012	
NH (2)	44.4	CA (10)	31.0	NH (2)	53.6	NH (2)	31.1
CA (6)	40.3	NH (2)	29.9	OR (14)	43.2	VT (7)	20.8
OH (6)	30.6	OH (10)	28.2	OH (10)	42.4	WI (11)	18.7
NY (6)	25.4	WI (9)	24.6	VT (10)	40.7	SC (3)	17.6
MD (6)	25.2	MD (10)	16.6	CA (6)	40.0	MI (6)	16.5
WI (10)	22.7	MA (10)	15.1	MT (16)	38.7	GA (7)	15.8
SC (4)	20.2	OK (3)	14.5	MA (6)	38.2	OK (7)	14.7
MI (5)	19.8	MO (3)	12.9	IN (12)	37.3	PA (12)	14.6
MO (6)	18.6	TX (11)	11.0	WI (9)	37.1	OH (7)	14.0
IL (9)	18.6	TN (7)	10.9	FL (5)	34.0	DC (11)	13.7
IA (1)	6.8	IA (1)	6.1	IA (1)	16.1	IA (1)	6.5

Source: US Elections Project, George Mason University.
Note: (N) = Sequence number of contest.

but as mentioned earlier, voters who register as Undeclared can choose which primary they wish to vote in. This can change the complexion of a primary electorate as Undeclared voters tend to be less ideological and somewhat less partisan than either registered Republicans or Democrats. In the 2012 Republican primary, 60 percent of registered Republicans identified as conservative, while only 30 percent of Undeclareds voting in the Republican primary said they were conservative. The 2008 GOP electorate was similar: 56 percent of registered Republicans said they were conservative, while 45 percent of Undeclareds voting in the primary said they were conservative. Over the past four primary cycles, the percentage of the Republican electorate consisting of registered Republicans has fluctuated considerably, reaching a high of 89 percent in 2004, when there was no contested Republican primary, to a low of 60 percent in 2012, when there was no contested Democratic primary (Figure 8.1).

Similarly, the makeup of the Democratic primary electorate has also fluctuated depending on whether both parties have contested primaries. The percentage of registered Democrats reached a high of 82 percent in 2012, when President Obama faced no serious challengers, and a low

Table 8.2. Number of Voters Voting and Percent Turnout in New Hampshire Primary by Party Registration, 1996–2012

Number Voting	1996[1]	2000	2004	2008	2012
Total Vote	304,897	396,385	290,723	529,711	311,311
Reg. Republican	210,211	171,031	61,712	165,517	150,428
Reg. Democrat	93,044	114,341	125,675	167,157	50,459
Reg. Undeclared	64,171	111,013	103,336	197,037	110,424
(In GOP Primary)	—	(68,492)	(7,702)	(75,522)	(99,106)
(In DEM Primary)	—	(42,521)	(95,634)	(121,515)	(11,318)
Percent Turnout[2]	1996	2000	2004	2008	2012
Reg. Republican	—	59.8	25.0	61.0	57.9
Reg. Democrat	—	54.0	63.0	64.6	22.3
Reg. Undeclared	—	38.9	38.3	55.1	48.7
Total Turnout	44.3	50.6	40.6	59.7	39.3

[1]In 1996, there were 1,642 votes cast in the Libertarian primary. The number of Undeclared voters voting in the Republican or Democratic primaries was not reported in 1996, just the total number voting.

[2]Turnout for this table is based on the number of voters voting and the number of registered voters in each party designation based on New Hampshire secretary of state voting records. This is not based on voting eligible population (VEP).

of 57 percent in 2004, when there was no Republican primary to draw away Undeclared voters (Figure 8.2). And like Republicans, Undeclareds voting in the Democratic primary are less ideologically extreme than registered Democrats — 48 percent of registered Democrats identified as liberals in 2008 compared with 22 percent of Undeclareds voting in that primary.

There are several interesting things to observe about Undeclared voters and how they behave in the primary. Of greatest importance is to recognize that most of them are not truly independent. If they were independent, it would make no sense for so many to vote in uncontested primaries. In fact, most Undeclared voters are quite partisan, as evidenced by their high turnout in 2004 and 2012. A second important observation about Undeclared voters is that in years when there is only one contested primary, the Undeclared voters can theoretically have a greater impact

Figure 8.1. New Hampshire GOP primary electorate by voter registration, 2000–2012.

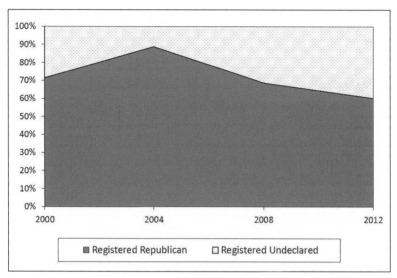

Source: New Hampshire Secretary of State.

Figure 8.2. New Hampshire Democratic primary electorate by voter registration, 2000–2012.

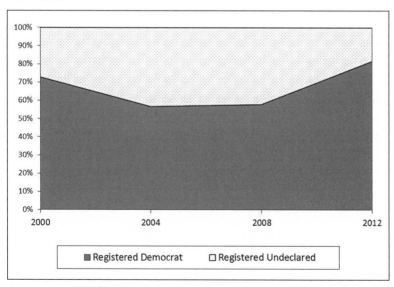

Source: New Hampshire Secretary of State.

on who wins the election by deciding to vote in the contested primary, even if they actually lean toward the other party. Nevertheless, as discussed more fully in Chapter 7, the composition of registered voters in a primary electorate has little impact on who actually wins.

New Hampshire GOP Primary Electorate

Because of relatively high turnout in New Hampshire, the presidential primary electorate more closely resembles a general election electorate than most states. Indeed, in 2008, turnout in the New Hampshire primary (54 percent) was higher than the turnout in Arkansas (53 percent) and Hawaii (49 percent) for the general election. The high turnout means that the New Hampshire primary electorate consists of a much lower percentage of ideological voters than does other states. This is most evident when looking at the Republican primary electorate and comparing New Hampshire to other early primary states. In both 2008 and 2012, the Republican primary electorate in New Hampshire had the third-highest percentage of self-described moderate or liberal voters among all the contested primaries (Table 8.3).[1]

There has been little change in the ideological makeup of New Hampshire Republican primary voters over the past thirty years. In each contested primary since 1980, about half of those voting have described themselves as moderates.[2] Interestingly, this does not correspond to the trend regarding whether there are two contested primaries or only one that year, as the percentage of self-described moderates and liberals was lowest in 1996, when there was no Democratic primary to attract more moderate Undeclared voters, but 5 percentage points higher in 2000 when both primaries were contested. The 1996 primary, which saw the highest percentage of conservative voters in the Republican electorate, resulted in Pat Buchanan narrowly defeating Bob Dole in New Hampshire (Table 8.4).

Considering that states with the highest percentage of moderate to liberal Republicans in their primary electorates (New Hampshire, Massachusetts, Vermont, and New Jersey) seldom vote Republican in the general election, these states can be considered out of step with the rest of the

Table 8.3. Exit Polls: Political Ideology of Republican Primary Voters, 2008 and 2012, Percentage Moderate to Liberal

2008		2012	
MA	47	VT	53
NJ	46	MA	49
NH	45	NH	47
NY	44	MI	39
WI	43	WI	39
CA	39	IL	36
FL	39	OH	34
IL	39	VA	34
MD	39	AL	33
GA	34	SC	32
VA	35	FL	31
OH	35	MD	31
AZ	34	GA	29
MO	32	MS	29
SC	32	TN	27
TX	28	AZ	27
TN	26	OK	25
IA	12	LA	23
		NV	17
		IA	17

Source: National Election Pool exit polls conducted by Edison Research.

Table 8.4. Exit Polls: Political Ideology of New Hampshire Republican Primary Voters, 1980–2012

	1980	1984[1]	1988	1992	1996	2000	2004[1]	2008	2012
Moderate/ Liberal	56%	—	53%	45%	44%	49%	—	45%	47%
Conservative	44%	—	47%	55%	56%	51%	—	55%	53%

Source: National Election Pool exit polls conducted by Edison Research.
[1]No Republican primary exit polls were conducted in 1984 or 2004.

Republican Party when deciding on a nominee. Because New Hampshire has such a great impact in winnowing the field, conservative Republicans often grouse that the kind of candidate who can win New Hampshire really doesn't represent the ideological views of Republicans elsewhere in the country. This is a valid criticism. The only Republican candidates thought of as "movement conservatives" who have won the New Hampshire primary since the 1968 reforms are Ronald Reagan (1980) and Pat Buchanan (1996). Gerald Ford (1976), George H. W. Bush (1988), John McCain (2000 and 2008), and Mitt Romney (2012) have all been regarded with some suspicion by the conservative wing of the party.

Perhaps the most important reason that the New Hampshire GOP electorate differs so dramatically from other states is the relative unimportance of religion and the lack of evangelical Protestants. Once again, Republicans from New Hampshire (and other northeastern states) are much different from Republicans in other states, particularly the southern states that make up the core of the party's general election base. In 2012, Mitt Romney, a Mormon, lost in all of the contested Southern primaries, except for Florida and Virginia, which are the southern states with the lowest percentage of born again Christians in the Republican electorate (Table 8.5). But Romney faced few problems winning among New Hampshire's much less religious voters.

The practical importance of these characteristics of the New Hampshire Republican primary electorate is that it is out of step with the southern and western states on social issues.

Dave Carney, another long-time Republican campaign consultant, says the New Hampshire Republican presidential primary electorate is "made up of two pretty distinct types of voters. One group, perhaps 30 to 40 percent, are very focused on non-fiscal issues such as guns, life, property rights and freedom issues. The second group, which is about 50 to 60 percent, are focused on fiscal issues like taxes and spending."[3]

Polls show that economic problems and jobs, fiscal issues (especially those involving taxes), and issues about the size and scope of government are all typically of greater importance to New Hampshire Republicans than social issues. In 2012, 61 percent of GOP primary voters told exit pollsters that the economy was the most important issue, followed by

Table 8.5. Exit Polls: Percentage Born Again or Evangelical Christians of Republican Primary Voters, 2008 and 2012

2008		2012	
MA	14	MA	16
NJ	16	**NH**	**22**
NY	19	VT	27
NH	**23**	NV	28
MD	34	MD	38
CA	35	WI	38
AZ	38	AZ	42
WI	38	MI	42
FL	39	IL	43
IL	41	VA	46
OH	44	FL	47
VA	46	OH	49
MO	55	IA	57
SC	60	LA	61
TX	60	SC	65
IA	60	GA	68
GA	62	OK	74
TN	73	TN	76
		AL	80
		MS	83

Source: National Election Pool exit polls conducted by Edison Research.

the budget deficit (24 percent). Only 6 percent said that abortion, the top social concern among Republicans for decades, was the most important issue. In a pre-primary poll conducted for the *Boston Globe* in June 2011, the UNH Survey Center asked likely GOP primary voters—using an open-ended question—to name the most important problems that candidates needed to address. Thirty-six percent cited the economy and 20 percent mentioned unemployment and jobs. Fiscal issues, such as the budget deficit (8 percent) and the national debt (6 percent) were next.

Less than 1 percent mentioned any social issue, including abortion, illegal immigration, religion, gun ownership, the environment, or morality.[4]

To be fair, the 2012 Republican campaign was being waged in the wake of the Great Recession of 2008, so it is not surprising that more people mentioned economic or fiscal issues than social issues. But even during the 2000 campaign, when the country had a budget surplus and the economy was relatively strong, and before the 2001 terrorist attacks and the subsequent wars in Afghanistan and Iraq, only 21 percent of New Hampshire's GOP primary voters said that social issues (abortion, morality, gun control) were the most important battles of the campaign, while 20 percent cited taxes and 14 percent named the economy as the most important issues.[5]

The importance of economic and fiscal issues compared to social issues means that Republicans who are seen as social or religious conservatives typically fare poorly in New Hampshire, while they perform much better in other early contests. In the past two primaries, social conservatives Mike Huckabee and Rick Santorum won the Iowa caucuses, but only got 11 percent and 9 percent, respectively, of the vote in New Hampshire.

Candidates who hold very conservative positions on social issues, such as Rick Santorum and Newt Gingrich in 2012 and Mike Huckabee in 2008, tend to do well in states with religious electorates, but not in New Hampshire. Perhaps the most important litmus test among Republicans is whether a candidate opposes legal abortion. Looking just at the early primaries in 2012, 62 percent of New Hampshire primary voters say they have a moderate or liberal position on social issues such as abortion. While an identical question was not asked on exit polls in other states, only 35 percent of South Carolina and 37 percent of Florida Republican primary voters think that abortion should be legal. In 2012, New Hampshire GOP primary voters were more likely to say that abortion should be legal in all circumstances (32 percent) than was the country as a whole (25 percent).[6] Perhaps the second most visible social issue today is the legalization of gay marriage. New Hampshire was the first state to legalize gay marriage through an act of the legislature signed by the Governor (in 2009). While Republican presidential candidates have strongly opposed gay marriage for the nation, more than one-third of New

Table 8.6. Support for the Tea Party among 2012 New Hampshire Republican Primary Voters

Question Text: "Which of the following best describes you: you are an active member of the Tea Party movement; you support the Tea Party movement, but you are not an active member; you have no view of the Tea Party one way or the other; or you oppose the Tea Party movement."

	Dec. 2011	Jan. 2012
Active Tea Party Member	2%	1%
Support Tea Party	37%	34%
No view	44%	49%
Oppose Tea Party	17%	16%

Question Text: "Overall would you say you support the political movement known as the Tea Party, you oppose the Tea Party, or that you neither support nor oppose it?"

	July 2011	Oct. 2011	Nov. 2011
Support Tea Party	47%	49%	34%
Neutral / don't know	41%	32%	39%
Oppose Tea Party	12%	19%	20%

Source: UNH Survey Center Polls.

Hampshire Republicans (37 percent) oppose repeal of New Hampshire's gay marriage law.[7]

Following the 2008 election, the Tea Party rose as a force within Republican politics, and it had considerable impact in New Hampshire Republican primaries in 2010. However, very few GOP primary voters were actively involved in a Tea Party organization during the 2012 primary campaign. Most Republican primary voters were generally supportive of the Tea Party or at least indifferent, although support waned somewhat as the campaign wore on (Table 8.6).

As another long-time Republican strategist, Rich Killion, said, "Social conservatives [in New Hampshire] are not represented in significantly high numbers, but do have a bloc that should not be ignored. . . . Center-right coalitions win Republican primaries in New Hampshire and they are largely generated by fiscal conservatives."[8]

New Hampshire Democratic Primary Electorate

While the New Hampshire Republican primary electorate may be more moderate than those in most other states, the New Hampshire Democratic electorate is less moderate than comparable electorates in most other primary or caucus states. More than 4 in 10 (43 percent) of 2008 New Hampshire Democratic primary voters said they were either moderate or liberal in their political ideology. Only comparable voters in New York (42 percent) and Massachusetts (41 percent) have a lower percentage of moderates or conservatives (Table 8.7).

New Hampshire has not always had a liberal Democratic electorate. The percentage of moderates to conservatives voting in the New Hampshire Democratic primary has decreased significantly since 1980, when two-thirds of the Democratic primary electorate identified as moderate or conservative. A look at exit poll data from 2008 shows that 57 percent of Democratic primary voters identified as liberals, a 10-percentage-point increase from 2004. But this is not because New Hampshire Democrats became significantly more liberal in four years, but rather because more moderate Undeclared voters made up a larger percentage of the Democratic electorate in 2004 than in 2008. Still, the overall trend is that the New Hampshire Democratic primary electorate has become more liberal over time.

The composition of New Hampshire Democrats is quite different today than it was in the 1970s and 1980s when Mayer wrote, "There is a hole in the middle of the New Hampshire Democratic electorate. It has New Politics [white collar liberal supporters of George McGovern] and Conservative voters [blue collar conservative Wallace supporters], but is conspicuously short of Regulars [Humphrey and Muskie backers]."[9] Today that hole in the middle is gone. There are plenty of mainstream Democrats, and even more progressives. The hole is on the right, where there are very few conservative Democrats (Table 8.8).

Dante Scala has looked at New Hampshire Democrats in terms of "mainstream" and "elite" voters, which roughly corresponds to moderate Democrats and liberal Democrats. While recognizing Sullivan's comment that "nothing is set in stone," he found that different candidates

Table 8.7. Exit Polls: Political Ideology of Democratic Primary
Voters, 2008, Percentage Moderate to Conservative

2008			
KY	63	PA	50
TX	62	VA	50
IN	61	CA	50
OH	59	FL	50
NC	58	NJ	49
TN	58	MD	48
MO	58	IA	46
SC	56	OR	43
WI	54	**NH**	**43**
GA	52	NY	42
AZ	51	MA	41
IL	51		

Source: National Election Pool exit polls conducted by Edison Research.

Table 8.8. Exit Polls: Political Ideology of New Hampshire Democratic
Primary Voters

	1980	1984	1988	1992	1996	2000	2004	2008	2012[1]
Liberal	32%	29%	38%	43%	45%	54%	47%	57%	—
Moderate/ Conservative	68%	71%	62%	57%	55%	46%	53%	43%	—

Source: National Election Pool exit polls conducted by Edison Research.
[1]No Democratic primary exit polls were conducted in 2012.

appeal to different wings of the Democratic coalition. Elite (more liberal
voters) were more attracted to candidates like Gene McCarthy (1968),
George McGovern (1972), Ted Kennedy (1980), Gary Hart (1984), Michael Dukakis (1988), Paul Tsongas (1992), and Bill Bradley (2000), while
mainstream (moderate) Democrats went for LBJ (1968), Ed Muskie (1972),
Jimmy Carter (1980), Walter Mondale (1984), Dick Gephardt (1988), Bill
Clinton (1992), and Al Gore (2000).[10] We can add Howard Dean to this

list of candidates attractive to elite voters in 2004 and John Kerry to the list of moderate candidates.

The 2008 primary does not fit cleanly into this dichotomy, as both Clinton and Obama were equally attractive to the wings of the party, and voters obviously had a difficult time choosing between the two, as the polling controversy surrounding the 2008 primary indicates. This is discussed more fully in Chapter 9.

New Hampshire does have fewer minority voters in the Democratic primary electorate than any other state, which has led to the criticism that it is too white. Only 5 percent of voters in the 2008 New Hampshire Democratic primary were minorities (see Table 7.2), the same percentages as in 2004 and quite similar to Democrats in the Iowa caucuses. New Hampshire is certainly out of step on this measure.

Similar to the New Hampshire Republican electorate, New Hampshire Democrats are decidedly less religious than their fellow Democrats in other states. According to 2008 exit polls, 37 percent of voters in the New Hampshire Democratic primary said they never attend religious services, the highest of any state. But the corresponding lack of religiosity among New Hampshire Democrats is seldom commented on, even though it does impact the kind of candidates who are attractive to some voters. For example, in 2004, Howard Dean ran 8 percentage points better among voters who never attend religious services than among those who did so weekly. Conversely, John Kerry did 7 percentage points better among weekly churchgoers than with those who never attend services. Some of the lack of religiosity can be attributed to the lack of minorities, either African American or Hispanic, who are typically more likely to attend religious services than whites, but it is also related to levels of education. Polls conducted by the UNH Survey Center regularly show that Granite Staters with postgraduate degrees are more likely to never attend church services and are more likely than others to say they have no religious preference. In 2008, more than half (54 percent) of Democratic primary voters told exit pollsters they had at least a college degree, just a small percentage of whom were regular churchgoers (Table 8.9).

New Hampshire Democrats also differ from their compatriots in other states in that they are less likely to be union members. Outside southern

Table 8.9. Exit Polls: Religious Attendance and Race among Democratic Primary Voters, 2008, Percentage Who "Never Attend Religious Services" and Percentage White

	Percent "Never"		Percent White
NH	**37**	**NH**	**95**
OR	34	IA	93
AZ	29	KY	89
MA	28	WI	87
NY	27	MA	85
CA	27	OR	85
FL	22	PA	80
NJ	19	IN	78
MO	19	MO	76
VA	19	OH	76
OH	18	NY	70
WI	18	AZ	68
IN	17	TN	67
MD	17	FL	66
PA	17	NC	62
IL	15	VA	61
GA	13	NJ	59
TX	13	IL	57
TN	12	MD	53
NC	12	CA	52
KY	11	TX	46
SC	9	GA	43
IA	Not asked	SC	43

Source: National Election Pool exit polls conducted by Edison Research.

states, which are much less welcoming to unions compared to other parts of the country, New Hampshire has the lowest percentage of union members (only 20 percent in 2008 and 23 percent in 2004) in the Democratic primary electorate (Table 8.10). However, this is certainly not to say that organized labor is not important in the New Hampshire primary; it still

Table 8.10. Exit Polls: Union Household Residents as a Percentage of
Democratic Primary Voters, 2004 and 2008

2004		2008	
OH	44	NC	42
NY	43	NY	40
MO	39	IL	38
WI	35	IN	36
CT	34	NJ	35
RI	34	WI	35
CA	33	OH	34
MA	33	CA	31
DE	29	PA	31
MD	29	MA	27
TN	25	MO	27
LA	24	OR	26
VT	24	MD	24
IA	23	IA	22
NH	**23**	**NH**	**20**
FL	22	TN	19
MS	22	AZ	16
AZ	21	VA	14
OK	21	GA	13
TX	21		
GA	20		
VA	18		
SC	12		

Source: National Election Pool exit polls conducted by Edison Research.

provides much of the organizational muscle for campaigns. Both Al Gore
and John Kerry got critical organizational and boots-on-the-ground support from the Professional Firefighters of New Hampshire, which greatly
contributed to their wins in the Granite State.[11]

So how can we best characterize New Hampshire Democrats? They
are white, highly educated, relatively nonreligious, and not likely to be

union members. There are definitely two wings to the party, an upscale liberal wing and a more moderate wing. This correlates with an electorate that is more liberal than Democrats in other states, but not as out of step ideologically with Democrats in the rest of the country as are New Hampshire Republicans when compared with Republicans nationally.

It is difficult to tell whether the issues that are important to New Hampshire Democratic primary voters are the same as those of importance to Democrats nationwide, because New Hampshire Democrats are typically polled in the midst of the primary campaign while the rest of the country is not. But there have been some occasions that a polling organization asked the same question in both places at the same time, such as in early December 2007 when a *LA Times*/Bloomberg poll asked adults nationwide, as well as New Hampshire primary voters, "What issue or problem do you consider the top priority for candidates running for president to address this election?" Table 8.11 shows that at least in late 2007, New Hampshire Democratic primary voters were remarkably similar to national Democrats. The percentage citing health care issues was 9 percentage points higher among New Hampshire Democrats, but that is likely due to the centrality of the issue in the New Hampshire campaigns. Another example of the similarities between New Hampshire and national Democrats comes from primary and general election exit polls, although these cannot be compared directly. The most important issue to New Hampshire Democratic primary voters were health care (28 percent), the economy (22 percent), the war in Iraq (19 percent), and education (10 percent). Ten months later, the most important issues for Kerry voters were the economy (33 percent), the war in Iraq (23 percent), moral issues (8 percent), and education (6 percent). Health care was not included on the national exit poll, but the other issues were of similar magnitude to national Kerry voters as they were to New Hampshire primary voters.

There are many reasons why New Hampshire Democrats are quite similar when it comes to issue importance and issue positions despite being demographically different from the national Democratic electorate. Most importantly, the New Hampshire primary campaign is waged by candidates with an eye toward the broader Democratic electorate. The

Table 8.11. Top Issues for Democratic Primary Voters and National Registered Democrats, December 2007

	NH	US
War in Iraq	42%	43%
Health care issues	35%	24%
The economy	26%	28%
Education	7%	10%

Source: LA Times/Bloomberg Polls.
Note: Two responses possible, percentages sum to more than 100%.

issues they campaign on and which they address in their campaign ads are those that are generally important to Democratic voters anywhere. Second, New Hampshire, unlike Iowa, does not have a unique state industry that candidates must support. While candidates in Iowa must talk about farming and ethanol, New Hampshire presents no such parochial economic issues. And third, because the high turnout in the New Hampshire primary more closely resembles a general election electorate, issues that are only important to activists are typically overwhelmed by issues of interest to the broader electorate.

So where do New Hampshire Democratic primary voters stand on other issues? Generally, they hold very liberal positions on social issues — two-thirds think that abortion should be legal in all circumstances, and more than 80 percent support legalizing gay marriage.[12]

On the major domestic policy issues, New Hampshire Democrats take typical Democratic positions: 80 percent of 2008 Democratic primary voters said that providing health care is the responsibility of the government, supported repealing the Bush tax cuts to fund expanded health care, and believed that health care was one of the most important issues in the campaign. They believe that Social Security should be strengthened by raising the level of income subject to Social Security taxes rather than via privatization or raising the retirement age.[13]

On foreign policy issues, New Hampshire Democrats have generally been opposed to US military interventions going back to at least the McCarthy campaign against LBJ in 1968. More recently, they strongly opposed the wars in Iraq in both 2004 and 2008, and have generally approved of the Obama administration's handling of foreign policy. Opposition to the war Iraq was central to both the Dean and Obama insurgencies in New Hampshire and made those candidates very attractive to the more liberal wing of the party.

Does voter ideology have an impact on which candidate Democratic voters support? Kathy Sullivan, who served as chair of the New Hampshire Democratic Party from 2000 to 2008, certainly thinks so. She describes the New Hampshire Democratic Party as having two wings: "There is a moderate to liberal or pragmatic progressive wing and a smaller, more liberal wing. But this is still a sizable group which likes more outspokenly progressively partisans, which is why President Obama, Howard Dean, and Bill Bradley all did OK."[14] In fact, in 2004 Howard Dean lost to John Kerry by 19 percentage points among conservative Democrats, by 25 percentage points among moderates, and by only 1 percentage point among liberals. This was not the case in 2008, when Hillary Clinton and Barack Obama did equally well among voters of all ideological stripes.

WHAT KIND OF candidates appeal to New Hampshire voters? On the Republican side, the most attractive candidates are those who are moderate on social issues or who at least don't make social issues the center of their campaign. The New Hampshire Republican electorate has stayed moderate to conservative over the past twenty years, and this has left it somewhat out of step with the national Republican Party, especially on social and moral issues. Candidates are much better off appealing to New Hampshire Republicans by emphasizing opposition to taxes, calling for smaller and more limited government, and championing a strong national defense. But as Rich Killion points out, successful candidates must build coalitions so that they are not strongly opposed by social conservatives in the state, but it's best for the candidates not to wear the socially conservative positions on their sleeves.

Historically, New Hampshire has favored mainstream Democrats such as Clinton, Gore, and Kerry — except in years when a Republican incumbent looked hard to beat. In those elections, more liberal candidates like

Gary Hart (1984) and Michael Dukakis (1988) had a much better chance at knocking off the mainstream candidate. This may be changing as the Democratic primary electorate has become increasingly liberal, making it possible for more progressive candidates to win the Granite State. The past three primaries resulted in close calls for the progressive candidate, with Bill Bradley losing to Al Gore by only 6,000 votes, Howard Dean leading John Kerry for much of late 2003 before collapsing in Iowa and losing by 27,000 votes, and most recently, Barack Obama surging into a lead after his win in Iowa before being beaten by only 4,000 votes. In 2016, Hillary Clinton looks to be the prohibitive favorite and is leading among all wings of the party.[15] However, should she decide not to run, look for progressive candidates to again do well in the New Hampshire Democratic primary.

9

Myths about New Hampshire and the Primary

By reading media coverage of the New Hampshire primary, a casual observer might conclude that Granite State voters resemble an ideal form of the American electorate — knowledgeable, highly engaged in politics (especially the primary campaign), regularly going to hear candidates speak, and carefully weighing the policy and personal characteristics of the candidates. They are, in short, independent political thinkers. And while there is a kernel of truth to many aspects of this caricature, it is primarily myth. In truth, the voters of New Hampshire are not much different from voters in other states, especially voters in states that also have early primary contests. This chapter explores several myths about New Hampshire and the New Hampshire primary, tries to dispel them where appropriate, but also illuminates the attitudes and behaviors that are at the core of these myths.

The Independent Voter

Perhaps the most enduring myth about the New Hampshire primary, and one of the favorite story lines of reporters covering the primary, is of the abundance of independent voters in the state. This is also one of the most frequently cited reasons that backers of the New Hampshire primary give for why the state should remain first in the nation — that New Hampshire residents are somehow less influenced by partisanship than people in other states. It is also a source of much misguided speculation about the likely success of presidential candidates in the primary, that they can win New Hampshire by winning the independent voters.

There are two related ways that independent voting in New Hampshire is described. First, that a plurality of New Hampshire voters are registered "independent," and second, that this reflects a thoughtful, practical, and even nonpartisan nature possessed by the New Hampshire electorate.

The first of these explanations does have a basis in fact, although it is misleading. As described in Chapter 7, New Hampshire citizens can register to vote as Democrats or Republicans, or they can choose not to identify with a party when they register. In that case, they are by default Undeclared. (In the mid-1990s, it was possible to register as a Libertarian, but this ended in 2000 when Libertarian candidates in state elections were unable to achieve the 4 percent bar that allowed them to be considered an official party in New Hampshire.)[1] At the time of the 2012 New Hampshire primary, 38 percent of registered voters in New Hampshire were registered Undeclared, 33 percent were registered as Republicans, and 29 percent were registered as Democrats. These figures would lead one to believe that nearly 4 out of 10 New Hampshire voters do not side with either the Democratic or Republican party—that they are politically independent. However, if we look at the voters who are registered Undeclared, it becomes evident that most of them lean toward one of the major parties when asked a standard party identification question. Polling data collected regularly since 1999 provide a more accurate view of New Hampshire voters, showing that approximately 40 percent are Republicans, 45 percent Democrats, and 15 percent truly independent. These proportions vary somewhat from poll to poll, but they have been stable over the past decade. There has been a slow but steady uptick in those identifying as Democrats and a slight decline in Republicans, but the percentage of truly independent voters has stayed remarkably consistent, approximately 15 percent of the electorate (Figure 9.1).

When the New Hampshire electorate is seen from the perspective of party identification, rather than party registration, it is no more independent than other states. American National Election Studies (ANES) consistently shows approximately 10 to 15 percent of the American public being truly independents, no different from what we see in New Hampshire.[2]

Figure 9.1. Party registration and identification of New Hampshire undeclared voters: 1999–2014.

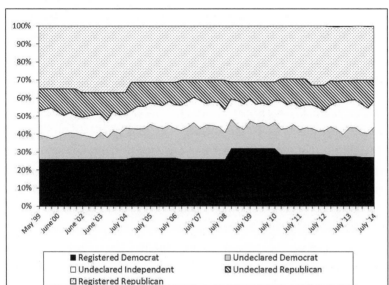

Source: UNH Survey Center Polls and New Hampshire Secretary of State.

So why then does the myth of the New Hampshire independent persist? Most of the problem lies with the label used by New Hampshire politicos as well as state and national journalists, who continue to call Undeclared voters "independents" when they clearly are not. Most of New Hampshire's "independents" are as partisan as those who register as party members. They just don't want to be identified as partisans. But the story of the "independent voter" is so attractive to local and national journalists alike that they continue to use the term, and to write the same story, election after election.

To further emphasize that the informal label "independent" is the source of this problem, it is useful to compare New Hampshire to Massachusetts, its neighbor to the south. In 2012, 36 percent of Massachusetts voters were registered Democrat, 11 percent registered Republicans, less than 1 percent other, and 53 percent "Unenrolled."[3] Unenrolled is the Massachusetts equivalent of Undeclared, voters who don't want to be publicly known as Democrats or Republicans. Massachusetts had 10 percentage points more of these independent voters than did New Hampshire in 2012, but no pundit would think to call Massachusetts, which elects almost exclusively Democrats, a state dominated by independents.

Characteristics of New Hampshire "Independents"

But are there any measures by which Undeclared voters differ from registered Republicans or Democrats? The most politically important difference is that the rates of turnout are consistently lower among the Undeclared than among registered Republicans or Democrats. For example, in the hotly contested 2008 primary, Undeclared voters' turnout was 55 percent compared to 61 percent for registered Republicans and 65 percent for registered Democrats. Since 1996, turnout of Undeclared voters has averaged 45 percent, while Democrats averaged 50 percent and Republicans averaged 55 percent. And this underestimates the difference between Undeclareds and registered partisans, as the calculation includes uncontested Democratic primaries in 1996 and 2012 and an uncontested Republican primary in 2004.[4] When these uncontested elections are removed, average primary turnout increases to 63 percent for registered Republicans and 61 percent for registered Democrats, 15 percentage points higher than Undeclared turnout.

A major reason Undeclared turnout is lower is that such voters report being less interested in politics in general than are registered partisans. At the conclusion of the 2008 primary, 15 percent of Undeclared voters who said they planned to vote reported that they were only somewhat or not very interested in the election, compared with 8 percent of registered Democrats and 10 percent of registered Republicans reporting the same thing. In 2012, just two days before the election, 49 percent of registered Republicans said they were very interested in the GOP primary, while only 35 percent of Undeclareds voting in the GOP primary said they were very interested.

In part because they are less interested, Undeclareds are also more likely to change their minds at the end of the campaign. In 2008, 62 percent of registered Democrats said they definitely knew whom they *planning to vote?*

were going to vote for, while only 40 percent of Undeclareds voting in the Democratic primary had definitely made up their minds.

Impact of "Independent" Voters on the Primary

The most important reason for being registered Undeclared in New Hampshire is that one can then vote in either party's primary (as can people who register to vote on Election Day). This quirk in New Hampshire's election law is the reason the media focuses on the New Hampshire "independent" voter. Because Undeclareds make up more than 4 in 10 registered voters, they can potentially have a significant impact on the outcome of the primary in one of two ways: by voting disproportionally in one party's primary, or by heavily favoring one candidate within a primary. In the run up to the 2008 primary, this was a common theme in media coverage, exemplified in this story from CNN: "Candidates are making their closing arguments as they try to win over New Hampshire voters, but the results of the first-in-the-nation primaries could come down to one thing: who can woo the Independents."[5]

But there is little evidence that this actually happens, and certainly not to the extent that it sways the outcome of the primary. There are indeed several examples in recent years when Undeclared voters have broken heavily to one primary, but those are years in which there was only one competitive primary. This happened most recently in 2004, when 93 percent of Undeclared voters cast ballots in the Democratic primary, and again in 2012, when 90 percent voted in the Republican primary. The reason for this is obvious — there was only one competitive primary in those years, so the Undeclared voters who were closet Republicans stayed home in 2004, as did the closet Democrats in 2012. When both parties have competitive primaries, such as in 2000 and 2008, Undeclared voters split more evenly — 62 percent voted in the Republican primary in 2000, and 62 percent voted in the Democratic primary in 2008.

In years with two competitive primaries, the proportion of the Undeclared electorate that votes in a particular primary seems to be driven by two things: the underlying political leanings of Undeclared voters, and the intensity of the primary campaigns, which is related to the inevitability of the outcome. It is difficult to draw conclusions about what happens in these instances as both parties have had competitive primaries in 2000 and 2008 (and perhaps 1992 if one considers the Buchanan insurgency a serious campaign). In 2000, Undeclareds were slightly more likely to identify as Democrats (by about 3 percentage points), and this margin had grown to 5 percentage points by 2008.[6]

Other than the ongoing partisan realignment in New Hampshire, the second reason Undeclared voters choose one primary over the other is the relative competitiveness of the two primaries. Undeclared voters do have the option of voting where the action is and where their vote might matter more. For example, in 2000, then Vice President Al Gore was expected to sweep the early Democratic contests on his way to his inevitable nomination. He had only one serious challenger, former New Jersey Senator Bill Bradley, who had considerably less money and organization than Gore and who was not seen to have a serious shot at the nomination. That year, the Republican field was much more interesting and featured several big names: Governor George W. Bush (TX), Senators John McCain (AZ) and Orrin Hatch (UT), as well as publisher and 1996 candidate Steve Forbes, along with conservative activists Alan Keyes and Gary Bauer. The Bush-McCain battle was the more interesting contest in 2000 and, indeed, more people voted in the GOP than the Democratic primary (239,523 to 156,862) — and, unsurprisingly, so did more Undeclared voters (171,031 to 114,341). The 2008 primary was a different story, one in which the fight between Barack Obama and Hillary Clinton dominated the news (and advertising spending) compared to the rather uninspiring slog between John McCain and Mitt Romney. More people voted in the Democratic than the GOP primary in 2008 (288,672 to 241,039), and more of the Undeclared voters voted in the Democratic primary (121,515 to 75,522).

Do "Independents" Pick the Winner?

Typically, about two-thirds to three-quarters of the voters in each primary are registered partisans, and the remainder are registered as Undeclared voters. This varies depending on the level of competition in a primary, but it hovers near this mark. This extremely important fact often gets obscured by campaign coverage of the independent voter, but it is critical to understanding who is likely to win as it is much more important for a candidate to do well among his or her party's registered voters than among Undeclared voters. A look at the two most recent election cycles in which both parties had contested primaries illustrates this point.

Both John McCain and Bill Bradley won among Undeclared voters in 2000. McCain won 61 percent of the Undeclared who voted in the Republican primary while Bush won only 19 percent. However, McCain also won by 44 percent to 36 percent among registered Republicans. On the Democratic side, Bradley narrowly beat Gore among Undeclareds voting in the Democratic primary (52 percent to 47 percent) but lost 58 percent to 42 percent among registered Democrats, which resulted in Gore's win. Both Gore and McCain were victorious because they won among the roughly two-thirds of the voters in their primaries who were registered partisans, not because of their support (or lack thereof) among Undeclared voters. And contrary to some assertions made at the time, Bush did not lose the 2000 New Hampshire primary because of independent voters; he lost because registered Republicans favored McCain.

In 2008, Barack Obama edged Hillary Clinton among Undeclared voters (40 percent to 34 percent) but Clinton won 43 percent to 32 percent among registered Democrats, making her the overall winner. John McCain defeated Mitt Romney among both Undeclared voters (38 percent to 30 percent) and also among registered Republicans (37 percent to 33 percent).

Since exit polls began keeping records of how New Hampshire votes, no candidate has won their party's primary in New Hampshire without winning the plurality of registered partisans. "You can't come to New Hampshire and say, 'I'm the independent,'" said Steve Duprey, a former state party chairman who backed Mr. McCain and now, as a Republican National Committeeman, must stay neutral. 'You need to have your base within the party and then attract independents, not the other way around.'"[7]

This phenomenon has been recognized by scholars who emphasize that nominating candidates is the most important thing that parties do, and that it is the party membership, however loosely that might be defined, that does the selection.[8] But Duprey's advice is often ignored by campaigns. Many candidates, or at least their campaign advisors, have unfortunately based their strategies in New Hampshire on winning the independent vote. The most recent example of this was the campaign of former Utah governor Jon Huntsman. His New Hampshire strategy was tailored to appeal to independent voters who were disenchanted with the Obama administration but who were also not comfortable with the crop of more conservative Republican candidates. The goal was to first get them to vote in the Republican primary, and then to vote for Huntsman. "Today's primary is especially important for Huntsman. His 'Our Destiny' political action committee has spent the most money on advertisement in New Hampshire, hoping to draw in more moderate conservatives and the independent voters who make up a significant chunk of the electorate and can vote in the primaries."[9]

Huntsman finished a distant third place, behind eventual nominee Mitt Romney and Libertarian Ron Paul. The lesson for campaigns is that you have to win among partisans to win in New Hampshire.

Strategic Independents

Another regular news story about the impact of independent voters is repeated every four years — that Undeclared voters will strategically try to elect a weaker candidate in the primary of the party they don't support. The following quote is typical.

> Well over one-third of the tiny, snow-draped state's eligible voting population — some 275,000 people — are registered to vote as independents Tuesday. And while New Hampshire has always been known for its ornery, unpredictable electorate, the state's rule that allows Republicans and Democrats to register as independents and vote in each other's primaries has created a Machiavellian side show of significant proportions. And the plot of that captivating sideshow unfolds thusly: A good number of the state's Democratic sympathizers have registered as independents in an effort to head off the national juggernaut of the George W. Bush campaign. These intrigue-minded voters plan to cast their primary votes for Arizona Republican Senator John McCain,

who has campaigned hard in the Granite State in the hopes of getting a boost across the rest of the country with a first primary victory.[10]

While this makes for a titillating newspaper story, there is little evidence beyond anecdotes that this happens, and no evidence that it occurs in a systematic way. Linda Fowler and her colleagues at Dartmouth College, Dean Spiliotes and Lynn Vavreck, conclude that "taken as a whole, there is very little evidence that undeclared voters in New Hampshire behave much differently than registered party voters."[11] Exit polls from 2012 showed that 86 percent of 2012 Republican primary voters had voted in a Republican primary in the past.[12]

The Engaged New Hampshire Electorate

A frequent joke told during the New Hampshire primary goes something like this:

Reporter: "After hearing Senator X speak, are you going to vote for him?"
New Hampshire Voter: "Certainly not! I've only met him three times."

THE IMPLICATION OF this tale is that the New Hampshire primary voter is intensely interested in the election and the candidates, and believes that it is her civic obligation to seriously evaluate the candidates before casting her vote. Civic leaders in New Hampshire often use this image of the New Hampshire electorate as another reason that New Hampshire deserves to have the first-in-the-nation primary. But like the independent voter, the ultra-engaged New Hampshire primary voter is more myth than truth. There are many ways to evaluate voter engagement, including behavioral measures such as voter turnout or attendance at campaign events, as well as attitudinal measures such as interest in the campaign. These are discussed below.

As discussed in Chapter 8, New Hampshire almost always has the highest turnout in nomination contests. In fact, turnout in New Hampshire is typically much higher than even the other early states of Iowa, South Carolina, and Florida. Based on figures from the New Hampshire secretary of state's office, New Hampshire turnout has averaged just over 48 percent, with a high of 62 percent in 1992 and a low of 37 percent in 1984. By comparison, the highest turnout for the Iowa caucuses was 19 percent in 1988. In competitive primaries, when both parties had two or more viable candidates, turnout averaged 54 percent. And even in years without two competitive primaries, turnout averaged 42 percent. Since 1996, only California (in 2004) had higher turnout than New Hampshire in a presidential primary (see Table 8.1).

New Hampshire does indeed have an engaged primary electorate when measured simply by turnout, but this is most likely due to the attention given to an early contest, the amount of money spent on primary campaigns in New Hampshire, the length of the campaign, and the sheer dominance of the primary in local media. It is almost impossible not to be impacted by the primary. During the final month of the campaign, television, radio, newspapers, and highways are covered with candidate advertisements, and the news coverage is dominated by the campaign. In the last week of 2008, more than 3,800 television ads were run on New Hampshire and Boston television stations by candidate campaigns — more than five hundred a day![13] Radio and newspaper ads are much more difficult to quantify, but they too are omnipresent. And while ads for the candidates (and against their opponents) run continuously in the final weeks of the campaign, there are also hundreds of ads sponsored by outside groups seeking to influence the election.

But what about our voter waiting to hear from candidates multiple times? Does this actually happen? Since 2000, the UNH Survey Center has asked New Hampshire adults about their engagement in the primary campaign, and there is indeed evidence that New Hampshire voters engage with candidates at extremely high levels, but the great majority of adults do not, in fact, attend campaign events or meet candidates. In the four primary campaigns since 2000, an average of 19 percent of adults said they had attended a rally, speech, or other event on behalf of a candidate for president during the primary campaign. And over these cycles, an average of 12 percent said they had actually shaken hands with a candidate during the primary campaign. Voters in larger states than New Hampshire probably envy the opportunity that New Hampshire voters

Figure 9.2. Attend rally, speech, other event (percent "yes").

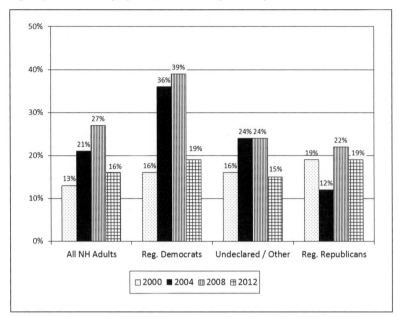

Source: UNH Survey Center Polls.

have to meet a candidate, even if most New Hampshire voters do not take advantage of the opportunity.

Perhaps the most interesting information that Figure 9.2 displays is that more than 10 percent of Granite Staters whose party did not have a competitive primary still attended a campaign event, including 12 percent of registered Republicans in 2004 and 19 percent of registered Democrats in 2012 — indicating that there is a sizeable segment of the population who are "political junkies." Furthermore, 9 percent of registered Republicans in 2004 and 10 percent of registered Democrats in 2012 said they had shaken hands with a presidential candidate in a year in which their party had no competitive primary (Figure 9.3). This can be looked at in two ways. The first is that most voters in New Hampshire do not have personal interactions with a candidate or even attend campaign events. This should not be surprising, as only a small proportion of voters anywhere are truly interested in politics enough to go to a rally.

Figure 9.3. Personally shake hands with candidate (percent "yes").

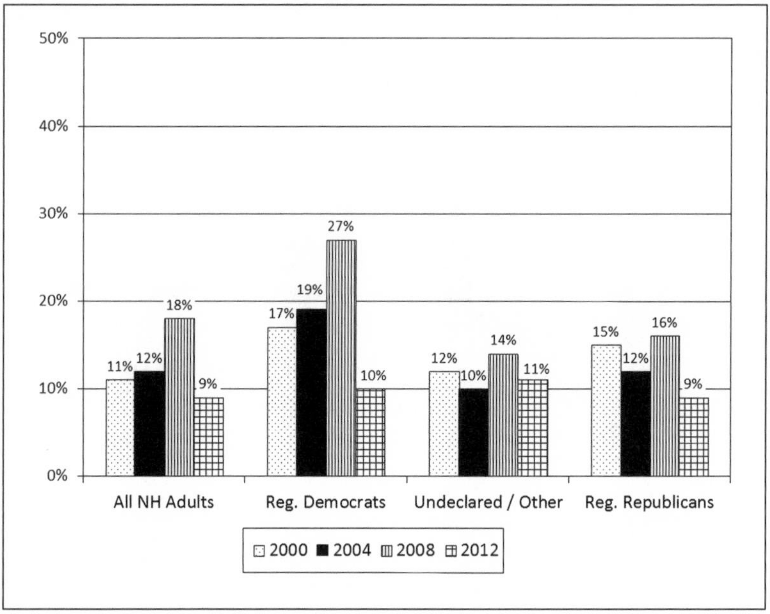

Source: UNH Survey Center Polls.

Another way to look at the figures is to recognize that having one in ten New Hampshire voters personally meet a presidential candidate (shaking hands) indicates an extraordinary level of access to candidates compared with other states.

Grassroots Campaigning

A related myth to the engaged electorate, and part of the allure of the New Hampshire primary, is the image of candidates interacting with voters face-to-face, listening to their concerns and telling them why they deserve to be the next president. Perhaps the best example of this type of campaign in recent years was John McCain's 2000 run, when he spoke to more than one hundred town hall-type meetings, public meetings that consisted of a short address followed by plenty of time for questions and answers. The national media loved McCain in 2000 and covered his

Straight Talk Express extensively. On the basis of national media stories about New Hampshire, one would get the idea that this is how most voters in New Hampshire get their information about candidates and how they decide whom to support.

But in reality, face-to-face campaigning is typically done by candidates who don't have the money to mount a traditional media campaign. When Jimmy Carter ran for the presidency in 1976, he did spend considerable time campaigning in the state, but typically to very small groups of people. It was not until his unexpectedly good showing in Iowa that people began coming to his events in larger, but still modest, numbers.

Ever since Carter's day, successful candidates have understood the need to mount a traditional media campaign. But media campaigns take money, and in recent years candidates with money are spending less and less time in New Hampshire in order to focus on other early contests. Today when a candidate says he will be spending all of his time campaigning face-to-face in New Hampshire, that is typically a sign that he has little money and even less chance of winning. In 2003, Connecticut Senator Joe Lieberman practically moved to New Hampshire for the final month of the campaign in an attempt to endear himself to New Hampshire voters. "I feel like I'm running for a statewide office in some sense," he said. "I intend to do it that way. I'm going to reach out to every voter I can meet personally — town hall meetings, diners, supermarkets, house parties, wherever we find folks that want to hear my case for my candidacy for president."[14] Unfortunately for Senator Lieberman, a month is not enough time to meet enough voters to win the New Hampshire primary; he finished a distant fifth.

More recently, in 2011, former Louisiana governor Buddy Roemer "moved" to New Hampshire to boost his grassroots campaign. This move had no impact on his nonexistent standing in the polls, and it certainly did not increase his chances of winning the New Hampshire primary (he finished with .4 percent of the vote). Jon Huntsman was a much more established candidate than Roemer, and he also counted on winning New Hampshire by holding more campaign events than his rivals. He did, but he still lost.

As Dante Scala and Andrew Smith noted in their study of the 2008 primary, the candidates who spent the most money on television advertising finished at the top of the heap. Hillary Clinton, the winner, spent $4,005,517; Barack Obama spent $4,909,000 and finished a close second; John Edwards, who finished third, spent $1,185,000. Among the Republicans, the top spenders were Mitt Romney ($6,662,000), eventual winner John McCain ($2,659,349), and Rudy Giuliani ($2,115,000). None of the other candidates spent more than $600,000 on television ads in 2008, and all finished well back in the pack.[15]

Endorsements

One of the earliest signs of an emerging primary campaign is the announcement of endorsements by national and local political leaders. Candidates believe endorsements are important to their potential success, and they are supported in that belief by political scientists who have studied the nomination process.[16] The evidence suggests that numerous endorsements from key national leaders often help a candidate's campaign, and, at the very least, serve as a critical "score card" during the invisible primary period. Generally, the more support they receive from political leaders, the easier it is for a candidate to receive media attention, raise funds, create campaign organizations, and appeal to the rank-and-file party voters. The research in this area, however, has focused mostly on endorsements by well-known national political figures. Much less attention has been paid to local endorsements, which are more numerous and less documented and thus more difficult to analyze in a systematic fashion than those at the national level.

Still, the anecdotal evidence and testimony of several local politicos whom we asked about the impact of endorsements, suggest a rather nuanced view about the importance of endorsements, at least in New Hampshire.[17] The consensus of these experts seems to be that while endorsements from well-known leaders can help a campaign in the beginning and give a candidate credibility (and thus more media coverage and fund-raising ability), such indications of support don't seem to be critical in affecting the eventual outcome of the primary.

Jim Merrill, a senior advisor to the 2012 Romney campaign, notes that "endorsements in a presidential campaign can establish the credibility of a candidate. And early endorsements create a sense of momentum." Tom Rath, an advisor to Republican candidates for several decades, agrees. "You often start out with a lot of unknown candidates. One of the things you have to do is define yourself and you use endorsements to help do that." Ned Helms, co-chair of the 2008 Obama campaign and former Democratic Party chair echoes these sentiments: "Endorsements are a way for voters to verify a candidate. It takes a certain level of credibility to get a congressman or senator to endorse you. This is important for the press, and for the second level of campaign volunteers. [An endorsement] makes it easier to get someone to come to a house party."

Another take is provided by former ambassador George Bruno, also a former state Democratic Party chair, who suggests that "voters in New Hampshire often consider candidate endorsements in light of the endorser's support of candidates in prior primaries. So if endorsers of Bill Clinton start endorsing John Kerry, that means it is OK for other Clintonites to support John Kerry, even though Kerry might be slightly more liberal than Clinton."

The number of endorsements a candidate gets, regardless of how well-known the endorsers are, can also be important. "Lots of endorsements look like you're building momentum," said Kathy Sullivan, former chair of the Democratic Party and a 2008 Hillary Clinton supporter. Joe Keefe, former state Democratic Party chairman reinforces this view, saying "I don't think individual endorsements are vitally important in most instances, although cumulative endorsements or the ability to show broad support among elected office holders and party activists can show momentum and seriousness. Also, the media can pick up on this momentum and it can translate into higher visibility and improved fundraising."

But the media bounce from an endorsement is typically limited. Tom Rath believes a "big league" endorsement "gives a candidate a one- or two-day media bump." Former ambassador Terry Shumaker, an early Bill Clinton backer and early supporter of Hillary Clinton in 2008 and 2016, concurs: "You might get a one-day story on wmur when you get the governor's endorsement. But what good is that when the election comes?"

In many states, top political leaders have extensive campaign organizations, so that when they endorse a candidate, they also provide the
candidate with access to that organization. But, as Tom Rath notes, "most
politicians in New Hampshire don't really have organizations. There
aren't many organizations . . . because of the lack of opportunities for
patronage in the state. Our politicians can't or don't nurture their organizations, they don't do the care and feeding of political workers the way
folks in other states do." Joe Keefe agrees: "Some [well-known people]
simply don't have strong organizations to deliver."

Still, there are some New Hampshire organizations that can deliver
more than just verbal support. For Republicans, county sheriffs are important endorsements, said Rath. "They run in every town of their county
and have good relations with law enforcement groups, which tend to vote
Republican." For Democrats, Rath points out, one of the most important
endorsements is the Professional Fire Fighters of New Hampshire, whose
endorsement brings with it the support of hundreds of firefighters from
across the state, and from neighboring states, who will actively work for
campaigns.

In the end, it's unclear whether endorsements provide the key to victory in the New Hampshire primary. "Warren Rudman's 1996 endorsement of Phil Gramm went nowhere," notes George Bruno. "And despite
the full support of the New Hampshire Democratic Party establishment
for Walter Mondale in 1984, Gary Hart still won."

The scholarly literature shows similar skepticism. While endorsements appear to be very important for the first contest in Iowa, they are
much less important in New Hampshire. The correlation between the
number of politically weighted endorsements a candidate receives and
the candidate's vote share in the primary appears to be significant, when
no other factors are taken into account. But when the results of the Iowa
caucuses are included in a statistical analysis, "the relationship between
endorsements and vote share . . . lapses into non-significance."[18]

One way to interpret such findings is to recognize that endorsements
by political leaders have a large impact on how well a candidate does in
the very first contest, the Iowa caucuses, but once the campaign moves to
New Hampshire, what's more important than endorsements is how well

the candidate did in that first contest. In subsequent primaries, we would expect the same result: what's generally most influential is how well the candidate performed in previous contests, for those results become the ultimate endorsements — by the voters themselves.

The Underdog

In 1976, Jimmy Carter came out of nowhere to win the New Hampshire primary. The underdog had, despite the odds, managed to pull out a win in New Hampshire — and the eventual nomination. Carter's win began the myth of New Hampshire being the place where an underdog could mount a grassroots campaign and win. This myth was seemingly confirmed in 1984 when Gary Hart knocked off Vice President Walter Mondale to win New Hampshire (though not the nomination). And in 1996, Pat Buchanan squeaked by Bob Dole to win the Republican primary. John McCain also defeated early favorite and eventual nominee George W. Bush in 2000. Carter went on to win the White House, but Hart eventually lost to Vice President (and early front-runner) Mondale, and Buchanan lost the Republican nomination to Senate Majority Leader (and early front-runner) Dole.

Given these examples, it is no surprise that in every primary cycle, the media try to identify the underdog who can knock off the front-runner. But these four examples are the only times since the McGovern-Fraser reforms that a true underdog has won a New Hampshire primary. More often than not, the big dog gets the bone.

But how do you identify the front-runner in New Hampshire? In some cases this is easy: Carter in 1980, and George H. W. Bush in 1992, were incumbent presidents. Similarly, Mondale (1984), Bush (1988), and Gore (2000) were sitting vice presidents. But outside of the obvious criteria for these candidates, there is not a consistent method for figuring out who the front-runner is, other than using public opinion polls. But even this method has difficulties, especially in the early years of the primary. Back then, candidates did not typically start campaigning in earnest until the year the primary was held, and because there was no campaigning going on, no one bothered to conduct polls until the final weeks or months of the primary. But a poll conducted two weeks or even two months before the election doesn't really identify an early front-runner. With some caveats, early polls have been conducted from 1984 on, certainly enough to determine who the early front-runner was, even if it was only a year or so before the election. There have been only twelve competitive primaries in New Hampshire since 1984, and it is clear that the early identified front-runner has had a distinctly greater chance of winning in New Hampshire. Overall, the early front-runner in polls after all the major candidates had thrown their hats in (or decided not to run) have won nine of the twelve New Hampshire primary elections in since 1984 (the lines in bold type in Table 9.1). The early front-runners clearly won seven times — in 1988 (when Bush defeated Buchanan), in 1992 (when Bush defeated Buchanan), in 2000 (when Gore defeated Bradley), in 2004 (when Kerry defeated Dean), in 2008 (when McCain defeated Romney and Clinton defeated Obama), and in 2012 (when Romney handily defeated Ron Paul). The front-runner clearly lost three times — in 1984 (when Hart defeated Mondale), in 1996 (when Buchanan defeated Dole), and in 2000 (when McCain defeated Bush). The pattern is less clear in two other cases — in the 1988 and 1992 Democratic primaries, when New York Governor Mario Cuomo tantalized Democrats who hoped he would run, only to decide to forgo the battle. After Cuomo dropped out in 1988, Dukakis became the front-runner and won, and in 1992, Tsongas became the front-runner after Cuomo again decided not to run, and also won.

But — and this is important — it would be folly to suggest that voters have actually decided early in the contest for whom they will eventually vote. We demonstrated that nearly half of all likely primary voters had not definitely decided whom to vote for as late as the Sunday before the 2008 New Hampshire primary.[19] Being the early front-runner does give candidates significant advantages in fund-raising and in media coverage. As long as a candidate does not make significant gaffes during the campaign, such as Bush's not-ready-for-prime-time start in 1999, or does not fall victim to significant discontent within his party, such as Mondale (1984) and Dole (1996) experienced, the virtuous cycle of good poll numbers, significant media coverage, and strong fund-raising is likely to operate smoothly, enabling the early front-runner to win.

Table 9.1. Early Poll Results and Final Results in New Hampshire Primary

Year and Party	Poll Date	Polling Organization	Front Runner (F.R.)	F.R. %	NH Winner	Winner %	Percent Difference F.R. vs. Winner %
1984 DEM	3/83	WMUR/UNH	Mondale	41	Hart	37	—
1988 DEM	1/87	WCVBTV	Hart	42	Dukakis	36	—
1988 DEM[1]	2/87	*Boston Globe*	Dukakis	41	Dukakis	36	+5
1988 GOP	**1/87**	**WMUR/UNH**	**Bush**	**40**	**Bush**	**38**	**+2**
1992 DEM	3/91	McGuire	Cuomo	18	Tsongas	34	—
1992 DEM[2]	**12/91**	***Concord Mon.***	**Tsongas**	**25**	**Tsongas**	**34**	**−9**
1992 GOP	**12/91**	***Concord Mon.***	**Bush**	**58**	**Bush**	**52**	**+6**
1996 GOP	2/95	*Boston Globe*	Dole	42	Buchanan	27	—
2000 DEM	**9/98**	**WMUR/RKM**	**Gore**	**41**	**Gore**	**50**	**−9**
2000 GOP	9/98	WMUR/RKM	Bush	29	McCain	48	—
2000 GOP[3]	5/99	WMUR/UNH	Bush	37	McCain	48	—
2004 DEM	12/02	Marist	Gore	31	Kerry	38	—
2004 DEM[4]	**2/03**	**WMUR/UNH**	**Kerry**	**37**	**Kerry**	**38**	**−1**
2008 DEM	**2/05**	**WMUR/UNH**	**Clinton**	**28**	**Clinton**	**39**	**−9**
2008 DEM[5]	**2/07**	**WMUR/UNH**	**Clinton**	**35**	**Clinton**	**39**	**−4**
2008 GOP	**2/05**	**WMUR/UNH**	**McCain**	**40**	**McCain**	**38**	**+2**
2012 GOP	**2/09**	**WMUR/UNH**	**Romney**	**47**	**Romney**	**39**	**−8**

Note: **Bold** text indicates years when an early front-runner was clearly identified and won.
[1]After Cuomo dropped out.
[2]After Cuomo and Bradley dropped out.
[3]After McCain entered the race.
[4]After Gore dropped out.
[5]After Obama entered the race.

These results seem paradoxical—voters don't decide whom they will actually support until the very end of the campaign, often not until they are actually in the voting booth; but at the same time, the early front-runner, more often than not, ends up winning the New Hampshire primary—and usually his or her party's nomination. It seems that the early favorite is often seen as a logical candidate for president by the national press, and consequently, by potential voters. Front-runners are front-runners because of their past political experience, their success in other races, and the skill with which they have telegraphed their intention to run for president.

The Money Primary

A final myth about New Hampshire — and one that is often cited as a reason that it fights so hard to maintain its first-in-the-nation status — is that the primary is an enormous moneymaker for the state. A recent example of this meme was a segment broadcast on CBS the week before the 2012 primary entitled "How New Hampshire 'Firsts' Bring It Big Bucks."[20] Despite the staying power of this myth, there has only been one economic impact study done on the primary. During the 2000 cycle, beginning in 1997 when campaigns were getting organized, until the primary in February 2000, a study by the New Hampshire Political Library estimated the primary generated about $260 million, either directly and indirectly, for the state.[21] Adjusted for inflation, this would be about $350 million today, certainly a significant amount of money, but in a state with a gross domestic product of almost $60 billion (in 2009), the amount generated by the primary is modest indeed.

Certainly there are examples of how the primary has helped specific businesses in the state. Hotels are packed the week between the Iowa caucuses and the primary, and caterers, restaurants, and other companies that provide support services to the campaigns do well. And local television (and Boston TV) make out handsomely. The 2000 economic impact study estimated that 80 percent of the direct spending in the 2000 cycle went to television. WMUR, the ABC affiliate in Manchester and the state's only network station, opened a new building in 1999 known locally as the "house that Steve Forbes built," in recognition of the millions of dollars Forbes had spent on ads in the 1996 primary.

More important than money coming into the state is the visibility the primary gives the state and the attention it garners for New Hampshire's other attractions, such as its beautiful beaches, mountains, and lakes. To put the economic impact of the primary in context, New Hampshire has two NASCAR races each year that generate about $180 million annually.[22]

Who knows how many of those NASCAR fans would not have come to the race had their attention not been drawn to New Hampshire in the first place by the primary?

The independent voters, strategic voters, exceptionally informed voters, grassroots campaigning, the underdog, and the big bucks: these are all myths about New Hampshire that get repeated with each cycle and which will be dusted off again in 2016. And as we have shown, there is a kernel of truth to each of these myths, but they are more often than not exaggerated by the press and by campaigns. An underdog candidate hearkens back to Carter, Hart, and McCain to keep his chances alive. The press likes a good story. As Carleton Young says to Jimmy Stewart in *The Man Who Shot Liberty Valance*, "When the legend becomes fact, print the legend."

The Cracked Crystal Ball

POLLING AND THE PRIMARY

Hillary Clinton was the early front-runner in New Hampshire in 2008, but by primary day her campaign seemed to have collapsed. In the wake of her unexpected third-place finish in the Iowa caucuses, her once-commanding lead in New Hampshire polls had plummeted to an average 7-percentage-point lead for Obama in final election polls (Table 10.1). Some polls showed a closer race, but many had Obama winning by a wide margin. But as the votes came in on the evening of the primary, it became clear that Clinton would pull off an incredible upset; she eventually won a narrow 2-point victory.

Pollsters (including the UNH Survey Center) were hammered in the press and even by their professional colleagues. Gary Langer, then director of polling for ABC News, claimed that "it is simply unprecedented for so many polls to have been so wrong."[1] The American Association for Public Opinion Research (AAPOR), the major professional organization for survey research, called for a special investigation of the polling catastrophe, which some put on par with the famous 1948 "Dewey Defeats Truman" polling debacle.[2] They concluded that

> polling in primary elections is inherently more difficult than polling in a general election. Usually there are more candidates in a contested primary than in a general election, and this is especially true at the beginning of the presidential selection process. For example, there were a total of 15 candidates entered in the Iowa caucuses and more than 20 names on the New Hampshire primary ballot. Since primaries are within-party events, the voters do not have the cue of party

identification to rely upon in making their choice. Uncertainty in the voters' minds can create additional problems for pollsters. Turnout is usually much lower in primaries than in general elections, although it varies widely across events. Turnout in the Iowa caucuses tends to be relatively low compared to the New Hampshire primary, for example. So estimating the likely electorate is often more difficult in primaries than in the general election. Furthermore, the rules of eligibility to vote in the primaries vary from state to state and even within party; New Hampshire has an open primary in which independents can make a choice at the last minute in which one to vote. All of these factors can contribute to variations in turnout, which in turn may have an effect on the candidate preference distribution among voters in a primary election.

These are all meaningful observations, but were the 2008 primary polls so bad that they merited such an investigation? They did do a remarkably good job predicting the Republican field, somewhat underestimating support for both McCain and Romney, but accurately estimating the margin between the top two candidates (Table 10.2).

Additionally, polls were fairly accurate at predicting the percentage of the electorate that would vote in each primary, as the AAPOR report noted. But it was the prediction of an Obama victory that stuck in the craw of the media and political pundits. Perhaps 2008 looked especially bad because the polls in the 2004 Democratic primary were so good — not only accurately predicting that John Kerry would win, but also nailing the actual vote that Kerry and Dean received. Nevertheless, observers did not have to look back very far to see problematic predictions in previous New Hampshire primaries. As recently as 2000, none of the polls predicted the magnitude of John McCain's victory over George W. Bush. And that wasn't the only time that polls produced inaccurate pictures of the electorate.

Historic New Hampshire Primary Polling Gaffes

Since the advent of polling in the New Hampshire primary, the results have been at best erratic. While it is difficult to get a solid feel for the

Table 10.1. 2008 New Hampshire Democratic Primary Final Polls and Final Vote, Percentages

Pollster	Dates	N=[1]	Clinton	Edwards	Obama	Richardson	Obama Margin
Actual vote			**39**	**17**	**37**	**5**	**-2**
Average poll results			**30**	**19**	**37**	**6**	**+7**
Research 2000	1/4–5/08	400	33	23	34	4	+1
Mason-Dixon	1/2–4/08	600	31	17	33	7	+2
Franklin Pierce/RKM	1/4–6/08	403	31	20	34	6	+3
Fox/Op. Dynamics	1/4–6/08	500	28	18	32	6	+4
Suffolk/WHDH	1/6–7/08	500	34	15	39	4	+5
Rasmussen	1/5–7/08	1774	30	19	37	8	+7
CBS	1/5–6/08	323	28	19	35	5	+7
CNN/WMUR/UNH	1/5–6/08	599	30	16	39	7	+9
Marist	1/5–6/08	636	28	22	36	7	+9
ARG	1/6–7/08	600	31	20	40	4	+9
Strategic Vision (R)	1/4–6/08	600	29	19	38	7	+9
USA Today/Gallup	1/4–6/08	778	28	19	41	6	+13
Reuters/CSPAN/Zogby	1/5–7/08	862	29	17	42	5	+13

[1]Number of likely voters interviewed.

Note: These figures do not include allocation of undecided voters.

Table 10.2. 2008 New Hampshire Republican Primary Final Polls and Final Vote, Percentages

Pollster	Dates	N=[1]	Giuliani	Huckabee	McCain	Paul	Romney	McCain Margin
Actual vote			**9**	**11**	**37**	**8**	**32**	**+5**
Average poll results			**9**	**12**	**33**	**8**	**28**	**+5**
CNN/WMUR/UNH	1/5–6/08	492	10	13	31	10	26	+5
Marist	1/5–6/08	477	5	13	35	8	31	+4
USA Today/Gallup	1/4–6/08	776	8	13	34	8	30	+4
Suffolk	1/6–7/08	500	11	13	26	5	30	–4
ARG	1/6–7/08	600	13	14	31	9	24	+7
Fox	1/4–6/08	500	9	11	34	5	27	+7
Strategic Vision (R)	1/4–6/08	600	8	13	35	7	27	+8
Reuters/CSPAN/Zogby	1/5–7/08	859	9	10	36	9	27	+9
Franklin Pierce	1/4–6/08	409	8	9	38	7	29	+9
Rasmussen	1/5–7/08	1549	8	10	32	8	31	+1

Note: These figures do not include allocation of undecided voters.

[1] Number of likely voters interviewed.

magnitude of polling errors in those earlier elections, in recent cycles there have been at least eight organizations that did public polling in the days before the primary, making it fairly easy to assess their accuracy. Internet sites like RealClearPolitics, pollster.com, and FiveThirtyEight do a good job collecting and archiving polls. But despite the relative lack of polls during those first primaries when polling existed, it is still clear that surprises were not infrequent.

Arguably the most significant surprise in the history of the New Hampshire primary was Eugene McCarthy's "victory" over then President Lyndon Johnson in 1968. Polls before the election were showing Johnson with a significant lead over McCarthy, and he indeed won the popular vote narrowly (by 9 percentage points), although he lost the delegate count to McCarthy. Johnson's "loss" and, more importantly, the fact that the president got a far lower share of the vote than expected, inspired Robert Kennedy to enter the race for president — which in turn led Johnson to quit his quest for reelection. "By 11:40 on the evening of March 12th it was obvious that Eugene McCarthy would do far better than the Gallup Polls had predicted in January (12 percent); better than Johnson's private polls had told him in February (18 percent); better than Governor King had predicted in the first week of March (25 percent to 28 percent)."[3]

Maine Senator Edmund Muskie was significantly hurt in 1972 when he underperformed expectations. Polls prior to the election had Muskie winning as much as 60 percent of the Democratic primary vote, and — because he was a New Englander from neighboring Maine — the expectations were that he would win easily over South Dakota Senator George McGovern. But late events in the campaign, such as the "Canuck letter" and Muskie's possibly crying in a snowstorm defending the honor of his wife, hurt Muskie. While he won the primary, he did so by only a 9-percentage-point margin (46 percent to 37 percent), much worse than expected. That Muskie underperformed in New Hampshire, favorable turf for him, was seen as a sign of his weakness as a candidate and gave a boost to McGovern, who went on to win the nomination.

In the 1980 primary, Ronald Reagan easily beat George H. W. Bush 50 percent to 23 percent. A CBS pre-election poll showed Reagan winning (58 percent to 13 percent), but its margin was considerably larger (45 percentage points) than the actual margin (27 points). That same year, CBS greatly underestimated Edward Kennedy's challenge to Jimmy Carter. Its final poll showed Carter with a 19 point lead (55 percent to 26 percent) over Kennedy, but Carter won by just a 10-point margin (47 percent to 37 percent).

The 1984 Democratic primary was initially seen as a fight between former vice president Walter Mondale and Ohio Senator John Glenn. But Colorado Senator Gary Hart unexpectedly finished second in Iowa, ahead of Glenn, and thus, in the eyes of the national media, became Mondale's foremost challenger. Hart garnered enough media attention from his unexpectedly strong Iowa showing to put him over the top in New Hampshire a week later. Polls showed support for Hart increasing in the week between Iowa and New Hampshire, moving him from 23 percent to 35 percent in the *Washington Post*/ABC News poll during this period. But final polls showed Mondale either tied with or leading Hart — 30 percent to 30 percent in the *Washington Post*/ABC Poll and 38 percent to 32 percent in a CNN poll. The final vote was Hart 37 percent, Mondale 28 percent. There was a larger error in predicting the 1984 primary than in 2008 — polls were off in the final 1984 projections by an average of 12 percentage points, compared with an average error of 9 percentage points in 2008. In the wake of the 2008 primary, however, this earlier error, though larger, was not mentioned by the press or even by AAPOR in its analysis.

Another memorable surprise occurred in 1988. Gallup's final preprimary poll showed Kansas Senator Bob Dole, fresh off a huge win in the Iowa caucuses, leading George H. W. Bush by 8 percentage points, 35 percent to 27 percent. The *Washington Post*/ABC poll had Dole leading 33 percent to 30 percent, while other polls (CBS, *Boston Globe, Boston Herald*/WBZ, *Los Angeles Times,* and NBC) showed Bush narrowly defeating Dole in New Hampshire. Gallup and ABC were both wrong in their predictions as Bush defeated Dole handily 38 percent to 29 percent.[4]

The 1992 New Hampshire primary provided two dramatic stories. First, Bill Clinton recovered from damaging stories about his relationship with Gennifer Flowers and his "draft dodging" letter to finish second to Massachusetts Senator Paul Tsongas by a respectable 8 percentage points.

Outperforming the polls led Clinton to dub himself the "Comeback Kid." The final CNN/USA *Today* poll had Tsongas leading 32 percent to 20 percent, while the *Boston Globe*/WBZ poll showed a somewhat tighter race, but Clinton outperformed both. Also in 1992, Pat Buchanan launched his assault on George H. W. Bush, finishing in a much-closer-than-expected second place by only 16 percentage points.

In 1996, Buchanan again launched an outsider campaign against Bob Dole, who had easily won the Iowa caucuses. Buchanan narrowly won the New Hampshire primary by one percentage point, 37 percent to 36 percent (4,000 votes), but the final CNN /*Time* poll had Dole winning 36 percent to 21 percent, and the American Research Group poll just before the election had Dole winning by 7 percentage points. None of the pre-election polls predicted a Buchanan victory.

The 2000 Republican primary also resulted in an unexpected outcome when John McCain beat George W. Bush by 19 percentage points. As mentioned earlier, on average the polls showed McCain defeating Bush by 8 percentage points (40 percent to 32 percent), 11 percentage points smaller than the actual margin of victory. The error was larger than the error in the 2008 Democratic primary, but — like the 1984 error — it was never mentioned in the 2008 post-election analysis.[5]

Why Polling in Primaries Is More Problematic Than in General Elections

This review of New Hampshire polls raises the question of why polls are so inaccurate in predicting the primary. The major reason is that the partisan cues that dominate voter decisions in general elections are largely absent in primaries, especially in instances where both parties have competitive primaries. Political scientists have long known that in general elections, upwards of 90 percent of voters who consider themselves either Democrats or Republicans will vote for the candidate of their party. But in a primary, all candidates are of the same party, rendering partisan cues irrelevant.

Since the candidates in a primary are all of the same party, they often take similar positions. In multi-candidate contests, it's almost certain that two or more candidates will have similar issue positions, making it difficult for voters to decide among the candidates on the basis of policy differences. For example, in 2008, Clinton, Edwards, and Obama all favored significant overhauls of the country's health care system, favored withdrawing troops from Iraq, favored closing the Guantanamo prison facility, and had similar positions on many other issues as well. Trying to tease out the nuanced differences among the specifics of their policy proposals was of interest only to the most dedicated voter.

So if voters can't reasonably be expected to differentiate between candidates on the basis of policy, how do they choose? Candidate qualities such as experience, honesty, and general-election electability are often much more important. But these factors are rather vague and can be easily overcome by the release of unflattering material about a candidate's past (like the Gennifer Flowers incident discussed above), a major gaffe on the campaign trail, an unflattering interview, or a particularly poor debate performance (for example, Texas governor Rick Perry's "oops" moment, when he was unable to name three federal agencies his campaign said they would close should he be elected).

In New Hampshire in 2008, the big three Democratic candidates were all well liked by the Democratic electorate, as can be seen in the net favorability ratings from CNN/WMUR/UNH polls (Figure 10.1). The choice of a candidate was, for many voters, not one that required a great deal of thought. It certainly wasn't likely that many voters would actively vote *against* one of the top three Democratic candidates. Evidence for this is that most New Hampshire Democrats voted for Obama in November, regardless of whom they voted for in the primary. As early as September 2008, more than 80 percent of Democrats in a UNH Survey Center poll said they planned to vote for Obama, regardless of whom they voted for in the primary.[6]

For many voters, the choice of a candidate is analogous to choosing one flavor of ice cream from among many that they like. The decision is likely to be made at the last minute, and if somehow their choice is not available, they'll be content with another. Similarly, in political primaries, where there is often little difference among candidates, many voters don't give prolonged thought to their vote choice, often making up their

Figure 10.1. 2008 New Hampshire Democratic candidate net favorability ratings.

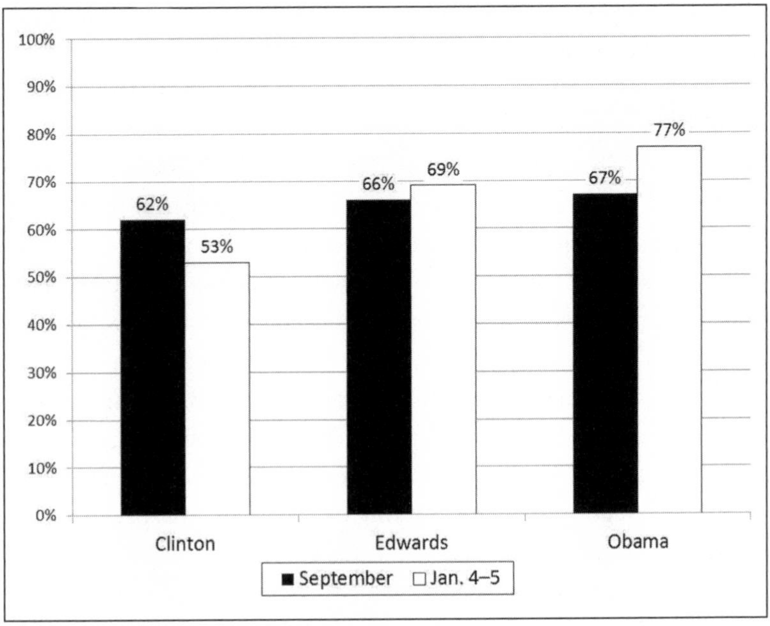

Source: UNH Survey Center Polls.

minds only days, or even hours, before the election. In the New Hampshire primary, about 15 percent of voters say they make up their mind on the way to the polls or even in the polling booth. Exit polls have consistently shown that 25 percent or more of voters said they made up their minds within the final three days before the election (Table 10.3). Such last-minute decisions can wreak havoc on polling results, which appear to measure a decided electorate but in fact contain top-of-mind responses that can easily change with the wind.

Polling by the UNH Survey Center during the 2008 primary campaign showed this phenomenon of voter indecision to be even more pronounced in the months before the elections. From July through the election in January, UNH included a question in its polls (sponsored by CNN, WMUR and the *Boston Globe*) before the trial heat question that asked "Have you definitely decided who you will vote for in the New Hampshire primary, are you leaning toward someone, or have you considered some candidates but are still trying to decide?"[7] Figure 10.2 shows just

Table 10.3. Time of Decision in Recent Primaries

	When did you make up your mind?	
	Today (Election Day)	Final 3 days[1]
2012 NH Republican Primary	21%	46%
2008 NH Democratic Primary	17%	38%
2008 NH Republican Primary	19%	39%
2004 NH Democratic Primary	—	35%
2000 NH Republican Primary	14%	26%
2000 NH Democratic Primary	15%	26%

Source: NEP/NES Exit Polls. Table from AAPOR's evaluation of 2008 primary polling.
[1]Includes respondents reporting that they decided "today."

Figure 10.2. Voter indecision—likely 2008 New Hampshire Democratic primary voters.

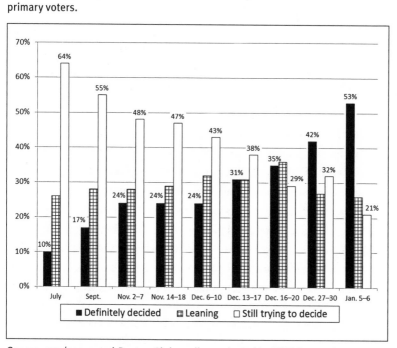

Source: cnn/wmur and *Boston Globe* polls conducted by UNH Survey Center.

Figure 10.3. Voter indecision—likely New Hampshire 2008 general election voters.

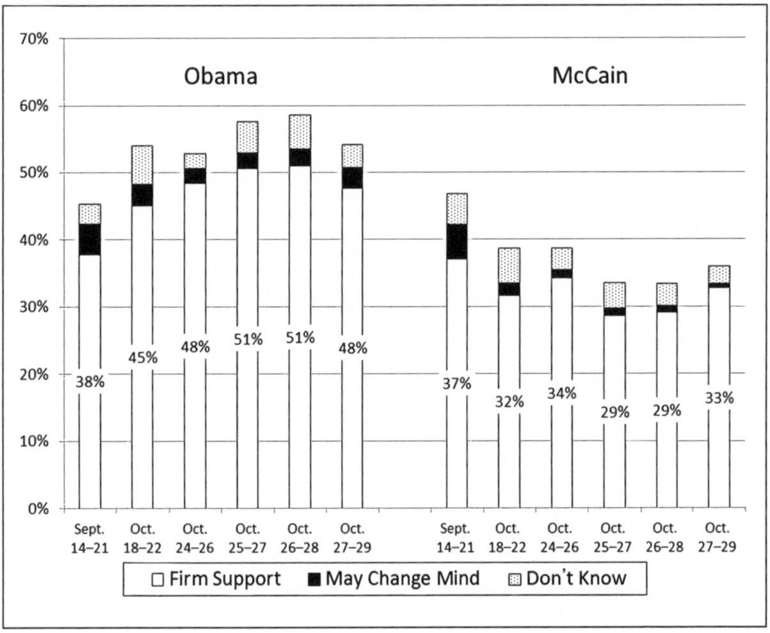

Source: CNN/WMUR and *Boston Globe* polls conducted by UNH Survey Center.

how late in the 2008 primary campaign voters said they decided whom they would vote for, with 21 percent of final pre-election poll respondents saying they had not yet decided and another 26 percent saying they were only leaning toward a candidate, only *two days* before the election.

Compare the results from this question with those of a similar one from the 2008 general election in New Hampshire (Figure 10.3). The data on this table reflect answers to a somewhat different poll question — after the trial heat question, respondents were asked, "Are you firm in your choice or could you change your mind?" In a general election context, the great majority of voters (75 percent) said they were firm in their choice for either Obama or McCain a full two months before the election.

Because all the candidates are from the same party, primary voters make their decisions much later and are therefore much more susceptible to late-term campaign events. New Hampshire Democrats saw several of these events in 2008 that are worth mentioning and that may have led to

Clinton's surprise win. The first major event was an ABC debate held at St. Anselm College on Saturday, January 5, three days before the election. At this debate, Scott Spradling, political anchor for WMUR-TV (the ABC affiliate in Manchester, New Hampshire) asked Clinton:

> The University of New Hampshire Survey Center has been consistently trying to probe the minds of New Hampshire voters and get a sense of what they think about all of you. I'd be happy to report that the experience vs. change debate seems to be sinking it. And what I'd like to get to is this: New Hampshire voters seem to believe that, of those of you on this stage, you are the most experienced and the most electable. In terms of change, they see Senators Obama and Edwards as the agents of change, in the New Hampshire mindset. My question to you is simply this: What can you say to the voters of New Hampshire on this stage tonight who see a resume and like it, but are hesitating on the likability issue, where they seem to like Barack Obama more?[8]

Clinton responded with feigned distress, "Well, that hurt my feelings," prompting laughter, to which Obama commented, "You're likeable enough, Hillary." After the debate, contrary to what Spradling expected, the Clinton campaign was pleased that he had asked the question, believing that it marked the turning point in the debate, and possibly in the campaign.

The second significant event occurred the following day, a Sunday, two days before the election. Clinton was filmed apparently choking back tears in a Portsmouth coffee shop while responding to a question from a voter on how she keeps going during the campaign. Her emotional response to this question was shown over and over on local and national television for the next two days — on Monday and then on Election Day itself. Several political writers speculated that these two events humanized her in the eyes of many voters who heretofore had seen her as unlikeable. "Hours before New Hampshire voters go to the polls, Clinton has finally showed 'the real Hillary,' the one advisers always insisted was there, the one the campaign tried to sell in a clunky road show in Iowa, where longtime friends were rolled out to tell endearing stories, the one I witnessed on numerous trips abroad during Clinton's years as

First Lady: an engaging, warm and witty woman, a first-class road-trip companion who seemed to spring to life as soon as her plane left U.S. airspace."[9] Taken together, these two events seemed to have a powerful effect on women voters in New Hampshire. Women supported Obama by a 4-point margin (38 percent to 34 percent) in the final CNN/WMUR/ UNH Survey Center poll but exit polls showed women actually voting for Clinton by a 12-point margin (46 percent to 34 percent).[10]

The third significant event was how the Obama and Clinton campaigns operated in the final days before the election. Clinton campaigned hard in those closing days while the Obama campaign, buoyed by polls showing him ahead by 9 percentage points, coasted home. On Election Day, Clinton shook hands at large polling places across southern New Hampshire. Later in the afternoon, the Clinton campaign called WMUR-TV at five o'clock and asked the news desk if they would send a film crew to a Manchester polling place where Clinton would be shaking hands with last-minute voters. Obama, by contrast, held only 4 events on Monday and only one on Election Day — a rally with supporters in Hanover, home of Dartmouth College and an Obama stronghold. He then left for Manchester to prepare for the apparent victory party.[11]

Campaigning until the very end can make a difference. As mentioned earlier, exit polls in New Hampshire have consistently shown that 25 percent or more of voters say they make up their minds in the last three days before the election, with more than 15 percent saying they make up their mind on Election Day (Table 10.3). These figures are similar to those shown in UNH pre-election polling (Figure 10.2) and provide strong evidence that the primary electorate is waiting until the last minute to decide.

Table 10.3 summarizes the fundamental problem with primary polls — pollsters (the authors included) ask respondents how they plan to vote, using a forced-choice format that does not explicitly offer a "don't know" option. This format subtly pressures respondents to come up with a choice, even if they are actually uncertain at the time of the poll. The results give the impression of a mostly decided electorate (typically, polls show only 5 percent to 10 percent undecided), when in fact the percentage of undecided voters is much greater. Often, the late deciders reflect the same pattern of responses as the early deciders, and in that case the polls "accurately" reflect voter intentions. But in many cases, the late deciders are influenced by late-breaking events and may well vote differently from what the polls suggest. The public is caught off guard, surprised at how volatile the electorate appears to be and (rightfully) critical of polls for an inaccurate picture of public opinion.

The AAPOR study that examined the 2008 New Hampshire primary polls barely recognized this fundamental problem. The study was useful in refuting some of the more disturbing criticisms of the 2008 polls. There did not appear to be significant methodological flaws, for example, that explained the shift to Clinton. Furthermore, there was no evidence that respondents were lying to pollsters about their intention to vote for an African American candidate. It is commendable that AAPOR took the criticisms seriously enough to undertake the study, but it addressed what we see as the crucial problem only tangentially:

> We found that decision timing — in particular, late decisions — may have contributed significantly to the error in the New Hampshire polls, though we lack the data for proper evaluation. The fact that Clinton's 'emotional moment' at the diner occurred after nearly all the polls were complete adds fuel to this speculation, as does the high proportion of New Hampshire Democratic primary voters who said they made up their minds during the final three days. It is also true that the percentages of voters reporting they made up their minds on Election Day or in the three preceding days are not substantially different from historical levels.[12]

The report failed to recognize the elephant in the room — that pollsters pressure respondents to give a choice, when many genuinely haven't yet made up their minds. Then pollsters treat the forced, top-of-mind responses as though they predict how the respondents will actually vote. But, in fact, such responses can't be trusted. A voter can't accurately tell a pollster whom they will vote for when they don't yet know themselves.

Second, the AAPOR analysis illustrates just how different primary elections are from general elections — in primaries, voters decide later, and the absence of party cues means that voters are much more likely to be influenced by last-minute campaign events. This is a problem for pollsters, who face an incredibly difficult task of getting it right, but it should be comforting for students of American politics because it shows that campaigns do matter, and that what happens during the campaign, particularly during the final days when voters close in on their decision, can indeed change the outcome of an election.

What to Do?

It is clear that reporters will continue to rely heavily on polls for their stories about the primary campaign. For the 2012 New Hampshire Republican primary, four years after the Obama-Clinton mis-prediction, the press frequently referred to poll results provided by six organizations. Much to the relief of pollsters, those polls proved to be reasonably accurate, estimating that Mitt Romney would get 38 percent of the vote and Ron Paul 18 percent. Romney won with 39 percent, though Paul somewhat over-performed, ending up with 23 percent of the vote. In 2016, there is no doubt there will be numerous pre-primary polls.

If historically polls have been inaccurate about as often as they have been accurate, how should they be used by journalists covering the primary? And how should average citizens, who generally have even less experience with survey methodology than journalists, decide how to interpret the results? While the horse race is certainly important to report, our experience leads us to believe that the same amount of time and coverage should be devoted to describing the state of indecision within the electorate as there is to describing the way voters are leaning. This would provide a much clearer picture of the actual state of the electorate. We would also want coverage to include, of course, the favorability and name recognition of candidates; candidates' personal and professional characteristics; which candidate voters say they will *not* vote for under any circumstances; and which candidate voters think will win.

Favorability ratings and name recognition questions have been used for decades to help explain elections. In primary polling they are somewhat less useful as most major candidates are well known, and relatively well liked, by voters, especially in the final days of the campaign.

However, early primary polls, especially those conducted years before the election, reflect only name recognition and are less valuable. What is useful to focus on is whether a candidate has a high percentage of "unfavorable" ratings. This is a strong indicator that they will likely be unable to expand beyond their core supporters. For example, Newt Gingrich was viewed unfavorably by 36 percent of likely Republican primary voters in late November 2011, strong evidence that he would not enjoy much success in New Hampshire.

A similar measure is to ask voters which candidate they would not vote for under any circumstances. The idea behind this is to further understand which candidates have a serious chance of winning and which candidates are likely campaigning for a cabinet position or a talk show slot. In 2012, Herman Cain and Michelle Bachman held the undesirable distinction of being the candidates New Hampshire Republican primary voters would not support, ever. And they didn't.

Because candidates have similar positions on most issues, we do not find these measures on issue preferences as useful as understanding how voters view other characteristics of the candidates. Characteristics such as honesty, experience, the capacity to bring about change, and the ability to relate to "people like you" are all typical candidate qualities that can be measured and which give reporters a better understanding of how they are perceived by voters. And perhaps the most important candidate characteristic, especially for stronger partisans, is which candidate has the best chance of winning in November. For many voters, electability is a crucial consideration. Including more lengthy discussions of these poll questions in media reports would help the public better understand the "true" state of the election.

A related measure is to ask voters, "Regardless whom you plan to vote for, which candidate do you think will win the New Hampshire primary election?" Public opinion researchers David Rothschild and Justin Wolfers have found in extensive historical research that this question is a better predictor of who will win an election than the standard horse race question.[13] The theory behind why this works is that voters will bring more than their own preferences into this calculation. What friends and co-workers think about the candidates, what they read in the papers or see on television, even the number of yard signs and bumper stickers they encounter, are all factored into respondents' estimation of public support for a candidate. The UNH Survey Center began asking this question in October 2011 and found that two months before the primary, 65 percent of likely Republican primary voters believed Mitt Romney would win the primary, even though he had the support of only 37 percent of likely voters at that time.

For better or worse, polls are the measure used by the public and the press for who is winning in New Hampshire, and it sets the bar for the expectations they need to meet. Paul Tsongas won in 1992, but because he met expectations or perhaps slightly underperformed, his victory was not in the spotlight. The light shone on Bill Clinton instead, because he convinced reporters, on the basis of earlier polling, that he had exceeded expectations, making him the real "winner." Lyndon Johnson in 1968, Edmund Muskie in 1972, Robert Dole in 1988, George H. W. Bush in 1992, and Barack Obama in 2008 are all examples of politicians who failed to meet expectations and whose campaigns were damaged as a consequence. But often the expectations themselves are unrealistic, drawn from polls that provide misleading results. Clearly, caution is necessary when interpreting pre-election polls in primary contests. As Richard Morin and Claudia Deane of the *Washington Post* observed, New Hampshire is a "snowy graveyard for pols and polls."[14]

Future of the New Hampshire Primary

IS THERE A BETTER WAY?

It's clear that the current nomination system, which favors Iowa and New Hampshire plus (more recently) the other two "carve-out" states of Nevada and South Carolina, is not fair. For the past forty years, however, various state officials and political leaders have been unsuccessful in trying to nullify New Hampshire's outsize influence in the nomination process. In fact, the two parties have seemingly moved in the opposite direction, solidifying the "rights" claimed by Iowa and New Hampshire to hold their contests before any other. This movement reflects the failure of numerous reform proposals to gain sufficient support to be adopted. Of course, there are alternative methods that would make the process fairer, if by that we mean moving to a process that would provide more equality of influence for voters living in different states. But typically such proposals come with other disadvantages that many see as worse than the current system. Nevertheless, it's worthwhile to examine what potential reforms have been proposed.

Reform Proposals

In addressing the voter fairness issue, several proposals have focused either on changing the order in which states vote, or on replacing the sequential primary system with a one-day national primary. Calls for reform have accelerated with the increasing front-loading of states in the 1990s and 2000s, and political scientists group these reforms into three general categories: a series of sub-national primaries, one national primary, and modifications to the current system of "window-based" primaries. The sub-national primaries include three types: regional primaries, based on geographical location; population-based primaries; and characteristic-based primaries.

Sub-National Regional Primaries

Proposals for regional primaries seek to increase fairness by rotating geographical groups of states to start the nomination process. In any given year, the region that went first would enjoy increased attention from candidates, have more attention paid to regional policy issues, and presumably have a greater influence in choosing the eventual nominee. That would not be fair to the other regions, of course, but for the next election cycle a new region would get the premier position. This process would ensure that in the long run, all regions of the country would get a chance to be at the head of the line.[1] Such a plan was proposed in 1996 by Senators Slade Gorton (R-WA) and Joe Lieberman (D-CT), which specified four regions of the country—Northeast, South, Midwest and West. Each region would hold a primary on the first Tuesday of the month, with the first region starting in March and the last ending in June of the presidential election year. In subsequent years, the last region (the one that held its primary in June the previous cycle) would move up to March, and each of the other regions would move back a month. The bill received two readings and was sent to the Senate Rules and Administration, where it died.

That year, the National Association of Secretaries of State (NASS) introduced its own regional primary plan. It was similar to the Gorton-Lieberman plan, except that it specifically allowed Iowa and New Hampshire to hold their events prior to the regional primaries. The point of the exceptions was to allow for "retail politics" in the two small states that would not be possible in the subsequent states.[2] That the NASS plan included exemptions for Iowa and New Hampshire was not surprising, as New Hampshire's secretary of state, Bill Gardner, was then president of the association. The Council of State Governments and the *New York Times* supported the plan, but neither of the two political parties was persuaded to adopt it.

Another variation of the regional primary plan was introduced by former New Hampshire senator Bob Smith. In his "Fairness in Primaries" plan, there would be four regions, as with the other plans described, but there would be two lotteries each election cycle to determine (1) the order of voting for each region, and (2) the order of voting by states within each region. This process would spread out the voting over the primary season, rather than having just four regional primaries. Also, there would be no automatic rotation of regions because a new lottery would be conducted each quadrennium. A region that went first in one election cycle would have a one-in-four chance of going first the next cycle as well. Iowa and New Hampshire would always precede the first region, as had been the tradition, which would also allow for retail politics.[3] Smith submitted his plan to the Republican National Convention in 2000, but it was not passed.

Sub-National Population-Based Primaries

This second type of plan differs from regional primaries by recognizing the sequential nature of the nomination process and the importance of retail politics in smaller and earlier states. The Delaware plan, designed for the 2004 nomination, typifies this type of system. It called for grouping states, on the basis of their population size, into "pods." All states in each pod would vote on the first Tuesday of the month, starting in March and ending in June. The smallest twelve states (plus federal territories) would vote first in March (in order to allow for retail politics), followed by increasingly larger states. Importantly, the Delaware plan did not have exemptions for Iowa and New Hampshire. Although this plan was intended to give smaller states the influence that goes with being the first contests, in actual practice the plan would require candidates to campaign across the country, rather than in a geographically limited region, thus reducing the time that a candidate would have to engage in retail politics. For example, states in the first pod would include New Hampshire, Vermont, and Maine in New England; North Dakota, Montana, and Wyoming in the plains and mountains; and also Alaska and Hawaii. Travel time and cost alone would be prohibitive for all but the biggest and best-funded campaigns.

A variation of the Delaware plan, the Ohio Plan was adopted by the rules committee of the Republican National Committee (RNC) in 2004. It also grouped states by population size, but put Iowa and New Hampshire at the beginning of the process. New Hampshire would precede other state primaries, but by only four days, which would conflict with New Hampshire law requiring that its primary be at least seven days before any other. Although the RNC Rules Committee approved it, the plan was voted down by the 2004 Republican National Convention rules committee, which had final say (see Chapter 3).

Another variation was the California plan, which also let smaller states vote earlier, but introduced randomness to the selection process. It called for ten elections held at two-week intervals for a twenty-week nomination period, about the length of the current process.[4] The first group would consist of a random selection of states and territories whose total electoral votes would equal eight. Each subsequent week would increase the total electoral votes by eight. So, in week two, a random selection of the remaining states would vote in that week's primary, as long as they represented no more than 16 electoral votes. The tenth and final week would consist of states with 80 electoral votes, or about 20 percent of the vote. No state, including Iowa or New Hampshire, would be guaranteed a slot in the first group. The logic for this rather complicated plan is that it allows for retail politicking in the early rounds of elections by ensuring that a state (or combination of states) having no more than eight congressional seats could be included in the first round. The plan does not completely discriminate against larger states, as a state with up to 16 electoral votes could be selected to go as early as the second round. (In that case, of course, it would be the only state holding a primary that week, since the maximum electoral votes for the second week is 16.) The random construction of groups would mean that no state would have a lock on an early spot.

Sub-National Characteristic-Based Primaries

This third type of proposal creates groups of states from across the country that have similar characteristics. It explicitly avoids having smaller states go first, thus implicitly dismissing retail politics as a worthwhile goal. And this type of proposal explicitly rejects regional groupings, so that no one region of the country can influence the nomination process more than another.

One example is the Texas Plan, which — like the Ohio and Delaware Plans — divided the country into four groups, but based neither on population size nor on geographical location. Instead, they were based on producing groups "that as near as practicable have the same number of states, the same number of delegate votes, the same number of electoral votes, and the same ratio of Republican to Democratic states."[5] Group 1 states could vote anytime during the month of March, Group 2 in April, Group 3 in May and Group 4 in June. The groups would rotate the starting dates from one election cycle to the next.

A similar, though more complicated, approach was the Michigan Plan, which divided the country into six pods, each consisting of states with approximately the same number of electoral votes, and spread across the country. One pod, for example, contains Connecticut and Rhode Island in the East; West Virginia, Arkansas, and Georgia from the South; and Oklahoma, Idaho, Nevada, and Utah from the West — totaling 75 electoral votes.[6] The pods would start voting in March and end in June, with the pods rotating the starting dates from one election cycle to the next.

National Primary

This type of primary would elect delegates in each state on the same day. A national primary would have the advantage of not favoring any one state or states, as everyone in the country would vote at the same time. Retail politics, of course, would be impossible. Candidates simply could not afford the time to meet with small groups of voters in any one state. Also, a candidate would have to be well funded right from the beginning in order to have a chance to do well. Presumably, this would make dark-horse campaigns all but impossible. The national primary is one of the oldest nomination reform plans, first proposed by Theodore Roosevelt for the 1912 presidential election. This type of reform has considerable public support but has not received serious considerations by the parties or in Congress.[7] If no candidate received a majority of the vote, either the plurality winner would be declared the nominee, or there would be a run-off primary among the top two candidates. Another variation would be to set a threshold of victory at less than a majority — at, say, 40 percent — to avoid a run-off.

Another variation of the national primary is the National Primary/ Convention Plan. It also provides for the election of all delegates on the same day across the country. If no candidate wins a majority of the delegates, a very likely situation in most years, the convention would then choose the nominee from among those who have, say, at least 15 percent of the delegates (or some other minimum threshold). Typically, there would be several candidates who would arrive at the convention with significant numbers of delegates, but not a majority. The first official vote in the convention would confirm the relative standings of the candidates, and after that there would be bargaining among party leaders to come up with a nominee. This process would mean that conventions would once again have a meaningful and direct role to play in the selection of the party's nominee.

Variations of this plan include several possible methods for awarding delegates, although all methods would be based on the results of the national primary. One method of awarding delegates would be by proportional representation, based on the total number of votes received nationally. Winning 30 percent of the national vote would give the candidate 30 percent of the total delegates attending the convention. Another more likely method would be a proportional assignment of delegates within each state. A candidate winning 50 percent of the vote in New Hampshire, for example, would get half the state's delegates. That same candidate might end up with just 20 percent of the vote nationally, but that figure would be irrelevant for assigning delegates. Finally, some states might decide to award delegates on a winner-take-all basis, so that a candidate getting the most votes in a state — even if that were only, for instance, 35 percent of the total — would still get all the delegates. Whatever the method of awarding delegates, it would be rare for any non-incumbent candidate to arrive at the convention with a majority of votes, thus forcing the convention to come up with the nominee.

This National Primary/Convention Plan would achieve the goal of state and voter equality. It would also probably eliminate retail politicking as a realistic method of campaigning, and it would probably also result in the emergence of regional candidates. Both of these results harken back to the pre-reform period, when conventions played the decisive role in the nomination process. But the plan might also give even more influence to the rich than already exists, because of the great expense of waging a national campaign. On the other hand, it's possible the convention would be the method by which the delegates could help to nullify the advantages that wealthy donors enjoy right now. With delegates coming together at a national convention, there could be a greater recognition of the need for a national strategy involving compromise. Perhaps the convention would emerge as the firewall against a moneyed candidate who might be able to win the first several contests and coast to victory.

It's important to keep that ambiguity in mind whenever proposing reforms: The Unintended Consequences of Seemingly Good Ideas.

Evolution, Not Revolution, of the "Window-Based" Primaries

The most common type of reform has been the constant tinkering with the current system, typically adjusting the "window" within which the states must hold their contests, changing the date of the convention, and increasing sanctions against states violating calendar rules. Both parties have passed rules that governed the nomination process for an upcoming nomination, and then modified those rules for the subsequent nomination cycle (see Chapter 3). The Democratic Party has been much more active in making modifications to their process than have Republicans. In 1982, the Democratic Party Hunt Commission created super-delegates, also known as PLEOs (party leaders and elected officials), who had reserved spots at the convention as a way to regain some control of the nomination after the outsider wins by McGovern and Carter. The original Hunt Commission called for 30 percent of convention delegates to be super-delegates, giving party insiders a potentially powerful voting bloc. While this never happened, almost one-fifth of delegates to the 2008 Democratic National Convention were super-delegates (796 of the 4,419 delegates). Republicans have been more restrained in stocking the convention with party insiders, but each state and us territory represented at the convention gets three super-delegates — the national committeeman and national committeewoman as well as the current state party chair.

The most important change, from New Hampshire's perspective, has been the solidification of Iowa and New Hampshire as the first caucus and primary states, respectively, and the more recent insertions of South Carolina and Nevada into the group of "carve-out" states that can hold their contests before the rest. By giving preference to four early states from different regions of the country — including one state with a large Hispanic population, another with a large African American population, and another with strong unions — the parties have undercut the criticisms that important interests are excluded from a significant role in the early contests. These four relatively small states also allow for retail politics and give dark-horse candidates some hope of catching lightning in a bottle.

Of the several types of reforms discussed above, it is most likely that any new reform will consist of modifications to the current system rather than wholesale change. It is much easier, and certainly less risky, to make minor modifications to a system that candidates, parties, and voters are familiar with, rather than to get the broad agreement necessary to push more radical reform.

Obstacles to Reform

The most important obstacle to a national or sub-national primary is the lack of consensus among political leaders for any one of the proposals. There have been more than 300 bills introduced into Congress to reform the nomination process, but none has passed.[8] It is even questionable whether Congress has the constitutional authority to mandate how nominations are run. Should legislation pass, states would certainly object to such interference in their authority to regulate elections.[9] Laws in Iowa and New Hampshire, for example, specify that their contests must precede any others, and both states have shown they are willing to counter any efforts to undermine their prerogative. Other states have reasons they would not want to have specific voting dates imposed on them:[10]

- Elections are expensive, and to save money some states will schedule the presidential primary to coincide with their state primary.
- There may be other compelling reasons for a state to schedule its primary or caucuses on a particular date, such as legislative sessions or availability of facilities.
- Rotating primary dates every year, as required by some plans, could create problems for states that prefer to have a fixed date every year.

Unless there is a constitutional amendment that overrides state law, it is hard to see any state going along with a reform plan with which it disagrees.

Political parties, too, would resist such mandated reform as an encroachment on their private organizational rules. Past Supreme Court decisions have backed parties in this area. William Mayer noted several cases:[11]

- In 1981, the Court overruled the Wisconsin Supreme Court's attempt to assert the supremacy of that state's "open primary" law against national Democratic rules.
- In 1986, the Court allowed the Connecticut Republican Party to open up its primaries to independent voters, even though state law limited primaries to registered party members.
- In 1989, the Court invalidated California laws that dictated the organization and composition of party governing bodies and prohibited those bodies from making endorsements before a primary.
- In 2000, the Court declared that the state of California could not compel the Democratic and Republican parties to nominate their candidates through a so-called blanket primary.

If significant reform is to come, it will almost certainly happen within the parties themselves, and not necessarily with a grand agreement between the parties. The McGovern-Fraser Commission reforms applied only to the Democratic Party, though the Republican Party largely went along with the calendar of Democratic contests, since most states didn't want to have separate events. Similarly, the Republican calendar changes for the 2016 cycle have been largely accepted by Democrats. The GOP has gone even further in its determination to force states to comply, by stipulating severe penalties for states that violate the defined schedule. For example, a state with 30 delegates or more that holds its contest outside the specified time period will see its delegation reduced to nine. For states with fewer than 30 delegates, their delegations will be reduced to one third of their allotted size, or six delegates, whichever is smaller.[12] At least that is the threat, though parties often don't carry through with the threats at convention time.

Other new rules adopted by the GOP specify that states that hold their contests prior to March 15 must award delegates proportional to the candidates' support, while states holding contests after March 15 can award delegates based either on proportional representation or a winner-take-all method. The mandatory proportional method in the early contests makes it likely that multiple candidates can remain in the race for several weeks, giving plenty of opportunity for diverse positions to be debated. The switch to winner-take-all in the latter part of the schedule encourages states to help identify the eventual winner within a reasonable time period in order to avoid a strung-out competition that could hurt the party in the general election. The Republican National Convention will be moved up to June or early July, giving the eventual nominee more time to concentrate on the general election.

These rules do not represent radical change but rather provide an adjustment to the process that should enable it to avoid some of the pitfalls of the long, drawn-out process that occurred in 2012, which many Republican leaders believe hurt their party's chances in the November election. The Democratic Party has largely adopted the Republican calendar, but has its own rules for awarding delegates and sanctions for states that jump ahead in the schedule. And there is no indication as of this writing that the Democrats will follow the GOP lead in holding their national convention in June.

With the recent changes in the Republican calendar, and with Democrats in general agreement, 2016 looks to be as stable a primary as we have seen for decades. That is, until even a single state decides to ignore the consequences and move its primary out of order. As noted in Chapter 3, the Utah House of Representatives made just such an effort, passing a bill on March 10, 2014, that would have required the state's presidential primary to be held before any other state's primary or caucus. To overcome New Hampshire's strategy of waiting until close to the primary season before scheduling its primary, the bill required the Utah primary to be conducted by electronic ballot online. The bill ultimately failed in the state senate five days later, but the author, Republican state Representative Jon Cox, implied the issue could be taken up again in 2015. He said the current system is unfair and creates "second class states." What is significant about the effort is that Cox wasn't troubled by the penalty the GOP would impose on the state's delegation to the Republican National Convention. Instead of forty delegates, Utah would get only nine. But, as Cox noted, "New Hampshire gets 12 delegates. Their 12 matter a lot more than our 40, so for us to go to nine, that's not much of a penalty at all."[13]

As this case makes clear, the issue of unfairness continues to rankle. It just isn't logical that such a small state should be able to exert so much influence, regardless of its history. To this oft-asserted criticism, however, New Hampshire Secretary of State William Gardner observes, "An ounce of history is worth a pound of logic."

Appendix. New Hampshire Primary Election Results since 1952

March 11, 1952

Democratic "Beauty Contest"	Vote	Percent	Delegates
Estes Kefauver (TN)	19,800	54.6	12
Harry Truman (MO)	15,927	43.9	0
Douglas MacArthur (AK)	151	0.4	0
James Farley (NY)	77	0.2	0
Adlai Stevenson (IL)	40	0.1	0
Other	257	0.7	0
TOTAL	36,252	100	12

Republican "Beauty Contest"	Vote	Percent	Delegates
Dwight Eisenhower (KA)	46,661	50.2	14
Robert Taft (OH)	35,838	38.6	0
Harold Stassen (MN)	6,574	7.1	0
Douglas MacArthur (AK)	3,227	3.5	0
William R. Schneider (OR)	230	0.2	0
Other	335	0.4	0
TOTAL	92,865	100	14

March 13, 1956

Democratic "Beauty Contest"	Vote	Percent	Delegates
Estes Kefauver (TN)	21,701	84.6	8
Adlai Stevenson (IL)	3,806	14.8	0
Other	139	0.5	0
TOTAL	25,646	100	8

Republican "Beauty Contest"	Vote	Percent	Delegates
Dwight Eisenhower (KA)	56,464	98.9	14
Other	600	1.1	0
TOTAL	57,064	100	14

March 8, 1960

Democratic "Beauty Contest"	Vote	Percent	Delegates
John Kennedy (MA)	43,372	85.2	20
Paul Fisher (PA)	6,853	13.5	0
Adlai Stevenson (IL)	183	0.4	0
Wesley Powell (NH)	168	0.3	0
Estes Kefauver (TN)	164	0.3	0
Other	159	0.3	0
TOTAL	50,899	100	20

Republican "Beauty Contest"	Vote	Percent	Delegates
Richard Nixon (CA)	65,204	89.3	14
Nelson Rockefeller (NY)	2,745	3.8	0
Paul Fisher (PA)	2,388	3.3	0
John Kennedy (MA)	2,196	3.0	0
Henry Cabot Lodge (MA)	141	0.2	0
Styles Bridges (NH)	108	0.1	0
Other	249	0.3	0
TOTAL	73,031	100	14

March 10, 1964

Democratic "Beauty Contest"	Vote	Percent	Delegates
Lyndon Johnson (TX)	29,317	95.3	20
Robert Kennedy (MA)	487	1.6	0
Henry Cabot Lodge (MA)	280	0.9	0
Richard Nixon (CA)	232	0.8	0
Barry Goldwater (AZ)	193	0.6	0
Nelson Rockefeller (NY)	109	0.4	0
Adlai Stevenson (IL)	16	0.1	0
Hubert Humphrey (MN)	11	0.0	0
Other	132	0.4	0
TOTAL	30,777	100	20

Republican "Beauty Contest"	Vote	Percent	Delegates
Henry Cabot Lodge (MA)	33,007	35.5	14
Barry Goldwater (AZ)	20,692	22.3	0
Nelson Rockefeller (NY)	19,504	21.0	0
Richard Nixon (CA)	15,587	16.8	0
Margaret Chase Smith (MA)	2,120	2.3	0
Harold Stassen (MN)	1,373	1.5	0
William Scranton (PA)	105	0.1	0
Other	465	0.5	0
TOTAL	92,853	100.0	14

March 12, 1968

Democratic "Beauty Contest"	Vote	Percent	Delegates
Lyndon Johnson (TX)	27,520	49.6	4
Eugene McCarthy (MN)	3,263	41.9	20
Richard Nixon (CA)	2,532	4.6	0
Robert Kennedy (NY)	606	1.1	0
Paul Fisher (PA)	506	0.9	0
Nelson Rockefeller (NY)	249	0.4	0
George Wallace (AL)	201	0.4	0
John Crommelin (AL)	186	0.3	0
Richard Lee (NH)	170	0.3	0
Jacob Gordon (MA)	77	0.1	0
Other	154	0.3	0
TOTAL	55,464	100.0	24

Republican "Beauty Contest"	Vote	Percent	Delegates
Richard Nixon (CA)	80,666	77.6	14
Nelson Rockefeller (NY)	11,241	10.8	0
Eugene McCarthy (MN)	5,511	5.3	0
Lyndon Johnson (TX)	1,778	1.7	0
George Romney (MI)	1,743	1.7	0
Willis Stone (CA)	527	0.5	0
Harold Stassen (MN)	429	0.4	0
Ronald Reagan (CA)	362	0.3	0
Paul Fisher (PA)	374	0.4	0
Herbert Hoover (CA)	247	0.2	0
David Watumull (HI)	161	0.2	0
William Evans Jr. (NJ)	151	0.1	0
Elmer Coy (OH)	73	0.1	0
Don DuMont (IL)	39	0.0	0
Other	636	0.6	0
TOTAL	103,938	100	14

March 7, 1972

Democratic "Beauty Contest"	Vote	Percent	Delegates
Edmund Muskie (ME)	41,235	46.4	15
George McGovern (SD)	33,007	37.1	5
Sam Yorty (CA)	5,401	6.1	0
Wilbur Mills (AR)	3,563	4.0	0
Vance Hartke (IN)	2,417	2.7	0
Edward Kennedy (MA)	954	1.1	0
Richard Nixon (CA)	854	1.0	0
Hubert Humphrey (MN)	348	0.4	0
Edward Coll (CT)	280	0.3	0
Henry Jackson (WA)	197	0.2	0
George Wallace (AL)	175	0.2	0
Pete McCloskey (CA)	133	0.1	0
John Ashbrook (OH)	27	0.0	0
Pat Paulsen (CA)	19	0.0	0
Other	244	0.3	0
TOTAL	88,854	100	20

Republican "Beauty Contest"	Vote	Percent	Delegates
Richard Nixon (CA)	79,239	67.6	14
Pete McCloskey (CA)	23,190	19.8	0
John Ashbrook (OH)	11,362	9.7	0
Pat Paulsen (CA)	1,211	1.0	0
Wilbur Mills (AR)	645	0.6	0
George McGovern (SD)	555	0.5	0
Edmund Muskie (ME)	504	0.4	0
George Wallace (AL)	93	0.1	0
Sam Yorty (CA)	55	0.0	0
Vance Hartke (IN)	32	0.0	0
Edward Kennedy (MA)	28	0.0	0
Edward Coll (CT)	2	0.0	0
Other	292	0.2	0
TOTAL	117,208	100	14

February 24, 1976

Democratic Direct Primary	Vote	Percent	Delegates
James Carter (GA)	23,373	28.5	15
Morris Udall (AZ)	18,710	22.9	2
Birch Bayh (IN)	12,510	15.3	0
Fred Harris (OK)	8,863	10.8	0
Sargent Schriver (MD)	6,743	8.2	0
Hubert Humphrey (MN)	4,596	5.6	0
Henry Jackson (WA)	1,857	2.3	0
George Wallace (AL)	1,061	1.3	0
Ellen McCormack (NY)	1,007	1.2	0
Ronald Reagan (CA)	875	1.1	0
Arthur Blessitt (FL)	828	1.0	0
Gerald Ford (MI)	405	0.5	0
Stanley Arnold (NY)	371	0.5	0
Billy Joe Clegg (MS)	174	0.2	0
Bernard Schechter (CA)	173	0.2	0
Frank Bona (NY)	135	0.2	0
Robert Kelleher (MT)	87	0.1	0
Terry Sanford (SC)	53	0.1	0
Rick Loewenherz (OK)	49	0.1	0
TOTAL	81,870	100	17

Republican Direct Primary	Vote	Percent	Delegates
Gerald Ford (MI)	55,156	50.1	18
Ronald Reagan (CA)	53,569	48.6	3
Birch Bayh (IN)	228	0.2	0
James Carter (GA)	591	0.5	0
Fred Harris (OK)	225	0.2	0
Morris Udall (AZ)	421	0.4	0
TOTAL	110,190	100	21

February 26, 1980

Democratic Direct Primary	Vote	Percent	Delegates
James Carter (GA)	52,648	47.2	10
Edward Kennedy (MA)	41,687	37.3	9
Edmund Brown (CA)	10,706	9.6	0
Lyndon LaRouche (VA)	2,307	2.1	0
Ronald Reagan (CA)	1,958	1.8	0
John Anderson (IL)	932	0.8	0
Richard Kay (OH)	563	0.5	0
George H. W. Bush (TX)	415	0.4	0
Howard Baker (TN)	317	0.3	0
Philip Crane (IL)	61	0.1	0
John Connally (TX)	18	0.0	0
Robert Dole (KA)	3	0.0	0
TOTAL	111,615	100	19

Republican Direct Primary	Vote	Percent	Delegates
Ronald Reagan (CA)	72,983	49.8	15
George H. W. Bush (TX)	33,443	22.8	5
Howard Baker (TN)	18,943	12.9	2
John Anderson (IL)	14,458	9.9	0
Philip Crane (IL)	2,618	1.8	0
John Connally (TX)	2,239	1.5	0
James Carter (GA)	788	0.5	0
Robert Dole (KA)	597	0.4	0
Edward Kennedy (MA)	287	0.2	0
Edmund Brown Jr. (CA)	157	0.1	0
Lyndon LaRouche (VA)	19	0.0	0
Richard Kay (OH)	2	0.0	0
TOTAL	146,534	100.0	22

February 28, 1984

Democratic Direct Primary	Vote	Percent	Delegates
Gary Hart (CO)	37,702	37.3	10
Walter Mondale (MN)	28,173	27.9	12
John Glenn (OH)	12,088	12.0	0
Jesse Jackson (IL)	5,311	5.3	0
George McGovern (SD)	5,217	5.2	0
Ronald Reagan (CA)	5,058	5.0	0
Ernest Hollings (SC)	3,583	3.5	0
Alan Cranston (CA)	2,136	2.1	0
Reubin Askew (FL)	1,025	1.0	0
Stephen Koczak (DC)	155	0.2	0
Walter Buchanan (CA)	132	0.1	0
Martin Beckman (WA)	127	0.1	0
Edward O'Donnell Jr. (DE)	74	0.1	0
Gerald Willis (AL)	50	0.0	0
William King(FL)	34	0.0	0
Richard Kay (OH)	27	0.0	0
William Kreml (SC)	25	0.0	0
Hugh Bagley (CA)	24	0.0	0
Claude Kirk (FL)	24	0.0	0
Chester Rudnicki (NH)	21	0.0	0
Roy Clendenan (OH)	20	0.0	0
Cyril Sagan (PA)	20	0.0	0
Raymond Caplette (AZ)	19	0.0	0
TOTAL	101,045	100	22

February 28, 1984

Republican Direct Primary	Vote	Percent	Delegates
Ronald Reagan (CA)	65,033	86.4	22
Gary Hart (CO)	3,968	5.3	0
Harold Stassen (MN)	1,543	2.1	0
Walter Mondale (MN)	1,090	1.4	0
John Glenn (OH)	1,065	1.4	0
Ernest Hollings (SC)	697	0.9	0
Jesse Jackson (IL)	455	0.6	0
George McGovern (SD)	406	0.5	0
David Kelley (TN)	360	0.5	0
Gary Arnold (CA)	252	0.3	0
Benjamin Fernandez (CA)	202	0.3	0
Alan Cranston (CA)	107	0.1	0
Reubin Askew (FL)	52	0.1	0
Martin Beckman (WA)	5	0.0	0
Cyril Sagan (PA)	2	0.0	0
Walter Buchanan (CA)	1	0.0	0
Richard Kay (OH)	1	0.0	0
Gerald Willis (AL)	1	0.0	0
TOTAL	75,240	1000	22

February 16, 1988

Democratic Direct Primary	Vote	Percent	Delegates
Michael Dukakis (MA)	44,112	36.5	
Richard Gephardt (MO)	24,513	20.3	
Paul Simon (IL)	21,094	17.5	
Jesse Jackson (IL)	9,615	8.0	0
Albert Gore (TN)	8,400	7.0	0
Bruce Babbitt (AZ)	5,644	4.7	0
Gary Hart (CO)	4,888	4.0	0
William DuPont (IL)	1,349	1.1	0
David Duke (LA)	264	0.2	0
Lyndon LaRouche Jr. (VA)	188	0.2	0
William Marra (NJ)	142	0.1	0
Conrad Roy (NH)	122	0.1	0
Florenzo DiDonato (MA)	84	0.1	0
Andy Martin-Trigona (CT)	61	0.1	0
Stephen Koczak (DC)	47	0.0	0
William King (FL)	36	0.0	0
Edward O'Donnell Jr. (DE)	33	0.0	0
Cyril Sagan (PA)	33	0.0	0
Frank Thomas (CA)	28	0.0	0
Claude Kirk (FL)	25	0.0	0
Norbert Dennerll (OH)	18	0.0	0
Osie Thorpe (DC)	16	0.0	0
A. A. Van Petten (CA)	10	0.0	0
Stanley Lock (MI)	9	0.0	0
TOTAL	120,731	100	

February 16, 1988

Republican Direct Primary	Vote	Percent	Delegates
George H. W. Bush (TX)	59,290	37.7	
Robert Dole (KA)	44,797	28.5	
Jack Kemp (NY)	20,114	12.8	
Pierre DuPont (DE)	15,885	10.1	0
Pat Robertson (VA)	14,775	9.4	0
Michael Dukakis (MA)	585	0.4	0
Al Haig (VA)	481	0.3	0
Paul Simon (IL)	219	0.1	0
Richard Gephardt (MO)	180	0.1	0
Jesse Jackson (IL)	166	0.1	0
Harold Stassen (MN)	130	0.1	0
Albert Gore (TN)	111	0.1	0
Paul Conley (MD)	107	0.1	0
Mary Rachner (MN)	107	0.1	0
Bruce Babbitt (AZ)	100	0.1	0
Gary Hart (CO)	91	0.1	0
Robert Drucker (PA)	83	0.1	0
William Horrigan Jr. (CT)	76	0.0	0
Michael Levinson (NY)	43	0.0	0
William DuPont (IL)	22	0.0	0
David Duke (LA)	9	0.0	0
Lyndon LaRouche Jr. (VA)	7	0.0	0
William Marra (NJ)	6	0.0	0
William King (FL)	1	0.0	0
Conrad Roy (NH)	1	0.0	0
TOTAL	157,386	100	

February 18, 1992

Democratic Direct Primary	Vote	Percent	Delegates
Paul Tsongas (MA)	55,663	33.2	
William Clinton (AR)	41,540	24.8	
Robert Kerrey (NE)	18,584	11.1	0
Thomas Harkin (IA)	17,063	10.2	0
Edmund Brown Jr. (CA)	13,659	8.1	0
Mario Cuomo (NY)	6,577	3.9	0
Tom Laughlin (CA)	3,251	1.9	0
Ralph Nader (CT)	3,054	1.8	0
Charles Woods (AL)	2,862	1.7	0
George H. W. Bush (TX)	1,434	0.9	0
Patrick Buchanan (VA)	1,248	0.7	0
Lenora Fulani (NY)	402	0.2	0
Lawrence Agran (CA)	335	0.2	0
Patrick Mahoney Jr. (FL)	304	0.2	0
Eugene McCarthy (MN)	212	0.1	0
John Rigazio (NH)	187	0.1	0
Curly Thornton (MT)	126	0.1	0
Lyndon LaRouche (VA)	116	0.1	0
Douglas Wilder (VA)	107	0.1	0
Caroline Killeen (NY)	94	0.1	0
John Patrick Cahill (NY)	83	0.0	0

February 18, 1992 (*continued*)

Democratic Direct Primary	Vote	Percent	Delegates
Paul Fisher (IL)	82	0.0	0
Andre Marrou (AK)	70	0.0	0
Frank Bona (NY)	65	0.0	0
Karl Hegger (IL)	61	0.0	0
William Horrigan Jr. (CT)	53	0.0	0
Dean Curtis (CA)	43	0.0	0
Stephen Burke (NY)	39	0.0	0
Gilbert Holmes (WA)	39	0.0	0
Ron Kovic (CA)	36	0.0	0
Rufus Higginbotham (TX)	31	0.0	0
Chris Norton (NY)	31	0.0	0
Rose Monyek (NJ)	29	0.0	0
James Gay Jr. (TX)	28	0.0	0
Barry Deutsch (NY)	26	0.0	0
Cyril Sagan (PA)	26	0.0	0
Edward O'Donnell Jr. (DE)	24	0.0	0
Tom Shiekman (FL)	23	0.0	0
Stephen Schwartz (NY)	17	0.0	0
Other	40	0.0	0
TOTAL	167,664	100	18

February 18, 1992

Republican Direct Primary	Vote	Percent	Delegates
George H.W. Bush (TX)	92,271	53.2	
Patrick Buchanan (VA)	65,106	37.5	
Paul Tsongas (MA)	3,676	2.1	0
Ralph Nader (CT)	3,258	1.9	0
William Clinton (AR)	1,698	1.0	0
James Lennane (FL)	1,684	1.0	0
Mario Cuomo (NY)	799	0.5	0
Edmund Brown Jr. (CA)	773	0.4	0
Robert Kerrey (NE)	721	0.4	0
Pat Paulsen (CA)	603	0.3	0
Thomas Harkin (CA)	543	0.3	0
Richard Bosa (NH)	349	0.2	0
Charles Woods (AL)	284	0.2	0
Tom Laughlin (CA)	267	0.2	0
John Merwin (VI)	225	0.1	0
Harold Stassen (MN)	205	0.1	0
Paul Conley (MD)	120	0.1	0
Billy Joe Clegg (MO)	110	0.1	0
Andre Marrou (AK)	99	0.1	0
Georgiana Doerschuck (NH)	58	0.0	0
Paul Daugherty (SC)	53	0.0	0
Michael Levinson (NY)	45	0.0	0
Lowell Fellure (WV)	36	0.0	0
Paul Fisher (IL)	33	0.0	0
Vincent Latchford (NH)	32	0.0	0
Hubert Patty (TN)	31	0.0	0
George Zimmerman (TX)	31	0.0	0
Douglas Wilder (VA)	30	0.0	0
Thomas Fabish (CA)	29	0.0	0
Stephen Koczak (DC)	29	0.0	0
F. Dean Johnson (NH)	24	0.0	0
Norman Bertasavage (PA)	23	0.0	0
Jack Trinsey (NH)	22	0.0	0
Lenora Fulani (NY)	21	0.0	0
Other	116	0.1	0
TOTAL	173,404	100	23

February 20, 1996

Democratic Direct Primary	Vote	Percent	Delegates
William Clinton (AR)	76,797	84.4	20
Patrick Buchanan (VA)	3,347	3.7	0
Lamar Alexander (TN)	1,888	2.1	0
Steve Forbes (NJ)	1,294	1.4	0
Robert Dole (KA)	1,257	1.4	0
Pat Paulsen (CA)	1,007	1.1	0
Albert Gore (TN)	679	0.7	0
Carmen Chimento (NH)	656	0.7	0
Lyndon LaRouche (VA)	433	0.5	0
Richard Lugar (IN)	410	0.5	0
Caroline Killeen (AZ)	391	0.4	0
Heather Harder (IN)	369	0.4	0
Bruce Daniels (CT)	312	0.3	0
James Griffin (NY)	307	0.3	0
Alan Keyes (MD)	281	0.3	0
Colin Powell (DC)	280	0.3	0
Ralph Nader (CT)	187	0.2	0
Morris Taylor (IL)	167	0.2	0
Stephen Michael (DC)	94	0.1	0
Willie Carter (TX)	85	0.1	0
Robert Drucker (PA)	81	0.1	0
David Pauling (FL)	74	0.1	0
Vincent Hamm (CO)	72	0.1	0
Ted Gunderson (NV)	70	0.1	0
Frank Legas (CA)	63	0.1	0
Ronald Spangler (CA)	62	0.1	0
Michael Dass (PA)	57	0.1	0
Osie Thorpe (DC)	50	0.1	0
Ben Tomeo (TN)	47	0.1	0
Sal Casamassima (TX)	45	0.0	0
John Safran (MI)	42	0.0	0
Ross Perot (TX)	41	0.0	0
Phil Gramm (TX)	25	0.0	0
Robert Dornan (CA)	21	0.0	0
Other	35	0.0	0
TOTAL	91,026	100	20

February 20, 1996

Republican Direct Primary	Vote	Percent	Delegates
Patrick Buchanan (VA)	56,874	27.3	
Robert Dole (KA)	54,738	26.2	
Lamar Alexander (TN)	47,148	22.6	
Steve Forbes (NJ)	25,505	12.2	0
Richard Lugar (IN)	10,838	5.2	0
Alan Keyes (MD)	5,572	2.7	0
Morris Taylor (IL)	2,944	1.4	0
William Clinton (AR)	1,972	0.9	0
Phil Gramm (TX)	752	0.4	0
Colin Powell (DC)	649	0.3	0
Richard Dornan (CA)	529	0.3	0
Richard Bosa (NH)	216	0.1	0
Georgiana Doerschuck (NH)	154	0.1	0
Susan Ducey (PA)	151	0.1	0
Billie Joe Clegg (MS)	118	0.1	0
Ralph Nader (CT)	94	0.0	0
Richard Skillen (NC)	80	0.0	0
Jack Kemp (NY)	62	0.0	0
William Flannagan (FL)	48	0.0	0
Charles Collins (FL)	42	0.0	0
Russell Fornwalt (NY)	37	0.0	0
Michael Levinson (NY)	35	0.0	0
Albert Gore (TN)	33	0.0	0
John Hurd (OH)	26	0.0	0
Ross Perot (TX)	24	0.0	0
Gerald McManus (FL)	20	0.0	0
Hubert Patty (TN)	17	0.0	0
Pat Paulsen (CA)	8	0.0	0
Other	54	0.0	0
TOTAL	208,740	100	16

February 1, 2000

Democratic Direct Primary	Vote	Percent	Delegates
Albert Gore (TN)	76,897	49.7	13
William Bradley (NJ)	70,502	45.6	9
John McCain (AZ)	3,320	2.1	0
Steve Forbes (NJ)	998	0.6	0
George W. Bush (TX)	827	0.5	0
Alan Keyes (MD)	424	0.3	0
Charles Buckley (NH)	322	0.2	0
Heather Harder (IN)	192	0.1	0
Jeffrey Peters (NH)	156	0.1	0
John Eaton (MA)	134	0.1	0
Lyndon LaRouche (VA)	124	0.1	0
Morris Taylor (IL)	87	0.1	0
Mark Greenstein (NY)	75	0.0	0
Gary Bauer (VA)	44	0.0	0
Nathaniel Mullins (MA)	35	0.0	0
Edward O'Donnell Jr. (DE)	35	0.0	0
Willie Carter (TX)	30	0.0	0
Randy Crow (NC)	29	0.0	0
Vincent Hamm (CO)	22	0.0	0
Tom Koos (CA)	19	0.0	0
Michael Skok (NY)	18	0.0	0
Other	340	0.2	0
TOTAL	154,630	100	24

February 1, 2000

Republican Direct Primary	Vote	Percent	Delegates
John McCain (AZ)	115,606	48.5	10
George W. Bush (TX)	72,330	30.4	5
Steve Forbes (NJ)	30,166	12.7	2
Alan Keyes (MD)	15,179	6.4	0
Gary Bauer (VA)	1,640	0.7	0
Albert Gore (TN)	1,155	0.5	0
William Bradley (MJ)	1,025	0.4	0
Elizabeth Dole (NC)	231	0.1	0
Orrin Hatch (UT)	163	0.1	0
Dorian Yeager (NH)	98	0.0	0
Andy Martin (IL)	81	0.0	0
Samuel Berry Jr. (OR)	61	0.0	0
Kenneth Capalbo (RI)	51	0.0	0
Timothy Mosby (CA)	41	0.0	0
Mark Harnes (NY)	34	0.0	0
Richard Peet (VA)	23	0.0	0
Other	293	0.1	0
TOTAL	238,177	100	17

January 27, 2004

Democratic Direct Primary	Vote	Percent	Delegates
John Kerry (MA)	84,377	38.4	13
Howard Dean (VT)	57,761	26.3	9
Wesley Clark (AR)	27,314	12.4	0
John Edwards (NC)	26,487	12.1	0
Joseph Lieberman (CT)	18,911	8.6	0
Dennis Kucinich (OH)	3,114	1.4	0
Richard Gephardt (MO)	419	0.2	0
Al Sharpton (NY)	347	0.2	0
George W. Bush (TX)	257	0.1	0
Lyndon LaRouche (VA)	90	0.0	0
Willie Carter (TX)	86	0.0	0
Carol Moseley Braun (IL)	81	0.0	0
Edward O'Donnell Jr. (DE)	79	0.0	0
Katherine Bateman (IL)	68	0.0	0
Randy Crow (NC)	60	0.0	0
Vincent Hamm (CO)	58	0.0	0
Robert Linnell (NH)	49	0.0	0
Gerry Dokka (GA)	42	0.0	0
Caroline Killeen (NY)	31	0.0	0
Randy Lee (NY)	15	0.0	0
Harry W. Braun III (IL)	13	0.0	0
Mildred Glover (MD)	11	0.0	0
Other	92	0.0	0
TOTAL	219,762	100	22

January 27, 2004

Republican Direct Primary	Vote	Percent	Delegates
George W. Bush (TX)	53,962	79.8	29
John Kerry (MA)	2,819	4.2	0
Howard Dean (VT)	1,789	2.6	0
Wesley Clark (AR)	1,407	2.1	0
John Edwards (NC)	1,088	1.6	0
Joseph Lieberman (CT)	914	1.4	0
Richard Bosa (NH)	841	1.2	0
John Buchanan (FL)	836	1.2	0
John Rigazio (NH)	803	1.2	0
Robert Haines (NH)	579	0.9	0
Michael Callis (NH)	388	0.6	0
Blake Ashby (MO)	264	0.4	0
Millie Howard (OH)	239	0.4	0
Tom Laughlin (CA)	154	0.2	0
William Wyatt (CA)	153	0.2	0
Jim Taylor (MN)	124	0.2	0
Mark Harnes (NY)	87	0.1	0
Cornelius O'Connor (NH)	77	0.1	0
George Gostigian (NJ)	52	0.1	0
Dennis Kucinich (OH)	38	0.1	0
Al Sharpton (NY)	15	0.0	0
Other	973	1.4	0
TOTAL	67,602	100	29

January 8, 2008

Democratic Direct Primary	Vote	Percent	Delegates
Hillary Clinton (NY)	112,404	34.8	9
Barack Obama (IL)	104,815	32.5	9
John Edwards (NC)	48,699	15.1	4
Dennis Kucinich (OH)	38,911	12.1	0
Bill Richardson (NM)	13,269	4.1	0
John McCain (AZ)	932	0.3	0
Joseph Biden (DE)	638	0.2	0
Mitt Romney (MA)	611	0.2	0
Mike Gravel (AK)	404	0.1	0
Ron Paul (TX)	267	0.1	0
Richard Caligiuri (PA)	253	0.1	0
Mike Huckabee (AR)	243	0.1	0
Christopher Dodd (CT)	205	0.1	0
Rudolph Giuliani (NY)	161	0.0	0
Kenneth Capalbo (RI)	108	0.0	0
Darrell Hunter (TX)	95	0.0	0
William Keefe (MA)	51	0.0	0
Tom Laughlin (CA)	47	0.0	0
Randy Crow (NC)	37	0.0	0
Michael Skok (NY)	32	0.0	0
Oloveuse Savior (MN)	30	0.0	0
Henry Hewes (NY)	17	0.0	0
William Hughes (MO)	16	0.0	0
Fred Thompson (TN)	15	0.0	0
Caroline Killeen (AZ)	11	0.0	0
Tom Koos (CA)	10	0.0	0
Dal LaMagna (WA)	8	0.0	0
Duncan Hunter (CA)	8	0.0	0
Stephen Marchuk (NH)	5	0.0	0
Alan Keyes (IL)	4	0.0	0
Millie Howard (OH)	1	0.0	0
Other	270	0.1	0
TOTAL	322,577	100	23

January 8, 2008

Republican Direct Primary	Vote	Percent	Delegates
John McCain (AZ)	88,713	37.0	7
Mitt Romney (MA)	75,675	31.64	
Mike Huckabee (AR)	26,916	11.21	
Rudolph Giuliani (NY)	20,344	8.50	
Ron Paul (TX)	18,346	7.70	
Fred Thompson (TN)	2,956	1.2	0
Barack Obama (IL)	1,996	0.8	0
Hillary Clinton (NY)	1,828	0.8	0
Duncan Hunter (CA)	1,192	0.5	0
John Edwards (NC)	747	0.3	0
Bill Richardson (NM)	210	0.1	0
Alan Keyes (IL)	205	0.1	0
Stephen Marchuk (NH)	127	0.1	0
Tom Tancredo (CO)	63	0.0	0
Cornelius O'Connor (NH)	46	0.0	0
Millie Howard (OH)	43	0.0	0
Vermin Supreme (MA)	43	0.0	0
John Cox (CA)	39	0.0	0
Verne Wuensche (TX)	36	0.0	0
Hugh Cort (AL)	35	0.0	0
Daniel Gilbert (NC)	35	0.0	0
Jack Shepard (MN)	28	0.0	0
James Mitchell Jr. (IL)	26	0.0	0
Mark Klein (CA)	16	0.0	0
Dennis Kucinich (OH)	15	0.0	0
Neil Fendig Jr. (GA)	13	0.0	0
Mike Gravel (AK)	5	0.0	0
Other	94	0.0	0
TOTAL	239,792	100	12

Note: The number of delegates awarded in 2008 was reduced by 50 percent per Republican rules for moving out of the prescribed window for holding contests.

January 8, 2012

Democratic Direct Primary	Vote	Percent	Delegates
Barack Obama (IL)	49,080	80.9	28
Ron Paul (TX)	2,289	3.8	0
Mitt Romney (MA)	1,815	3.0	0
Jon Huntsman (UT)	1,237	2.0	0
Ed Cowan (NH)	945	1.6	0
Vermin Supreme (MA)	833	1.4	0
Randall Terry (MO)	442	0.7	0
John D. Haywood (NH)	423	0.7	0
Craig "Tax Freeze" Freis (NH)	400	0.7	0
Rick Santorum (PA)	302	0.5	0
Bob Ely (NH)	287	0.5	0
Newt Gingrich (GA)	276	0.5	0
Cornelius O'Connor (NH)	266	0.4	0
Darcy G. Richardson (LA)	264	0.4	0
John Wolfe Jr. (LA)	245	0.4	0
Edward T. O'Donnell Jr. (DE)	222	0.4	0
Bob Greene (NH)	213	0.4	0
Robert B. Jordan (NH)	155	0.3	0
Aldous C. Tyler (NH)	106	0.2	0
Buddy Roemer (LA)	29	0.0	0
Fred Karger (CA)	26	0.0	0
Rick Perry (TX)	17	0.0	0
Other	772	1.3	0
TOTAL	60,644	100	28

January 8, 2012

Republican Direct Primary	Vote	Percent	Delegates
Mitt Romney (MA)	97,591	39.3	7
Ron Paul (TX)	56,872	22.9	4
Jon Huntsman (UT)	41,964	16.9	1
Rick Santorum (PA)	23,432	9.4	0
Newt Gingrich (GA)	23,421	9.4	0
Rick Perry (TX)	1,764	0.7	0
Buddy Roemer (LA)	950	0.4	0
Michele Bachmann (MN)	350	0.1	0
Fred Karger (CA)	345	0.1	0
Barack Obama (IL)	285	0.1	0
Kevin Rubash (IL)	250	0.1	0
Gary Johnson (NM)	181	0.1	0
Herman Cain (GA)	161	0.1	0
Jeff Lawman (NH)	119	0.0	0
Christopher V. Hill	108	0.0	0
Benjamin Linn (NH)	83	0.0	0
Michael J. Meehan (MO)	54	0.0	0
Joe Story (FL)	42	0.0	0
Keith Drummond (TX)	42	0.0	0
Bear Betzler (PA)	29	0.0	0
Joe Robinson (MA)	25	0.0	0
Stewart J. Greenleaf (PA)	24	0.0	0
Mark Callahan (OR)	20	0.0	0
Andy Martin (NH)	19	0.0	0
Linden Swift (IN)	18	0.0	0
Verne Wuensche (TX)	15	0.0	0
Timothy Brewer (OH)	15	0.0	0
L. John Davis Jr. (CO)	14	0.0	0
Randy Crow (RI)	12	0.0	0
James A. Vestermark (KY)	3	0.0	0
Hugh Cort (AL)	3	0.0	0
Other	260	0.1	0
	24,8471	100	12

Note: The number of delegates awarded in 2012 was reduced by 50 percent per Republican rules for moving out of the prescribed window for holding contests.

Notes

1. Importance of the New Hampshire Primary

1. William G. Mayer, "The Basic Dynamics of the Contemporary Nomination Process: An Expanded View," in *The Making of the Presidential Candidates 2004*, ed. William G. Mayer (Lanham, MD: Rowman & Littlefield, 2004), pp. 83–132. For more detail on the importance of New Hampshire and how it has been changing, see William G. Mayer and Andrew E. Busch, "The Frontloading Problem," in *The Making of the Presidential Candidates, 2004*.

2. Mayer, *The Making of the Presidential Candidates, 2004*, p. 106–07.

3. Ibid., p. 112.

4. Randall Adkins and Andrew Dowdle, "How Important Are Iowa and New Hampshire to Winning Post-Reform Presidential Nominations?" *Political Research Quarterly* 54:431 (2001).

5. William G. Mayer and Andrew E. Busch, *The Front-Loading Problem in Presidential Nominations* (Washington, DC: Brookings Institution Press, 2004).

6. Jules Witcover, "A Reporter's Encomium to the New Hampshire Primary," in *Marathon: The Pursuit of the Presidency, 1972–1976* (New York: Signet Book New American Library, 1977), pp. 235–38.

7. Ibid., p. 89.

8. See the national poll averages for the 2008 Democratic nomination at Real Clear Politics, http://www.realclearpolitics.com/epolls/2008/president/us/democratic_presidential_nomination-191.html.

9. See the national poll averages for the 2008 Republican nomination at Real Clear Politics, http://www.realclearpolitics.com/epolls/other/2012_2008_gop_presidential_race_4_years_ago.html.

10. See the national poll averages for the 2012 Republican nomination at Real Clear Politics, http://www.realclearpolitics.com/epolls/2012/president/us/republican_presidential_nomination-1452.html.

11. The initial idea that party leaders had reasserted control appears to come from a series of papers by Wayne Steger, updated and expanded in his forthcoming book, *Citizen's Guide to Presidential Nominations: The Competition for Leadership* (New York: Routledge, forthcoming). Scholars Marty Cohen, David Karol, Hans Noel, and John Zaller take up Steger's early idea and exam-

ine it in light of their own data in *The Party Decides: Presidential Nominations before and after Reform* (Chicago: University of Chicago Press, 2008).

12. Wayne Steger, "Candidate Endorsements: The Under-Appreciated Role of the Political Party Establishments in the Presidential Nominating Process" (paper given at the Annual Meeting of the Midwest Political Science Association, Chicago, 2000), cited in Cohen, et. al., *Party Decides*, p. 279.

13. Cohen, et. al., *Party Decides*, p. 339.

14. Ibid., p. 346–47.

15. Ibid., p. 347–48.

16. Ibid., p. 278 (emphasis added).

2. Getting the Inside Track

1. Hugh Winebrenner, *The Iowa Precinct Caucuses: The Making of a Media Event,* 2nd ed. (Ames, Iowa: Iowa State University Press, 1988), p. 27.

2. Ibid., pp. 254–55.

3. Richard F. Upton, "Address at the New Hampshire Historical Society on the Opening of the Exhibition, *New Hampshire's Road to the White House: Franklin Pierce to the Presidential Primary,*" *Historical New Hampshire* 42, no. 3 (Fall 1987), p. 195; Hugh Gregg and Bill Gardner, *Why New Hampshire: The First-in-the-Nation Primary State* (Nashua, NH: RESOURCES-NH, 2003, p. 32.).

4. Gregg and Gardner, *Why New Hampshire*, p. 226.

5. Upton, "Address," pp.196–97.

6. Winebrenner, *Iowa Precinct Caucuses*, p. 32.

7. For a more detailed history of the Iowa caucuses in this time period, see ibid., pp. 25–56.

8. Secretary of State William Gardner, interviewed by the authors, November 7, 2013.

9. Gregg and Gardner, *Why New Hampshire*, pp. 226–30; Charles Brereton, *First in the Nation: New Hampshire and the Premier Presidential Primary* (Portsmouth, NH: Peter E. Randall, 1987), 136–37.

10. Brereton, *First in the Nation*, p. 136.

11. Gregg and Gardner, *Why New Hampshire*, p. 226.

12. Ibid., p. 229.

13. Ibid., pp. 230–31.

14. Winebrenner, *Iowa Precinct Caucuses*, p. 77.

3. Keeping the Inside Track

1. Steven Duprey, interviewed by the authors, March 5, 2014.

2. For a detailed look at this phenomenon, see William G. Mayer and Andrew E. Busch, *The Front-Loading Problem in Presidential Nominations* (Washington, DC: Brookings Institution Press, 2004).

3. For a more detailed account, see Niall A. Palmer, *The New Hampshire Primary and the American Electoral Process* (Westport, CT: Praeger, 1997), pp. 137–46.

4. Information for this section is based primarily on the authors' interviews with Secretary of State Bill Gardner, November 7, 2013, and November 22, 2013; Gregg and Gardner, *Why New Hampshire*, pp. 232–33.

5. Gardner, interview, November 7, 2013.

6. George Bruno, interviewed by the authors, November 22, 2013.

7. Ibid.

8. "Legal Aspects of National Convention Delegate Selection Process in the State of New Hampshire," document prepared for the New Hampshire secretary of state, 1983, pp. 1–2, cited in Palmer, *New Hampshire Primary*, p. 143.

9. Palmer, *New Hampshire Primary*, pp. 142–43.

10. Bruno, interview.

11. Emmett H. Buell Jr. and James W. Davis, "Win Early and Often: Candidates and the Strategic Environment of 1988," in *Nominating the President*, eds. Emmett H. Buell Jr. and Lee Sigelman (Knoxville: University of Tennessee Press, 1991), p. 5.

12. Ibid., p. 5.

13. Palmer, *New Hampshire Primary*, p. 78.

14. Ibid., pp. 146–157.

15. New Hampshire Revised Statute Annotated 653:9.

16. Duprey, interview.

17. Palmer, *New Hampshire Primary*, p. 148.

18. Gardner, interview, November 22, 2013.

19. William J. Clinton: "Teleconference Remarks to Ohio Democratic Caucuses," January 11, 1996, The American Presidency Project, Gerhard Peters and John T. Woolley, http://www.presidency.ucsb.edu/ws/?pid=52747.

20. The discussion in this section is based on the authors' interviews with Secretary of State Bill Gardner, November 7, 2013, and November 11, 2013; Gregg and Gardner, *Why New Hampshire*, pp. 240–247; Palmer, *New Hampshire Primary*, 148–57.

21. Tom Rath, interviewed by the authors, February 7, 2014.

22. Gregg and Gardner, *Why New Hampshire*, p. 257.

23. Ibid., p. 259.

24. Ibid., p. 260.

25. Ibid., p. 261.

26. Rath, interview.

27. Kathy Sullivan, interviewed by the authors, March 5, 2014.

28. Liz Sidoti, "South Carolina Pushes Up GOP Primary," *USA Today*, August 10, 2002.

29. Gardner, interview, November 22, 2013.

30. Kevin Coleman, "Presidential Nominating Process: Current Issues,"

Congressional Research Service, January 27, 2012, http://www.fas.org/sgp/crs
/misc/RL34222.pdf.

31. "New Hampshire Primary Election 2012: Date Set for January 10," Huffington Post, first posted November 2, 2011, updated January 2, 2012, http://
www.huffingtonpost.com/2011/11/02/new-hampshire-primary-election-2012
_n_1028289.html.

32. Mario Trujillo, "Clock Runs Out for Utah's 2016 Primary Hopes," The
Hill, March 15, 2014, http://thehill.com/blogs/ballot-box/presidential-races
/200914-utah-wont-become-first-presidential-primary-state.

4. History of the New Hampshire Primary prior to Party Reforms

1. In these chapters, we rely heavily on two books that have focused on the
events surrounding each of the New Hampshire primary contests. Charles
Brereton's *First in the Nation: New Hampshire and the Premier Presidential
Primary* (Portsmouth, NH: Peter E. Randall, 1987) gives detailed accounts for
the primaries from 1952 through 1984. Niall A. Palmer's *The New Hampshire
Primary and the American Electoral Process*
provides "Granite State Watersheds 1916–1996" (Chapter 1).

2. See above.

3. Brereton, First in the Nation, p. 6.

4. Herbert S. Parmet, *Eisenhower and the American Crusades* (New York:
Macmillan, 1972), cited in Brereton, p. 9.

5. Cited in Brereton, *First in the Nation*, p. 11.

6. Cited ibid., p. 15.

7. Cited ibid., p. 13–14.

8. For a more detailed description of the Democratic New Hampshire primary in 1952, see Robert B. Dishman, "New Hampshire in the Limelight: The
1952 Kefauver-Truman Presidential Campaign," *Historical New Hampshire* 42,
no. 3 (Fall 1987), pp. 214–252.

9. Jack Anderson and Fred Blumenthal, *The Kefauver Story* (New York: Deal
Press, 1956), pp. 168–169, cited in Dishman, "New Hampshire in the Limelight," p. 220.

10. "Truman Bars Test in New Hampshire," *New York Times,* February 1,
1952, http://query.nytimes.com/mem/archive/pdf?res=F40B1EFD395E107A93
C3A91789D85F468585F9.

11. Brereton, *First in the Nation*, pp. 25–26.

12. Current rules in both parties assign delegates to the candidates roughly
proportional to the popular vote. But in 1952, the popular vote (the "beauty
contest") and the votes for delegates were separate exercises, which allowed
for the possibility that a candidate could win the popular voter (or, in the case
of Truman, receive a significant proportion of the votes) and still not win any
delegates.

13. Brereton, *First in the Nation*, p. 31.

14. Cited ibid., p. 42.

15. Cited ibid., p. 47.

16. Brereton, *First in the Nation*, p. 49.

17. Ibid., p. 61.

18. See Chapter 5.

19. Cited in "1960: Kennedy's Opening Drive," *Union Leader*, May 3, 2011, http://www.unionleader.com/article/99999999/NEWS0605/110509968. The article appears to be a summary of many of the same points made by Brereton, in his chapter "1960 — Kennedy versus Nixon — Round One" (pp. 52–70), which we have relied on for our own summary.

20. Cited in Brereton, *First in the Nation*, p. 66.

21. Cited ibid., p. 67.

22. Cited ibid., p. 66.

23. Hugh Gregg, "New Hampshire's First-in-the-Nation Presidential Primary," State of New Hampshire Manual for the General Court (Department of State), No. 55, 1997, http://www.nh.gov/nhinfo/highlights.html.

24. Brereton, *First in the Nation*, p. 67.

25. Ibid., p. 98.

26. "The Guarded, Tranquil World Happy Rockefeller Is Giving Up," *People*, September 9, 1974, http://www.people.com/people/archive/article/0,,20064443,00.html.

27. Brereton, *First in the Nation*, pp. 77–78.

28. Ibid., p. 81. However, we suggest the paper was even more active on behalf of Ronald Reagan in 1980. See Chapter 5 for more details on how Loeb and his paper almost single-handedly saved the Reagan candidacy following Reagan's loss to George H. W. Bush in the Iowa caucuses.

29. Associated Press, "Rocky Raps Barry's Stand," *Sarasota Herald Tribune*, January 25, 1964, http://news.google.com/newspapers?id=ESMhAAAAIBAJ&sjid=uWUEAAAAIBAJ&pg=5178,5695896&dq=barry-goldwater&hl=en.

30. Louis Harris, "Goldwater Clings to Narrow Lead," The Harris Survey, *Deseret News and Salt Lake Telegram*, February 3, 1964, http://news.google.com/newspapers?id=eNBSAAAAIBAJ&sjid=4n8DAAAAIBAJ&pg=7157,223507&dq=goldwater&hl=en.

31. "Lodge a Candidate: In Oregon to Stay," *Boston Globe*, March 10, 1964.

32. "Biography of Allard K. Lowenstein," The Orville H. Schell, Jr. Center for International Human Rights at Yale Law School, http://www.law.yale.edu/intellectuallife/lowensteinbio.htm.

33. "This Day in History: March 2, 1967: Kennedy Proposes Plan to End the War," History.com, http://www.history.com/this-day-in-history/kennedy-proposes-plan-to-end-the-war.

34. Brereton, *First in the Nation*, p. 107.

35. Ibid., p. 131.

36. Cited ibid., p. 133.

37. Johnson later wrote, "I think most people were surprised that Senator McCarthy rolled up the vote he did. I was much less surprised when Bobby Kennedy announced his candidacy four days later. I had been expecting it." Lyndon Johnson, *The Vantage Point* (Holt, Rinehart and Winston, 1971), cited in Brereton, *First in the Nation*, p. 133.

38. "Nixon Hints that He's Available," *New York Times*, January 24, 1964, http://news.google.com/newspapers?nid=2206&dat=19640121&id=dX4yAA AAIBAJ&sjid=3-kFAAAAIBAJ&pg=3089,2261902.

39. Eric Black, "Politics by Gaffe: Recalling the 'Brainwashing' of George Romney," Eric Black Ink, MINNPOST.com, December 2, 2011, http://www .minnpost.com/eric-black-ink/2011/12/politics-gaffe-recalling-brainwashing -george-romney. The article includes a video of the actual interview.

40. Larry Sabato, "Media Frenzies in Our Time: George Romney's 'Brain-washing,'" *Washington Post*, March 27, 1998, http://www.washingtonpost.com /wp-srv/politics/special/clinton/frenzy/romney.htm.

41. Cited in Black, "Politics by Gaffe."

42. Cited in Brereton, *First in the Nation*, p. 117.

5. History of the New Hampshire Primary Contests

1. "This Day in History: July 19, 1969: Incident on Chappaquiddick Island," History.com, http://www.history.com/this-day-in-history/incident-on -chappaquiddick-island.

2. "Muskie Leads Kennedy in Survey of Democrats," *Des Moines Register*, January 23, 1972, cited in Winebrenner, *Iowa Precinct Caucuses*, p. 49.

3. Brereton, *First in the Nation*, p. 160.

4. Ibid., p. 156. According to Brereton, the two journalists who were closest to Muskie were Joe Zellner of the Associated Press and John Milne of United Press International, both based in Concord. Clips of parts of Muskie's "debate" against Loeb can be found on YouTube, neither of which reveals any hint that he might be crying. See "Ed Muskie Cries before New Hampshire Primary in 1972 (or Did He?)," YouTube.com, http://www.youtube.com/watch?v =LiLL8ZAXGys; see also "Edmund Muskie: Regarding the Canuck Letter (1972), YouTube.com, http://www.youtube.com/watch?v=nsRe2YHZYLg.

5. Carl Bernstein and Bob Woodward, "FBI Finds Nixon Aides Sabotaged Democrats," *Washington Post*, October 10, 1972, p. A01.

6. Brereton, *First in the Nation*, p. 161.

7. Ibid., p. 162.

8. Jules Witcover, *Marathon: The Pursuit of the Presidency, 1972–1976* (New York: Signet Book New American Library, 1977), pp. 135–36.

9. Ibid., p. 388.

10. Ibid., pp. 113–14.

11. "Public Trust in Government: 1958–2013," Pew Research Center for the People and the Press, October 18, 2013, http://www.people-press.org/2013/10/18 /trust-in-government-nears-record-low-but-most-federal-agencies-are-viewed -favorably/.

12. Bob Woodward, *Shadow: Five Presidents and the Legacy of Watergate* (New York: Simon and Schuster, 2000), pp. 41–42.

13. One of the authors, David Moore, personally viewed such an occasion, sometime in the fall of 1975, at a small room in the New England Center, a convention center near the University of New Hampshire campus, when Carter addressed a group of about forty people.

14. Witcover, *Marathon*, pp. 221–23.

15. David W. Moore, "Ford and Carter in New Hampshire — or Maybe Not," *The Real Paper,* February 26, 1972.

16. Winebrenner, *Iowa Precinct Caucuses,* p. 70.

17. Brereton, *First in the Nation*, p. 179.

18. Jules Witcover, *Marathon: The Pursuit of the Presidency 1972–1976*, pp. 38–112.

19. Cited by Witcover, p. 98.

20. Witcover, *Marathon*, p. 107.

21. Ibid., p. 109.

22. Ibid., pp. 420–21.

23. Winebrenner, *Iowa Precinct Caucuses*, pp. 73–75.

24. Witcover, Marathon, pp. 397–423.

25. Ibid., p. 419.

26. Cited in Brereton, p. 194.

27. Moore, "Ford and Carter in New Hampshire — or Maybe Not."

28. See the discussion of the Chappaquiddick incident in an earlier part of this chapter on the 1972 New Hampshire primary.

29. Jeffrey M. Jones, "Obama Job Approval Average Slides to New Low in 11th Quarter," Gallup.com, October 21, 2011, http://www.gallup.com/poll /150230/Obama-Job-Approval-Average-Slides-New-Low-11th-Quarter.aspx. Jones compares Obama's average approval rating with other presidents in their eleventh quarter in office. The table includes Carter — whose 31.4 percent is the lowest of any president since 1952.

30. T. R. Reid, "Kennedy," in *Pursuit of the Presidency 1980*, ed. *Washington Post* staff (New York: Berkeley Books, 1980), pp. 65–66.

31. See Gallup's historical figures on presidential approval at "Presidential Approval Ratings — Gallup Historical Statistics and Trends, Gallup.com, http://www.gallup.com/poll/116677/Presidential-Approval-Ratings-Gallup -Historical-Statistics-Trends.aspx#2.

32. Reid, "Kennedy," p. 69.

33. Ibid., p. 71.

34. Statement by Jeanne Shaheen, chair of Carter's New Hampshire campaign, cited in Brereton, *First in the Nation*, p. 210.

35. Reid, "Kennedy," p. 66.

36. Witcover, *Marathon*, pp. 415–16.

37. Kevin Nash, *Who the Hell Is William Loeb?* (Wilton, NH: Amoskeag Press, 1975), a highly critical account of Loeb's tenure as publisher of New Hampshire's only statewide newspaper. Cited in Witcover, *Marathon*, p. 416.

38. Lou Cannon and William Peterson, "GOP," in *Pursuit of the Presidency 1980*, ed. *Washington Post* staff (New York: Berkeley Books, 1980), p. 142.

39. Brereton, *First in the Nation*, p. 205.

40. Cited ibid., p. 205–206.

41. David W. Moore, "The *Manchester Union Leader* in the New Hampshire Primary," in Gary R. Orren and Nelson W. Pollsby, *Media and Momentum: The New Hampshire Primary and Nomination Politics* (Chatham, NJ: Chatham House Publishers, 1987), p. 115.

42. Ibid., p. 115.

43. "Caucus History: Past Year's Results, *Des Moines Register*, http:// caucuses.desmoinesregister.com/caucus-history-past-years-results/

44. Cited in Brereton, *First in the Nation*, p. 218.

45. Moore, "The *Manchester Union Leader* in the New Hampshire Primary," p. 117.

46. The coding project was overseen by David Moore. From the article:

> To assess the stories presented during the New Hampshire primary, a systematic analysis was made of Union Leader coverage between 1 January and 25 February 1980, the day before the primary election. Two people were trained to classify and record the information about each story and picture dealing with the candidates and their campaigns. The coders also rated the items as positive, negative, or neutral.
>
> Positive stories presented the candidate in a favorable light, which might attract readers to vote for him. Negative stories had the opposite effect. Neutral stories contained both positive and negative elements or were neither positive nor negative throughout. All stories dealing with the "horse-race" aspects of the campaign, such as factual reports about how well the candidates did in Iowa and who was leading in the latest scientific poll, were considered neutral. "The coders worked independently of one another and obtained agreement on the ratings for 92 percent of the items; where a disagreement occurred, the item was ultimately classified as neutral." Moore, "The *Manchester Union Leader* in the New Hampshire Primary," p. 112.

47. The back page of the last section was essentially a second front page, laid out similarly to the front page, giving the reader easy access to numerous top stories of the day.

48. Moore, "The *Manchester Union Leader* in the New Hampshire Primary," p. 115.

49. Ibid., pp. 117–18.

50. Ibid., p. 120.

51. The iconic moment is captured on YouTube. See "Ronald Reagan: 'I Am Paying for This Microphone' (1980)," YouTube.com, http://www.youtube.com /watch?v=Rd_KaF3-Bcw. Cannon and Peterson (*Pursuit of the Presidency*, pp. 141–42) claim Bush was unaware of the possible change in format, but Brereton (*First in the Nation*, p. 219) writes that the Bush campaign was aware and indicated no objections. Whatever the background, it is clear that Bush's decision to defer to Breen, instead of supporting the larger inclusion, made him look weak, while Reagan's performance made him look like a real leader. The "I am paying for this microphone" clip was shown again and again in the day and a half before election day.

52. Noted in Cannon and Peterson, *Pursuit of the Presidency*, p. 142.

53. Moore, "The *Manchester Union Leader* in the New Hampshire Primary," p. 117.

54. Gerald Carmen, interviewed by Andrew Smith, May 20, 2014.

55. Paul McCloskey, letter to the Honorable George Bush, March 14, 1980, copy provided to David Moore by Paul McCloskey, cited in Moore, "The *Manchester Union Leader* in the New Hampshire Primary," p. 125.

56. Winebrenner, *Iowa Precinct Caucuses*, p. 115–116.

57. David W. Moore, "The Death of Retail Politics in New Hampshire," *Public Opinion*, February/March 1985, pp. 56–57.

58. Brereton, p. 227.

59. Winebrenner, *Iowa Precinct Caucuses*, p. 112–13.

60. Ibid., p. 110.

61. Ibid., p. 121.

62. Brereton, *First in the Nation*, p. 224.

63. See especially Susan Casey, *Hart and Soul: Gary Hart's New Hampshire Odyssey . . . and Beyond* (Concord, NH: NHI Press, 1986). Casey was Hart's campaign manager in New Hampshire.

64. Cited in Brereton, *First in the Nation*, p. 232.

65. Jack Germond and Jules Witcover, *Whose Broad Stripes and Bright Stars: The Trivial Pursuit of the Presidency, 1988* (New York: Warner Books, 1989), p. 255.

66. Ibid., p. 266. The *Des Moines Register* Web site rounds the number to 0 percent. See "Caucus History: Past Years' Results," DesMoinesRegister.com, http://caucuses.desmoinesregister.com/caucus-history-past-years-results/.

67. Germond and Witcover, *Whose Broad Stripes and Bright Stars,* pp. 169–215.

68. Ibid., pp. 230–44.

69. Ibid., pp. 222–23.

70. Ibid., pp. 272–76.

71. Moore, "The *Manchester Union Leader* in the New Hampshire Primary," p. 124.

72. Germond and Witcover, *Whose Broad Stripes and Bright Stars,* pp. 275–76.

73. Ibid., p. 132.

74. Ibid., p. 140.

75. Ibid., p. 135.

76. See Chapter 8, Who Votes?: The New Hampshire Primary Electorate, which also makes some comparisons with the Iowa electorate.

77. Germond and Witcover, *Whose Broad Stripes and Bright Stars,* pp. 136–46.

6. The 1990s and Beyond

1. Initially, it appeared as though Mitt Romney had narrowly edged out Rick Santorum for first place, but a final count showed Santorum with 29,839 votes to Romney's 29,805 votes. See "GOP Caucus Results," DesMoinesRegister.com, http://caucuses.desmoinesregister.com/data/iowa-caucus/results/.

2. "Presidential Approval Ratings — Gallup Historical Statistics and Trends," Gallup.com, http://www.gallup.com/poll/116677/Presidential-Approval -Ratings-Gallup-Historical-Statistics-Trends.aspx. George H. W. Bush's re-cord rating was topped by George W. Bush's 90 percent figure in the wake of the 9/11 attacks.

3. For the saga of Cuomo's decision, see Jack W. Germond and Jules Wit-cover, *Mad As Hell: Revolt at the Ballot Box, 1992* (New York: Warner Books, 1993), pp. 113–129.

4. Germond and Witcover, *Mad as Hell,* pp. 92–93.

5. Ibid., pp. 158–159.

6. See Jacob S. Hacker, *The Road to Nowhere: The Genesis of President Clinton's Plan for Health Security* (Princeton, NJ: Princeton University Press, 1999). The first chapter is viewable at "The Rise of Reform," NYTimes.com, http://www.nytimes.com/books/first/h/hacker-nowhere.html.

7. Cited in Germond and Witcover, *Mad as Hell,* p. 191.

8. Nelson Schwartz, "No Matter How Well Tsongas Performs, Party Is Skeptical; Poll Numbers Improve, but Leaders Recall Dukakis," *The Baltimore Sun,* February 8, 1992, http://articles.baltimoresun.com/1992-02-08/news /1992039027_1_paul-tsongas-new-hampshire-tsongas-wins.

9. Ron Goldwyn, "Native Son Harkin Wins Iowa, But . . .", *Philadelphia*

Inquirer, February 11, 1992, http://articles.philly.com/1992-02-11/news/26041259
_1_harkin-presidential-straw-poll-today-gallup-poll.

10. Germond and Witcover, *Mad as Hell,* p. 204.

11. Ibid., pp. 208–209.

12. Ibid., pp. 135–36.

13. Ibid., pp. 132–34.

14. See Chapter 5 about the 1988 New Hampshire primary.

15. Steven A. Holmes, "The 1992 Campaign: Republicans; Bush Steps Up
Campaign as Buchanan Lays Out an Agenda," *New York Times,* February 11,
1992, http://www.nytimes.com/1992/02/11/us/1992-campaign-republicans-
bush-steps-up-campaign-buchanan-lays-agenda.html.

16. Associated Press, "Polls: Bush Leads 2–1; Democratic Race Tight," *Lud-
ington Daily News,* February 5, 1992, http://news.google.com/newspapers
?nid=110&dat=19920205&id=7PZPAAAAIBAJ&sjid=TlUDAAAAIBAJ&pg
=3628,2226992.

17. Cited in Germond and Witcover, *Mad as Hell,* pp. 147–48.

18. Associated Press, "Polls: Bush Leads 2–1; Democratic Race Tight."

19. Cited in Germond and Witcover, *Mad as Hell,* p. 138.

20. Ibid., p. 150.

21. See Chapter 5 for a fuller discussion.

22. Palmer, *The New Hampshire Primary and the American Electoral Process,* pp. 25–27.

23. David Moore was managing editor of the Gallup Poll at the time, over-
seeing with Lydia Saad the CNN/*USA Today*/Gallup tracking poll of GOP
primary voters.

24. Palmer, *The New Hampshire Primary and the American Electoral Process,* p. 26.

25. Ibid., p. 27.

26. Stephen J. Farnsworth and S. Robert Lichter, "The *Manchester Union
Leader*'s Influence in the 1996 New Hampshire Republican Primary," *Presidential Studies Quarterly* 33 no. 2 (June 2003), pp. 291–304. Two tables showing the
results are found on p. 298.

27. Ibid.," p. 295.

28. "Buchanan Win Means Trouble for the GOP," February 20, 1996, CNN
.com, http://cgi.cnn.com/ALLPOLITICS/1996/news/9602/20/nh.results/
analysis.shtml.

29. Andrew Smith, "New Hampshire 2000: Either Bush or Dole Top Bradley
or Gore," CNN/WMUR/UNH poll press release, University of New Hampshire Survey Center, May 5, 1999.

30. Don Van Natta, "The 2000 Campaign: The War Chest; Early Rush of
Contributions Opened the Floodgates for Bush," *New York Times,* January 30,
2000.

31. Dan Balz, "Bush's Campaign Strategy Sets the Pace for 2000," *Washington Post*, July 4, 1999.

32. "Poll: New Hampshire Voters Support Bush over Gore," CNN.com, May 5, 1999, http://www.studentnews.cnn.com/ALLPOLITICS/stories/1999/05/05 /president.2000/wmur.poll/.

33. Paul West, "Republican Rivals Attack Bush for Skipping Second N.H. Debate," *Baltimore Sun*, October 29, 1999.

34. Carin Dessauer, "New Hampshire Poll Shows Dole, Bush Leading GOP Pack," CNN.com, January 6, 1999, http://www.cnn.com/ALLPOLITICS/stories /1999/01/06/president.2000/poll/

35. Diana J. Schemo, "White House 2000/Republicans: Elizabeth Dole," *New York Times*, January 5, 2000.

36. Richard Berke, "Political Memo; Alliance Holds Risks for Bradley and McCain," *New York Times*, December 16, 1999.

37. "Federal Surplus or Deficit," report prepared by Federal Reserve Bank of St. Louis, updated October 15, 2014, http://research.stlouisfed.org/fred2/series /FYFSD.

38. John Broder, "Bradley Pulls Ahead of Gore in Latest Fund-Raising Lap," *New York Times*, September 30, 1999.

39. Richard Berke, "Clinton Admits Early Concern about Gore's Campaign," *New York Times*, May 14, 1999.

40. John King, "Gore Campaign Shuffles Staff. Coelho Puts Stamp on Organization." CNN, July 2, 1999, http://edition.cnn.com/ALLPOLITICS/stories /1999/07/02/president.2000/gore.staff/.

41. Michael Duffy, "The Gore Campaign: Out of Portugal, Questions for Coelho," *Time*, October 4, 1999.

42. "In Town Meeting, Gore Criticizes Clinton Behavior, Bradley Defends Senate Retirement," CNN.com, October 27, 1999, http://edition.cnn.com /ALLPOLITICS/stories/1999/10/27/debate/index.html.

43. John Broder and Kathleen Seelye, "Gore Campaign Responds to Money Crunch," *New York Times*, November 20, 1999.

44. Jack Germond and Jules Witcover, "Retooling Al Gore's Campaign," *Baltimore Sun*, October 13, 1999.

45. Keith Moore, "Down in the Trenches: Donna Brazile, the New Manager of Al Gore's Campaign, Has a Reputation as a Tenacious Political Attack Dog." *Salon.com*, October 11, 1999, http://www.salon.com/1999/10/11/brazile/.

46. Andrew Smith, "Gore Maintains Wide Lead over Bradley," WMUR/ CNN Poll press release, University of New Hampshire Survey Center, May 4, 1999.

47. Andrew Smith, "Bradley Closes Gap On Gore," WMUR/CNN Poll press release, University of New Hampshire Survey Center, September 13, 1999.

48. An American Research Group poll released December 23, 1999 had Bradley leading Gore by 48 percent to 36 percent.

49. Jeff Zeleny, "Feisty Gore Waves Off Slippage in Iowa Poll. Bring on Bradley for Debates, He Says," *Des Moines Register*, October 23, 1999.

50. Andrew Smith and Dennis Junius, "Kerry/Dean Lead Tight Field in New Hampshire," Granite State Poll press release, University of New Hampshire Survey Center, July 7, 2003, http://cola.unh.edu/survey-center/kerrydean-lead -tight-field-nh-772003.

51. For more on Casey's role in New Hampshire primary politics, see Casey, *Hart and Soul*.

52. Andrew Smith and Dennis Junius, "Inside the NH Primary Race," Granite State Poll press release, University of New Hampshire Survey Center, December 17, 2003, http://cola.unh.edu/sites/cola.unh.edu/files/research _publications/primary2004_demana1121703.pdf.

53. Andrew Smith and Dennis Junius, "Dean Widens Lead, Voters Think He'll Win in NH," Granite State Poll press release, University of New Hampshire Survey Center, December 16, 2003, http://cola.unh.edu/sites/cola.unh .edu/files/research_publications/primary2004_dem121603.pdf.

54. Dan Balz, "Clark Under Sharp Attack in Democratic Debate," *Washington Post*, October 10, 2003.

55. From ABC debate at the University of New Hampshire, December 9, 2003. Transcript available at http://www.gwu.edu/~action/2004/primdeb /deb120903tr.htm.

56. Alex Johnson, David Shuster, Peiya David and Michelle Jaconi, "Kerry Roars Back to Win Iowa," NBCNews.com, January 20, 2004, http://www .nbcnews.com/id/3999491/ns/politics/t/kerry-roars-back-win-iowa-caucuses /#.U6HRYrHLMg8.

57. Andrew Smith and Dennis Junius, "Kerry, Dean, Edwards," FOX/ WMUR/UNH tracking poll, January 26, 2004, http://cola.unh.edu/sites/cola .unh.edu/files/research_publications/primary2004_tr12604.pdf.

58. John Heilemann and Mark Halperin, *Game Change: Obama and the Clintons, McCain and Palin, and the Race of a Lifetime* (New York: HarperCollins, 2010), p. 78.

59. Patrick Healy, "Clinton Reminds New Hampshire, I'm with Bill," *New York Times*, February 13, 2007.

60. Wayne Semprini, in personal conversation with author Andrew Smith, 2007.

61. Andrew Smith, "Rudy Slips to Third in NH," CNN/WMUR/UNH primary poll, University of New Hampshire Survey Center, November 19, 2007, http://cola.unh.edu/sites/cola.unh.edu/files/research_publications/primary 2008_gopprim111907.pdf.

62. Adam Nagourney, "Giuliani Hits a Rocky Stretch as Voting Approaches," *New York Times*, December 24, 2007.

63. Dan Nowicki, "McCain Seeks Spark from Newspapers' Endorsement," *The Arizona Republic*, December 17, 2007.

64. Rebecca Sinderbrand, "Fred Thompson Is Done with New Hampshire," CNN, December 11, 2007, http://politicalticker.blogs.cnn.com/2007/12/11/fred -thompson-is-done-with-new-hampshire/.

65. Andrew Smith, "Romney Early Favorite in 2012 NH Presidential Primary," WMUR/UNH Survey Center poll press release, May 10, 2010, http:// cola.unh.edu/sites/cola.unh.edu/files/research_publications/ gsp2010_spring _primary51810.pdf.

66. Frank Phillips, "Romney Paves Way for Possible '12 Run. Bulk of PAC Fund Goes for Political Ambitions," *Boston Globe*, December 8, 2008.

67. Paul Steinhauser and Robert Yoon, "Romney Takes First Official Step Towards Running for President," CNN, April 11, 2011, http://politicalticker .blogs.cnn.com/2011/04/11/romney-forms-presidential-exploratory -committee/.

68. Nicholas. Confessore, "For Romney, Close Ties to Officials Bear Fruit," *New York Times*, January 9, 2012.

69. For more information on the impact of endorsements, see Wayne Steger, "Who Wins Nominations and Why? An Updated Forecast of the Presidential Primary Vote," *Political Research Quarterly* 60, no. 1 (March 2007), and Marty Cohen, David Karol, Hans Noel, and John Zaller, *The Party Decides* (Chicago: University of Chicago Press, 2008).

70. David Lightman, "Romney to Make It Official Thursday in Divided New Hampshire," McClatchy News Service, June 1, 2011, http://www.mcclatchydc .com/2011/06/01/115109/romney-to-make-it-official-on.html.

71. Alec McGillis, "Unremitting," *The New Republic*, November 3, 2011.

7. A Demographic and Political Profile of New Hampshire

1. Frances Martel, "Fox Anchor: Critics Suggest NH Primary 'Not Representative' For Being 'Primarily White,' Lightly Populated," Mediaite.com, January 7, 2012, http://www.mediaite.com/tv/fox-anchor-critics-suggest-nh-primary -not-representative-for-being-primarily-white-lightly-populated/.

2. Will Lester, "States Challenge New Hampshire's Primary Status," Bryan Times, March 13, 2003, http://news.google.com/newspapers?nid=799&dat =20030313&id=M8VOAAAAIBAJ&sjid=pEkDAAAAIBAJ&pg=2903,341783.

3. For more detail about the history of Manchester and its mills, see Tamara Hareven's *Family Time and Industrial Time* (Lanham, MD: University Press of America, 1982), and Tamara Hareven and Randolph Langenbach's *Amoskeag:*

Life and Work in an American Factory-City (Lebanon, NH: University Press of New England, 1995).

4. Michael Levenson, "Most Who Left State Don't Plan to Return," *Boston Globe*, May 14, 2006. Survey conducted by the University of New Hampshire Survey Center.

5. Statistics in this section come from the US census.

6. See http://taxfoundation.org/article/state-and-local-tax-burdens-all-states -one-year-1977–2009.

7. Kenneth Johnson, "New Hampshire Demographic Trends in the Twenty-First Century," University of New Hampshire Carsey Institute, http://www .carseyinstitute.unh.edu/publications/Report-Johnson-Demographic-Trends -NH-21st-Century.pdf.

8. Kenneth Johnson of the University of New Hampshire Carsey Institute has done important work examining the changing age structure of the New Hampshire population.

9. See Thomas H. O'Connor, *The Boston Irish: A Political History* (Boston: Back Bay Books, 1995).

10. From 2012 Granite State polls conducted by the University of New Hampshire Survey Center.

11. Ibid.

12. "Religious Landscape Survey: Affiliations," Pew Research Center Religion and Public Life Project, 2007, http://religions.pewforum.org/affiliations.

13. Frank Newport, "State of the States: Importance of Religion," Gallup .com, January 28, 2009, http://www.gallup.com/poll/114022/State-States -Importance-Religion.aspx.

14. From 2012 Granite State polls conducted by the University of New Hampshire Survey Center.

15. Frank Newport, "America's Church Attendance Inches Up in 2010," Gallup.com, June 2010, http://www.gallup.com/poll/141044/Americans-Church -Attendance-Inches-2010.aspx.

16. University of New Hampshire Survey Center, November 2, 2008, http:// www.unh.edu/survey-center/news/pdf/e2008_trk110208.pdf.

17. William Mayer, "The New Hampshire Primary: A Historical Overview," in *Medium and Momentum: The New Hampshire Primary and Nomination Politics*, eds. Garry Orren and Nelson Polsby (Chatham, NJ: Chatham House, 2007), p. 26.

18. See Hugh Gregg, *Birth of the Republican Party: A Summary of Historical Research on Amos Tuck and the Birthplace of the Republican Party at Exeter, New Hampshire* (Resources of New Hampshire: 1995).

19. See Walter Dean Burnham, *Critical Elections and the Mainsprings of American Politics* (New York: Norton, 1970), and James Sundquist, *Dynam-*

ics of the Party System: Alignment and Realignment of Political Parties in the United States (Washington DC: Brookings Institution Press, 1983).

20. See V. O. Key, "Secular Realignment and the Party System," *Journal of Politics* 21, no. 2 (1959).

21. See Charles S. Bullock III, Donna R. Hoffman, and Ronald Keith Gaddie, "Regional Variations in the Realignment of American Politics, 1944–2004," *Social Science Quarterly* 87, no. 3 (September 2006).

22. Kenneth Johnson, Dante Scala, and Andrew Smith, "Many New Voters Make the Granite State One to Watch in November," New England Issue Brief no. 9 (Fall 2008), University of New Hampshire Carsey Institute, http://www .carseyinstitute.unh.edu/publications/IB-NHVoter08.pdf.

23. New Hampshire Revised Statute Annotated 154:2 (1994).

24. New Hampshire Revised Statute Annotated 654:34 (amended 1993).

25. See Alan Abramowitz's *The Disappearing Center: Engaged Citizens, Polarization, and American Democracy* (New Haven, CT: Yale University Press, 2010).

8. Who Votes?

1. All exit polls referenced in this work, unless otherwise specified, were conducted by CBS/*New York Times* (1980), and media consortium exit polls conducted by Voter Research and Surveys (1984–1992), Voter News Service (1996–200), and Edison Media Research (2004–2012).

2. Caution must be used when comparing the ideology of voters as reported in exit polls with that reported in telephone surveys because of differences in question wording, question context, and mode of interviewing.

3. Dave Carney, email correspondence with the authors, July 13, 2012.

4. *Boston Globe* New Hampshire primary poll conducted by the University of New Hampshire Survey Center, June 2011.

5. Fox News/WMUR/UNH Primary tracking poll conducted by University of New Hampshire Survey Center, January–February 2000.

6. New Hampshire data from University of New Hampshire Granite State Poll press release, April 27, 2012, http://cola.unh.edu/sites/cola.unh.edu/files /research_publications/gsp2012_spring_legiss042712.pdf. National data from a Gallup Organization poll conducted May 3–6, 2012, http://brain.gallup.com /documents/questionnaire.aspx?STUDY=P1205006&p=2.

7. Andrew Smith, "NH Legislature Faces Tough Year, Difficult Issues," Granite State Poll Press Release, University of New Hampshire Survey Center, February 7, 2012, http://cola.unh.edu/sites/cola.unh.edu/files/research _publications/gsp2012_winter_legapp020712.pdf.

8. Rich Killion, email correspondence with the authors, July 18, 2012.

9. See William Mayer, "The New Hampshire Primary: A Historical Overview," p. 29.

10. See Dante Scala, *Stormy Weather: The New Hampshire Primary and Presidential Politics* (New York: Palgrave MacMillan, 2003).

11. See Michael McCord, "Firefighter's Endorsement on the Minds of Democrats," *Concord Monitor*, May 10, 2007. The Professional Firefighters of New Hampshire Director David Lang is a much-sought-after endorsement for Democrats running in the New Hampshire primary.

12. Granite State polls, conducted by the University of New Hampshire Survey Center.

13. *Boston Globe* New Hampshire primary polls conducted by the University of New Hampshire Survey Center, November–December, 2007.

14. Kathy Sullivan, email correspondence with the authors, July 22, 2012.

15. WMUR/UNH Survey Center polls have shown Clinton consistently getting more than 60 percent support from likely 2016 Democratic primary voters. Other candidates are struggling to achieve double-digits. See Andrew Smith and Zachary Azem, "Clinton Alone on Top in NH, No GOP Frontrunner," University of New Hampshire Survey Center, April 18, 2014, http://cola.unh.edu/sites/cola.unh.edu/files/research_publications/gsp2014_spring_primary041814.pdf.

9. Myths about New Hampshire and the Primary

1. New Hampshire Revised Statute Annotated 654.

2. American National Election Studies, "Time Series Cumulative Data File," Stanford University and the University of Michigan, 2010, http://www.electionstudies.org/studypages/cdf/cdf.htm. These materials are based on work supported by the National Science Foundation under grant numbers SBR-9707741, SBR-9317631, SES-9209410, SES-9009379, SES-8808361, SES-8341310, SES-8207580, and SOC77–08885. Any opinions, findings, conclusions, or recommendations expressed in these materials are those of the authors and do not necessarily reflect the views of the funding organizations.

3. Massachusetts Secretary of State, "The Commonwealth of Massachusetts: Enrollment Breakdown as of 10/17/2012," November 1, 2012, www.sec.state.ma.us/ele/ele12/06NOV2012_ST_Party_Enrollment_Stats_3.pdf.

4. From New Hampshire official voting statistics, calculated by the authors.

5. "New Hampshire in the Hands of Independents," CNN.com, January 7, 2008, http://articles.cnn.com/2008–01–07/politics/nh.guide_1_independent-voters-democratic-primary-voters-republican-region?_s=PM:POLITICS.

6. From WMUR/UNH Granite State Polls, University of New Hampshire Survey Center, analysis by authors.

7. Katherine Seelye, "Voters without a Party Splinter New Hampshire," *New York Times*, January 5, 2012.

8. See Cohen, et al., *"The Party Decides."*

9. Huma Khan, "New Hampshire Primary: Mitt Romney the Clear Front-Runner, Jon Huntsman Vies for No. 2 Spot," ABCNews.com, January 10, 2012, http://abcnews.go.com/Politics/hampshire-primary-mitt-romney-gaining -edge-jon-huntsman/story?id=15329628.

10. Ian Christopher McCaleb, "On Weekend before New Hampshire Primary, Independent Voters Relish Opportunity. But Some Take Umbrage to 'Cloak and Dagger' Voting Tactics," CNN.com, January 28, 2000, http:// edition.cnn.com/2000/ALLPOLITICS/stories/01/28/independent.cnn/index .html.

11. Linda L. Fowler, Constantine J. Spiliotes, Lyn Vavreck. "Sheep in Wolves' Clothing: Undeclared Voters in New Hampshire's Open Primary," *PS: Political Science and Politics* 36, no. 2 (April 2003), pp. 159–163.

12. 2012 Media Consortium New Hampshire Primary exit poll, http:// elections.nytimes.com/2012/primaries/states/new-hampshire.

13. Dante Scala and Andrew Smith, "Bet or Get Out: A Study of Campaign Ad-buy Strategies in the New Hampshire Primary" (paper presented at the annual meeting of the American Political Science Association, Boston, MA, August 28–31, 2008).

14. Diane Cardwell, "The 2004 Campaign: The Connecticut Senator; Lieberman Makes New Hampshire Home," *New York Times*, December 23, 2003, www.nytimes.com/2003/12/23/us/the-2004-campaign-the-connecticut -senator-lieberman-makes-new-hampshire-home.html.

15. Scala and Smith, "Bet or Get Out: A Study of Campaign Ad-buy Strategies in the New Hampshire Primary."

16. Randall Adkins, Andrew Dowdle, and Wayne Steger have done extensive research into this topic. See also Cohen, et al., *The Party Decides.*

17. The information from this section comes from the authors' conversations with George Bruno, Ned Helms, Joe Keefe, Jim Merrill, Tom Rath, Doug Scamman, Terry Schumaker, and Kathy Sullivan.

18. Cohen, et al., *The Party Decides*, p. 290.

19. David Moore and Andrew Smith, "Measuring Intensity of Opinion" (paper presented at the annual meeting of the American Association for Public Opinion Research, Chicago, IL, May 13–16, 2010).

20. "How New Hampshire 'Firsts' Bring It Big Bucks," CBSNews.com, January 4, 2012, http://www.cbsnews.com/news/how-new-hampshire-firsts -bring-it-big-bucks/.

21. Ross Gittell and Brian Gottlob, "Economic Impact of the New Hampshire Primary." Study commissioned by the New Hampshire Political Library, 2000.

22. Douglas Blais, "NASCAR — A Leading Economic Indicator?" Southern New Hampshire University, Department of Sports Management, July 27, 2011, www.snhu.edu/14467.asp.

10. The Cracked Crystal Ball

1. Langer's comments are particularly interesting. In private conversation with author Andrew Smith, he indicated that ABC would not be conducting polls in New Hampshire, in part, because it is so difficult to be accurate. Doug Schwartz, Director of Quinnipiac University's Polling Institute made a similar comment to Smith prior to the 2004 New Hampshire primary and also did not conduct polls in New Hampshire in 2008.

2. "An Evaluation of the Methodology of the 2008 Pre-Election Primary Polls, American Association for Public Opinion Research as Hoc Committee on the 2008 Presidential Primary Polling," American Association for Public Opinion Research, revised version, April 2009, http://www.aapor.org /AAPORKentico/AAPOR_Main/media/MainSiteFiles/AAPOR_Rept_FINAL -Rev-4-13-09.pdf.

3. Theodore White, *The Making of the President, 1968* (New York: Athenaeum, 1969).

4. Kenneth John, "Report: 1980–1988 New Hampshire Presidential Primary Polls," *Public Opinion Quarterly* 53, no. 4 (Winter 1989).

5. Andrew Smith, "The Perils of Polling in New Hampshire," in Mayer, *The Making of the Presidential Candidates 2004.*

6. Andrew Smith, "McCain With a Slight Edge — Many Voters Undecided," WMUR/UNH Granite State Poll press release, September 22, 2008, http:// www.unh.edu/survey-center/news/pdf/gsp2008_fall_nhpres92208.pdf.

7. David Moore and Andrew Smith, "Haven't You Made Up Your Minds Yet! Undecided Voters in the New Hampshire Primary" (paper presented at the annual meeting of the American Association for Public Opinion Research, New Orleans, LA, May 15–18, 2008).

8. ABC News, New Hampshire Primary Democratic Debate, January 5, 2008. http://abcnews.go.com/Politics/Vote2008/story?id=4091645&page=1.

9. Karen Breslau, "Hillary Tears Up: A Muskie Moment, or a Helpful Glimpse of 'The Real Hillary?" *Newsweek*, January 7, 2008, http://www .newsweek.com/id/85609.

10. See "Election 2008: New Hampshire Primary Results," *New York Times*, December 7, 2014, http://politics.nytimes.com/election-guide/2008/results /states/NH.html.

11. Special thanks to Karen Hicks, from the Clinton campaign, and Heather Quinn, of the Obama campaign, for providing campaign schedules.

12. "An Evaluation of the Methodology of the 2008 Pre-Election Primary

Polls, American Association for Public Opinion Research as Hoc Committee on the 2008 Presidential Primary Polling," p. 68.

13. David Rothschild and Justin Wolfers, "Forecasting Elections: Voter Intentions versus Expectations," Brookings Institution white paper, November 1, 2012, http://www.brookings.edu/research/papers/2012/11/01-voter -expectations-wolfers.

14. Rich Morin and Claudia Deane, "A Snowy Graveyard for Pols and Polls," *Washington Post,* January 26, 2004.

11. Future of the New Hampshire Primary

1. See Barbara Norrander, *Super Tuesday: Regional Politics and Presidential Primaries* (Lexington: University of Kentucky Press, 1992).

2. The NASS plan is described in Gregg and Gardner, *Why New Hampshire,* pp. 215–217.

3. Cited in Thomas Gangale, *From the Primaries to the Polls: How to Repair America's Broken Presidential Nomination Process* (Greenwood Publishing Group, 2008), p. 92.

4. Thomas Gangale, "The California Plan: A 21st-Century Method for Nominating Presidential Candidates," *PS: Political Science and Politics* 37, no. 1 (January 2004).

5. Elaine C. Kamarck, *Primary Politics: How Presidential Candidates Have Shaped the Modern Nomination System* (Washington, DC: Brooking Institution Press, 2009), p. 175.

6. Ibid., p. 177.

7. Caroline Tolbert, David Redlawsk, and Daniel Bowen, "Reforming Presidential Nominations: Rotating State Primaries or a National Primary?" *PS: Political Science and Politics* 42, no.1 (January 2009).

8. See Kevin Coleman, "Presidential Nominating Process: Current Issues," Congressional Research Service, October 6, 2011, http://fpc.state.gov /documents/organization/175965.pdf.

9. See William Mayer and Andrew Busch, "Can the Federal Government Reform the Presidential Nomination Process?" *Election Law Journal* 3, no. 4 (2004).

10. Kevin Coleman, "Presidential Nomination Process: Current Issues," Congressional Research Service, *CRS Report for Congress,* January 27, 2012.

11. Cited in Kamarck, *Primary Politics,* p. 181.

12. "The Rules of the Republican Party Amended by the Republican National Committee on April 12, 2013, January 24, 2014 and May 9, 2014," https:// cdn.gop.com/docs/2012_Rules_of_the_Republican_Party.pdf.

13. Mario Trujillo, "Clock Runs Out for Utah's 2016 Primary Hopes."

Index